THE
BILL OF RIGHTS

by the author of

THE SUPREME COURT IN
AMERICAN HISTORY

THE
BILL OF RIGHTS

Its Impact
on the American People

MARJORIE G. FRIBOURG

Macrae Smith Company : Philadelphia

ACKNOWLEDGMENTS

The author is most deeply grateful to Mr. Mark Woolsey, Managing Editor of *United States Law Week* for his careful editing and reviewing of this manuscript.

The author also thanks Trial Examiner Josephine H. Klein of the National Labor Relations Board and Thomas P. Healy, Associate Director of Information for the National Labor Relations Board, for their assistance in checking the accuracy of "Both Sides . . . Of The Labor Relation." My thanks also go to Dorothy V. Allport, the librarian for the United States Court of Military Appeals, and my special thanks to Commissioner Daniel F. Carney who carefully read the typescript of the military chapter. For the help I received with the property rights chapter my thanks go to William A. Blair, the attorney in the Griggs case; and to Francis Burns, City Solicitor of Pittston, Pennsylvania. The Negro chapter has been materially improved by the generous and careful going over it received from Mr. David L. Norman, Chief of the Appeals and Research Section of the Civil Rights Division of the Department of Justice. I am also indebted to the numerous attorneys involved in these cases who generously allowed me to interview them.

Copyright © 1967 by Marjorie G. Fribourg

Library of Congress Catalog Card Number 67-15809

MANUFACTURED IN THE UNITED STATES OF AMERICA

6706

SECOND PRINTING

Foreword

———— ◆ ————

That continuing struggle to maintain both liberty and order in a democratic society is the central theme of Marjorie Fribourg's provocative *The Bill of Rights*. It has been both a lonely fight and one that has enlisted the enthusiastic support of great masses of Americans.

Mrs. Fribourg tells us about individual heroes like John Milton, going almost blind in the writing of the *Areopagitica,* that seminal tract in favor of the freedom of the press. Again we are told of George Washington reminding his fellow Americans of the Jewish faith that toleration is an inherent natural right, not a favor granted by the majority. Mrs. Fribourg's portraits include as well single-minded lonely civil rights heroes of our own time. We see J. Garner Anthony of Honolulu tenaciously, and, in the end, successfully, defending the principle of the supremacy of civil over military authority. We are told how John Doar and his indefatigable staff of Justice Department attorneys labored through sixteen-hour days and seven-day weeks in one hostile southern county after another, gathering evidence to prove how Negroes had been fraudulently disenfranchised. Then, too, there is Lewis Schweitzer, whose VERA Foundation spearheaded efforts to reform the outmoded and unfair bail system.

The canvas also makes room for collective portraits, for numberless heroes of the civil rights struggle who remain anonymous, for the masses who supported the Montgomery bus boycott or who participated in the two notable marches—from Washington Monument to Lincoln Memorial in August of 1963, and from Selma to Montgomery in the spring of 1965.

The story of these civil liberties fighters and the war they waged makes for dramatic reading. But, as Mrs. Fribourg reminds us, the battle for civil rights is by no means won. Grievous problems in the administration of criminal justice and in the guarantee of a fair trial still plague the law enforcement authorities. Military and security problems have temporarily relegated civil liberties to a subordinate place. Even the most respected and seemingly established tenets of American constitutional law are tested anew in each generation. This is notably the case with the principle of the separation of church and state, a doctrine whose maintenance demands eternal vigilance. Indeed, as the author reminds us, the battle to achieve ordered liberty must still be pressed, for the achievement of these goals is central to the heritage of the American people.

RICHARD B. MORRIS

Columbia University

Contents

—————◆◆—————

Introduction		**9**

PART I   CITIZENS WHO WRITE, SPEAK, READ, OR LISTEN

"Silence Coerced by Law"	*13*
"Clear and Present Danger"	*22*
"To Err Politically"	*28*
"Constitutionally Intolerable"	*36*

PART II   CITIZENS WHO ORGANIZE FOR ACTION

"In the Eye of the Law Civilly Dead"	*49*
"Labor Must Do Its Best to Maintain Justice"	*59*
"Both Sides . . . of the Labor Relation"	*68*
"In this Case, the Wrongs Are Enormous"	*76*
"After Enduring Nearly a Century"	*88*

PART III   THE WORSHIPERS

"Make No Law Respecting an Establishment of Religion"	*109*
"A Pandora's Box"	*117*

PART IV   THE PROPERTY OWNERS

"Projected into Unexpected Abysses"	*139*
"By Federal Permission"	*145*
"The Particular Emergency"	*153*

PART V   SOLDIERS AND CIVILIANS

"Precisely What the Bill of Rights Outlaws"	*175*
"You Cannot . . . Run an Army That Way"	*185*
"Our Fundamental Aim is to Prevent Crime"	*198*

PART VI   ADULTS OR YOUTH ACCUSED OF CRIME

"The Purpose of Bail Is Not Punishment"	*212*

"I Didn't Shoot Manuel, You Did It"   222
"A Fair Trial and a Free Press"   233

Index   245

Introduction

A visitor from a distant planet would wonder whether the Bill of Rights was a new addition to the United States Constitution. There is always so much activity in the courts or before Congress over civil liberties that it would be hard for any stranger to believe that the Constitution could never have been adopted in 1788 had not the Founding Fathers promised to add a Bill of Rights.

The Constitution had been written in Philadelphia in the summer of 1787 by daring men who far exceeded their authority. They were there to patch up what was nothing more than a friendly alliance between the states—the Articles of Confederation. Instead, they sent their shattering proposal for a new and stronger federal government to the then existing Continental Congress.

Elections were called in the thirteen states. Delegates were chosen to attend state conventions that would pass on the proposed Constitution. A cry of opposition went up even before the first convention met: a guarantee of personal freedoms would have to be added to the document. It was no use for statesmen to argue that the new government could do only what the Constitution permitted, and that nowhere in the document was anyone given the power to control speech, the press, or the practice of religion. An overwhelming number of delegates wanted their safeguards against tyranny put in writing. Friends of the Constitution agreed that this should be done.

Therefore, in 1789, the first Congress under the new government framed the Constitution's first ten amendments, spelling out our liberties.

Charters of liberties due the citizenry were nothing new. The English Magna Carta went back to 1215, and England had had a Bill of Rights since 1689. However, Congressman James Madison of Virginia worded the American version in stronger terminology than had ever been used before. It was not a series of privileges granted by a powerful ruler to humble subjects. It was a series of orders from "We the People"—the sovereign people of the United States—to the elected representatives and public servants. As such, it was sent to the states for ratification and became part of the supreme law of the land in 1791. Since then, the American people have always considered the Bill of Rights one of their most precious possessions. And, because of the Fourteenth Amendment adopted in 1868, most of the bill binds the states as well as the Federal Government.

Since these rights are so old, so prized, and so unquestionably ours, the question arises: why all these court cases and all this agitation? The answer is partly that freedom is like a dike holding back the waves of oppression. It must be kept in repair or small holes will let the floods in to wash away the entire structure. Furthermore, each generation has seen a new group rise up and demand more of what it considered to be its fair share of American freedom. Above all, the answer is partly that Americans do not always agree on how far their freedoms go or which party to a dispute needs and should have protection.

In these pages are the struggles of men and women who felt they needed rights and the story of the justices and the lawmakers who had to deal with their demands. Who these people are and what their rights have turned out to be is the basis of this book.

It would not, however, be enough merely to relate that in 1961 the Supreme Court threw out a group of convictions based on illegally seized evidence or that Congress passed this or that act for civil rights or against advocating the violent overthrow of the government. How and why these decisions were reached—and what arguments and memories influenced the public, the justices, and the lawmakers—are the most important and exciting part of the story.

PART ONE

CITIZENS WHO

WRITE, SPEAK, READ,

OR LISTEN

"Congress shall make no law . . . abridging the freedom of speech, or of the press . . ."

—First Amendment

"The right of the people to be secure in their persons, houses, papers, and effects, against unreasonable search and seizures, shall not be violated . . ."

—Fourth Amendment

THE RIGHTS AND THE ISSUES

". . . it is robbing the human race," said John Stuart Mill describing censorship in his *Essay on Liberty*. "If the [suppressed] opinion is right," said Mill, "[men] are deprived of the opportunity of exchanging error for truth; if wrong, they lose, what is almost as great a benefit, the clearer perception and livelier impression of truth, produced by its collision with error. . . ."

No responsible group in the United States wants to suppress the mere academic discussion of ideas. What, though, should a free society do about other types of talk: words designed to trigger a brawl; words used as a call to violence, or revolution; words that are lies and are intended to destroy another's reputation; words that are so lewd that they arouse the morally sick and offend the decent? Legally stated, the question becomes: When does speech stop being protected by the First Amendment to the Constitution and become an indivisible part of forbidden action?

No question is more delicate, for obviously what is truth to one man may be the rankest damaging lie to another; what is beauty to some eyes is to others filth. What one debater sees as a blunt statement of fact, his opponent considers "fighting words." The question affects everyone, not only authors, newspaper reporters, booksellers, and outspoken public speakers. The reader and the listener are the most concerned. For them the question becomes: What is to be told and what withheld from man as he struggles to cope with the world around him? Here follows a series of human episodes in which Congress and the courts had to face this problem. They had to ask themselves: What do we mean by freedom of speech and press, and who needs First Amendment protection?

"Silence Coerced by Law"

ASSOCIATE Justice Brennan of the United States Supreme Court undoubtedly sighed as he adjusted his stocky frame in his office swivel chair and examined the papers before him. The fact had to be faced. The advertisement carried by the *New York Times* on March 29, 1960, did not in all its particulars accurately describe what had happened in Montgomery, Alabama. As a result the justices of the Supreme Court faced a difficult case.

The *Times* people wanted the High Court to overturn a $500,-000 libel judgment granted against them by the Alabama courts for the benefit of City Commissioner L. B. Sullivan. Could any paper survive judgments like that? Brennan doubted it. If not, and the judgment stood, Brennan could easily imagine all news commentators reporting under a pall of fear. The public would cease to get all the news.

On the other hand, Brennan wondered, how far should the Court go to protect the press in publishing a provably untrue statement —one that a public official felt injured his reputation? Brennan knew his brother justices were going to be deeply, possibly even vehemently, divided. Leaning forward, his round youthful face partially hidden by dark-rimmed glasses, he examined the ad many times.

HEED THEIR RISING VOICES, screamed the big type. Below the headline, the text described Negro youths singing "My Country, 'Tis of Thee" on the Alabama State Capitol steps. The youths, it was stated, were merely lobbying for their right to live in dignity as guaranteed by the United States Constitution and the Bill of Rights. However, the advertisement claimed, their nonviolent efforts were met by a "wave of terror." Armed policemen ringed their campus. Their leaders were expelled from Alabama State College, and when the students protested their dining room was padlocked. The ad went on, "Southern violators . . . have bombed his [Dr. Martin Luther King's] home. . . . They have arrested him seven times."

Now actually, as Brennan knew from the lower court records, nine civil rights workers had been expelled from Alabama State College, but not in connection with the demonstration on the capitol steps. There they sang the national anthem and not "My Country, 'Tis of Thee." The dining room had not been padlocked. Although on three occasions large numbers of police had been stationed near the campus, they had never ringed it. They were not there in connection with the singing. The police were not implicated in the bombing of King's home—if that could be inferred from the ad. In fact, the record stated, they had done all they could to find the culprit. And King had been arrested four times, not seven.

Sullivan brought his suit in the Alabama state courts because, he said, his duties as commissioner included supervising the police. On the witness stand he showed that he was not in office at the time of the bombing or during the first three arrests of King. He did not secure the fourth indictment (of which King was acquitted). However, much of what the ad described was supposed to have taken place during his term. He therefore contended that he was being falsely accused of ringing the campus with police, of having the dining room padlocked, and of causing the nonexistent arrests of King. He dragged into court not only the *New York Times* but also four Negro ministers whose names appeared as endorsing the ad.

The ministers emphatically denied having given anyone permission to use their names. Their attorney, Fred Gray, earnestly told the jury, "What happened to them could happen to you or anyone else."

Nevertheless the Alabama jury brought in its staggering verdict. The half-million-dollar judgment was awarded both against the ministers and the newspaper. Since the clergymen had nothing like that kind of money, the sheriff seized their automobiles and one preacher's land.

Brennan, mulling over the results of the trial, could readily anticipate the outraged reaction that Associate Justice Hugo L. Black would have. Black had come to the Court in 1937 as an Alabama Democrat. Only a trace of his southern drawl remained. He was now white-haired and seventy-eight, the oldest and, in stature, the smallest of the justices. But he was not the least vigorous. He still played tennis, and he still championed liberal positions. Of course, even Justice Black had to concede that at times the Supreme Court itself had upheld restrictions on speech and press. For example, it had upheld restrictions on obscene publication in a case called *Roth v. United States,* and in *Chaplinsky v. New Hampshire* it had allowed the state to punish "fighting words," likely to trigger a brawl. Just the same, Black contended, "An unconditional right to say what one pleases about public affairs is what I consider to be the minimum guarantee of the First Amendment." The power of the Government, then, to use libel laws—or any laws—to impose punishment for criticizing the way a public official performed his duties was "precisely nil."

The majority of the justices were not ready to go that far. They were prepared to accept some form of libel law. It bothered neither them nor Black that the First Amendment to the United States Constitution restricted only the Congress and not the states from abridging freedom of speech and of the press. They all felt that the Fourteenth Amendment, passed after the Civil War, extended the First Amendment to make its prohibitions binding on the states; it said: "nor shall any State deprive any person of life, liberty, or property, without due process of law." The justices all agreed that freedom of the press—as far as it should go—was one of the basic liberties referred to. It was essential to orderly representative government. To use their voting power effectively, people had to know what was going on. To fetter the press "is to fetter ourselves," said an earlier Court ruling.

Granting that, Justice Black found in the *Times* case a chilling warning. "There is no reason to believe," he said, "that there are not more such huge verdicts lurking just around the corner for *The Times* or any other newspaper or broadcaster which might dare to criticize public officials."

Black was all too correct. At the time sixteen libel suits were being brought against news media by Alabama local and state officials. Evidently, these verdict seekers were encouraged by the conclusions of the Supreme Court of Alabama. That judicial body did not think it mattered that Sullivan's name had never been mentioned in the ad. The ad had mentioned the police. Said the Alabama court, "We think it common knowledge . . . [that] police and firemen, and others, are under the control and direction of . . . a single commissioner. . . ." This finding made it easier for any official of a government agency, if he were so inclined, to prove libel.

As the Supreme Court justices had expected, other newspapers were worried. Lawyers for both the *Washington Post* and the *Chicago Tribune* asked the Supreme Court to let them send in briefs (written arguments) in support of their competitor, the *Times*. The Court welcomed their interest.

It was clear to the lawyers for the newspapers that the Alabama courts had relied heavily on earlier statements by the Supreme

Court that the Constitution of the United States did not protect libelous publications. They took hope, however, from the fact that these earlier statements did not refer to misstatements against public officials acting in their official capacities. That difference made this a special case. Certainly, errors of fact were often spouted by citizens and press alike in the heat of each campaign every November. Surely it was not desirable for these debates to be dampened.

The lawyers, like the justices, turned their minds back to the words and the experiences of the great libertarians who had been responsible for the Bill of Rights. Separately, they searched the past for what the Founding Fathers had in mind when they used the phrase "freedom of the press." What had they intended it to mean, and had the Alabama court violated that intent?

When several anxious lawyers for the *Tribune* tackled the problem, they likened the actions of the Alabama court to the Star Chamber of England. The comparison was not irrelevant. The Star Chamber was a special tribunal exercising the sovereign's power to punish slander against officialdom—to silence opposition. To that end the majestic judges of this court, seated under their star-studded ceiling, overlooked all the rules for the protection of the accused, rules that were the pride of English criminal law. The Star Chamber judges were not supposed to inflict the death penalty but, as the *Tribune* lawyers pointed out, they ordered branding and floggings, one man's ear sliced, another's nose cut open.

Were the Alabama courts similarly trying to silence agitators for integration by punishing them with a farfetched libel suit? Not only the *Tribune* lawyers but also other friends of the *Times* insisted they were.

They noted emphatically that the Star Chamber had been abolished in England in 1641. They could not deny that after the Chamber was gone a system of licensing publications was administered by censors. Into the case of *New York Times Co. v. Sullivan* marched ghosts of these censors of old, reminding everyone that in their day a printer submitted his work to them before publication.

To break the chain of *prior censorship* on free expression, the poet John Milton—later to go blind—strained his dimming eyesight to write *Areopagitica* in 1644. Milton said that "to keep a narrow bridge of licensing where the challenger should pass . . . is but weakness and cowardice in the wars of Truth . . . ; she needs no policies, . . . stratagems, . . . licensing . . . those are the shifts and the defences that Error uses against her power. . . ."

Milton's advice at last prevailed with Parliament, and our own Founding Fathers read his urgent plea in their student days. Then their tutors sent them off to burn their candles studying Blackstone's *Commentaries*. Sir William Blackstone—cold, reserved, and cautious—was the renowned legal authority of the mid-eighteenth century. Conceding Milton's point, Blackstone warily lectured to his well-born young English students that freedom of the press meant freedom from prior censorship. You could still be punished for what you said once it was in print. You could still get into trouble for criticizing the sovereign. The sovereign was still master over his subjects.

Of course Brennan, Black, and the others believed that American law had gone beyond Blackstone. They were well aware that the Founding Fathers had brought to life a newer wisdom. They all knew how James Madison had expressed it—that in a republic "the censorial power is in the people over the government, and not in the government over the people." Therefore, Madison reasoned, in republican America freedom of the press had to mean more than in royalist England. The sovereign was not master. The people were.

Nevertheless, those who wished to could point to the Alien and Sedition Acts passed in the administration of President John Adams and claim that at least some of the Founding Fathers had accepted Blackstone's definition of freedom of the press. They could also point out that the issue of the legality of the Alien and Sedition Acts had never been brought before the Supreme Court.

The nine justices considering the *Times* case found it necessary to take a fresh look at these acts. The Alien Act was to allow "enemy aliens" to be expelled or imprisoned. It was aimed mostly at the French. France was molesting our shipping. Relations between the two countries teetered on the brink of war. The Sedition Act was passed in the same overcharged atmosphere. It provided jail sentences and fines of $5,000 "if any person shall write, print, utter or publish . . . any false, scandalous and malicious writing or writings against the government of the United States, or either house of Congress . . . or the President." Libel, then, under this act, was not confined to smearing individuals but also included slurs against the Government or its branches.

The Sedition Act moved forward in only one way from earlier libel laws devised by rulers to suppress opposition: it conceded that the truth of one's statement could be used as one's defense. The newspapermen gratefully remembered how that improvement had come about.

It all happened when a courageous old Scotsman living in Philadelphia named Andrew Hamilton agreed to be the defending attorney for a little German immigrant printer, Peter Zenger. Struggling to stay in business for himself, Zenger printed a journal and made his New York print shop the outlet for a group of spirited writers using false names. These writers openly criticized Royal Governor Cosby. At the same time they cried out for more freedom of the press. Their attitude reflected that of a pair of secretive British libertarians who signed themselves *Cato*. Said Cato, "Only the wicked Governors of Men dread what is said of them. . . . [Freedom of Speech] is the Terror of . . . Oppressors." Cosby was such a governor, according to the journal.

After being cooped up in the darkness and stench of a colonial jail for nine months, Zenger finally saw the light of the courtroom. Then it was that Andrew Hamilton made his brilliant argument that truth should be a defense in a libel suit, saying that, if truth is no defense, "who is it that has not libeled the devil?"

This was a daring contention. Judges believed the truth was no defense. A true statement could do the Crown more harm than a false one. Hamilton was gambling everything on convincing the jury. "Men who injure and oppress the people under their administration," he said, "provoke them to cry out and complain, and then make that very complaint the foundation for new oppressions and prosecutions." He could not have known that two hundred years later Associate Justice Arthur J. Goldberg of the United States Supreme Court would be copying his words into an opinion in the case of *New York Times Co. v. Sullivan*. All he knew at that moment was that the jury listened to his novel plea. On August 4, 1735, they brought in a verdict of "not guilty."

Statesmen in President Adams' administration remembered Andrew Hamilton when they wrote the Sedition Act. They too allowed the truth.

However, as the Supreme Court justices reviewed the history of the Adams period, they read that the truth as a defense had not worked well in protecting the press. In the first place, when feelings were aroused against the French and for the President, the jury did not always distinguish between what was a false statement and what they believed a false opinion. In the second place, some things, though true, were impossible to prove. As John Locke had pointed out years before, ". . . where is the man that has uncontestable evidence of the truth of all that he holds, or of the falsehoods of all he condemns?"

Unfortunately, the Adams administration did not come to the

same conclusion Locke did. Said Locke, "[The] blindness we are in, should make us more busy and careful to inform ourselves than contain others." On the contrary, the containing went on. Anti-administration editors, of course, feared they could not prove the truth to the satisfaction of a judge appointed by the President and a jury picked by the administration's marshal. They were, therefore, effectively silenced.

At last, matters relevant to the Sedition Act came to a head over a congressman from Vermont known as that "wild Irishman," Matthew Lyon. When Lyon had an opinion, he felt strongly—strongly enough on one occasion to get into a fist fight on the floor of the House. He was, besides, a Jefferson Republican (they later became the Democrats and, at the time, opposed Federalist President John Adams). Lyon's "wild Irish" temper was boiling over at the idea of a law to enforce acceptance of presidential policy. In addition, he accused the President of "ridiculous pomp, and selfish avarice."

In October of 1789, the Alien and Sedition Acts were just off the press. Lyon was running for re-election. Even had he been willing, he could not have campaigned successfully without condemning these presidential measures which he had already voted or argued against, including the President's handling of our relations with France. Lyon thought Adams was rapidly getting the country entangled in a needless war.

One infamous day Lyon found himself managing his campaign from inside a cold stone prison cell. Outraged, Thomas Jefferson and James Madison waged a war of words against the Sedition Act. An "alarming infraction of the Constitution . . . expressly and positively forbidden by one of the Amendments," they termed it. They said that "it is leveled against the right of freely examining public characters and measures." They hoped it would cause universal alarm. Astutely, they managed to get their opinions incorporated into resolutions passed by the General Assemblies of Virginia and Kentucky.

Their cry of alarm awakened the American people in 1800. The Federalist administration was voted out of office forever. The Alien and Sedition Acts, when they lapsed in 1801, were not again made the law of the land. Lyon won his re-election from jail and left his cell to return to Congress.

Newly elected President Jefferson, of course, pardoned those convicted under the Sedition Act. He considered it, he said, "as palpable as if Congress had ordered us to fall down and worship a golden image."

No, Brennan admitted, after he had reviewed all these facts, the

Supreme Court had not ruled on the validity of the Sedition Act, but, he said, Madison's and Jefferson's "attack upon its validity has carried the day in the court of history." The American people had decided that in the election of 1800.

Brennan did not think there was any force to the argument in Sullivan's lawyer's brief that Jefferson felt the Sedition Act was invalid only because it was a federal law, and the states were not similarly restricted. The Fourteenth Amendment had changed that. Besides, Madison obviously believed that every republic must have a free press.

At last, on March 9, 1964, the justices were ready to announce their conclusions. Accordingly, on that Monday morning they took their appointed seats on that high mahogany platform in their courtroom that lawyers call "the bench." Chief Justice Earl Warren was seated in the middle of the group. He nodded to Brennan, far on his right. Brennan was to speak.

Brennan sometimes used his own words and sometimes quoted justices of an earlier day. It was the Supreme Court's policy, Brennan said, to guard against the suppression of public debate. Whenever possible, he explained, the Court would use the principle it had outlined in *Roth v. United States*. The First Amendment "was fashioned to assure the unfettered interchange of ideas for the bringing about of political and social changes desired by the people." To explain why, he added a quote from a case called *Stromberg v. California:* "to the end that government may be responsive to the will of the people and that changes may be obtained by lawful means. . . ."

Brennan then reminded the ladies and gentlemen in the courtroom of the words of the revered Judge Learned Hand of the Court of Appeals: "right conclusions are more likely to be gathered out of a multitude of tongues, than through any kind of authoritative selection."

To further demonstrate the Court's deep responsibility toward free expression, Brennan recited the words of a great liberal justice of almost half a century before—lean and bushy-haired Justice Louis Dembitz Brandeis. "Those who won our independence believed . . . that political discussion is a public duty. . . . They recognized the risks. . . . But . . . they eschewed silence coerced by law. . . ."

This, then, was what the Founding Fathers considered when they provided for freedom of speech. They wanted unfettered public debate. They wanted the citizens fully free to exchange information. They wanted all men free to air their grievances. They knew that the wicked governors of men "dread what is said of them." From their own past experience, they could foresee and dread the possibility of a dictatorlike creature or group in America. To keep America free, their descendants also must "eschew silence coerced by law," as Brandeis had said.

Brennan knew that in heated debate some erroneous statements are inevitable. They must be protected if public debate is to remain robust and vigorous, as it must if a self-governing people is to be able to make the best decisions and to air its grievances peacefully.

Commissioner Sullivan felt his public image was marred. The interest of the public had to outweigh the interest of any individual in a case such as this, a case involving criticism of an official acting in his official capacity. If not, the people would cease to be masters of their own fate and would revert to their Colonial status. Then, the sovereign was their master and no one could criticize him. This was unthinkable in present-day America.

"Whatever is added to the field of libel is taken from the field of free debate," Brennan quoted from another lower court case.

Was there then no limit to the extent to which a man's reputation could be damaged? Sullivan and his lawyer were not alone in wondering about this.

Yes, Brennan said, there was a limit. A libel judgment was possible if a public official could prove that a statement made against him was made with actual malice—that is, with knowledge that it was false or with reckless disregard of whether it was false or not. Months later the justices clarified this. Brennan said in a later case that the public official would have to prove that the harmful statement was made with a high degree of knowledge of its probable falsity. Justice Byron R. White told a group of young lawyers in a Florida hotel that the evidence must show that a deliberate liar was spreading a known and damaging falsehood.

In the *Times* case, Brennan ruled, there was no such evidence. Even if it could be proved that the ministers had lent the use of their names, there was no evidence whatsoever that they knew the statements were false.

The evidence against them and the *Times* was constitutionally defective in another way as well. Sullivan's name had not been mentioned in the ad, nor had he been in any way described. No impersonal statement against government operation could thus be judged a personal attack. It was unconstitutional, Brennan said. The Alabama court was reversed. All the justices agreed to the reversal.

The case went back to the lower courts where it was dropped.

"Sullivan," said a lawyer for the *Times*, "knew he could not prove malice." The reporters put a heading in the paper: UNANIMOUS RULING EXPECTED TO WIDEN PRESS FREEDOM IN COVERING THE SOUTH.

Justice White said the case was a "major development, [for] anyone who wants to talk or write about his public servants." He hoped that public-spirited citizens would be made aware of it.

This then is where the United States stood in 1964. Freedom of speech and press was not absolute. It was, however, so important for all the people that it was to be given preferred status over almost every other consideration. Nine vigilant justices made it clear they were determined to see to that. And, in fact, in the months that followed, they found themselves compelled to protect freedom of communication for a strange assortment of individuals.

"Clear and Present Danger"

IN April of 1964, a month after the *New York Times* ruling involving reporters, advertisers, and newspaper readers, the Supreme Court justices heard the arguments in *Garrison v. Louisiana*. Here was a controversy brought on by a vigorously outspoken district attorney. Jim Garrison was the district attorney for Orleans Parish, Louisiana. The parish prison was overcrowded and a retired judge, William J. O'Hara, blamed Jim for the number of prisoners awaiting trial. On November 1, 1962, O'Hara issued a statement to the press saying, "any lag in the disposition of [court] cases is a direct result of inadequate operational methods of the district attorney's office."

During the events that followed, a reporter from a New Orleans evening paper commented, "I have . . . heard him [Jim] blast the Judges, so it is a sort of a tie. . . ." The reporter was R. J. Dempsey—called Jack. Jack's city editor thought he sensed a series of news items in the controversy. Since Jack was occupied, the city editor sent Jack's colleague, reporter Bert Hyde, to the criminal court building to get the next installment in the story—Jim's answer to O'Hara.

Hyde was standing outside Jim's door when he spotted the tall, lean frame of the district attorney coming up the front steps. It was a pleasing sight for more than one reason. People have said that dashing Mr. Garrison looked like a vigorous enforcement officer in a TV script. Perhaps Bert Hyde thought so too. After a while, Hyde was let into Jim's meticulously kept office and Jim obligingly said, "Sit down and I'll give you a statement."

Hyde noticed that the district attorney was calm and that he doodled on a piece of paper as he talked. Jim first spoke of the problem of inmates awaiting trial month after month in the parish prison. "It is incredible . . . in this country in 1962. . . ." The fault, he insisted, lay with the judges. They took too much time off.

Jim had another complaint. The judges, he said, were "tying the purse strings" on his vice investigations. They had stopped him from using money from fines to pay his undercover agents. That, he said, blocked his investigation of the "clip joints" on Canal Street. At one point, Hyde, pushing his pencil as fast as it would go, asked Garrison to "slow down." Jim was cooperative, and the reporter was able to take down his words. "The judges have now made it eloquently clear where their sympathies lie in regard to aggressive vice investigations. . . ." At another point he told Hyde, "They do not want the district attorney's office to investigate anything." Before he finished, Jim made the statement that really got him into trouble: "This raises interesting questions about the racketeer influence on our eight vacation-minded judges."

Later Dempsey himself talked to Jim and decided that, by "influence," Jim meant something quite indirect, not that the judges were tied up with racketeers or that they listened to racketeers in the conduct of their office. Dempsey's reaction to the whole dispute was, "I guess we have got a pretty good fight going, yes, sir."

Yes, sir, they had! Early in January Jim was in court, neatly dressed in a blue suit and a striped tie. This time he was not helping to bring a case. This time he was the defendant in a criminal libel suit.

The judges, when they testified, were in a position to bring out that not all their time away from court was vacation. Both careful research and careful writing is involved in handing down decisions. Besides, while their courtrooms were dark and empty they were working out innumerable problems in chambers—issuing warrants, fixing bail, or settling cases out of court. Moreover, as most lawyers will agree, trial hearings should not go on for long, unbroken periods. If weary judges or overtired members of the jury only half hear what is said, justice may miscarry.

The testifying judges were also ready to make their position clear on Jim's fine money. The district attorney's undercover agents were not members of the police force. Therefore, under Louisiana's constitution, as retired Judge O'Hara explained it, "The District Attorney's office had no legal authority to use [them] . . . to detect vice."

Meanwhile, Jim had added to the case by a talk he gave at St. Anthony's Church auditorium. He started out, wisely enough, talking about free speech. Then he told his audience, "I will not be stopped. What I said was, essentially, true and they don't work enough. . . . I will never back down."

The trial judge, the Honorable William H. Ponder, thought differently. Jim was convicted of libel and ordered to pay a $1,000 fine. The state supreme court upheld the conviction. Jim took his case to the United States Supreme Court.

The justices may have been startled by getting a criminal libel suit. Most libel cases are civil suits—that is, they are between individuals. Usually, criminal cases are those which involve harm to the community.

That, however, was the way Louisiana's attorney general felt about it. "The integrity of the judiciary was involved," he said. By his reasoning, the case involved a question of serious public interest.

Brennan, on examining the case, reminded everyone of a letter written back in 1940 by Robert Jackson, then Attorney General of the United States and later a Supreme Court justice. Jackson said it was the policy of the federal Attorney General's office not to prosecute for criticism of public officials. Brennan sympathized with that policy. A policy, however, is not a statute. Brennan scrutinized Louisiana's criminal libel law. It was hardly what he would call a narrowly drawn law. It was not limited to controlling speech likely to lead to public disorder or to a breach of the peace. He noted particularly that, as the law was applied to this case, there was no reliance on a concept called "the clear and present danger" test.

This important test was evolved during World War I. At the time socialists and anarchists mailed out propaganda or leaned out of windows and dropped their tracts on the crowd beneath. The leaflets urged young men to resist the draft, calling it a crime for American workers to fight the workers of other lands. As a result, Congress passed the Espionage Act of 1917 and outlawed speech that was intended to impede the war effort. The Supreme Court justices soon found themselves hearing arguments against the Espionage Act.

In order to protect both free speech and national defense, those two independent thinkers, Justices Oliver Wendell Holmes and Louis D. Brandeis, worked out a formula for judging inflammatory language.

Holmes read their formula from the bench in *Schenck v. United States*. "The question in every case is whether the words used are used in such circumstances and are of such a nature as to create a clear and present danger. . . ."

Brandeis further explained this position in another case called *Whitney v. California*. "If there be time to expose through discussion the falsehood . . . to avert the evil by the process of education, the remedy to be applied is more speech, not enforced silence. Only an emergency can justify repression."

Brennan was keenly aware that both Justice Douglas and Justice Goldberg wanted to apply Brandeis' formula of "more speech" to libel law. Public officials, such as these Louisiana judges, could answer a libel instead of punishing it. Douglas, besides, was ever wary in his attitude toward the "clear and present danger" test. It is not, he said, in the Constitution. Speech, he insisted, must be an inseparable part of illegal action before it can be subject to a penalty. When in 1951 the Court broadened the theory to cover probable *future* as well as clear and *present* danger, he strongly dissented. Brennan also knew of Black's view. Black did not believe that the liberties in the Bill of Rights could be abridged because of a superior public interest. "I cannot accept this approach to the Bill of Rights," he told a distinguished audience at New York University in 1960. The First Amendment forbids laws against freedom of speech or press, and Black said that the men who wrote it "meant their prohibitions to be 'absolutes' " for they knew firsthand the dangers of tyrannical government.

The mere fact that Jim's words were not likely to endanger the public safety, however, did not solve the justices' problems. The records showed that the Louisiana supreme court, in upholding Jim's conviction, had relied on a 1952 group libel case called *Beauharnais v. Illinois*. In that case the United States Supreme Court had ruled that judges need not consider "clear and present danger" in a libel suit. The Louisiana attorney general had carefully noted this in his brief.

Justice Douglas immediately wanted the Court to change its mind and overrule its own stand in *Beauharnais*. Justice Black agreed. The other justices did not want to abandon the *Beauharnais* case. The haunting memories involved in that issue were much more upsetting than in Jim's case.

At a meeting of the White Circle League, Joseph Beauharnais had passed around bundles of leaflets vilifying Negroes, calling them, among other things, robbers and carriers of knives. Under his instruction, volunteers handed out these leaflets on the streets of downtown Chicago. The city officials thought they had seen enough. A municipal judge fined the hate advocator $200. Illinois's criminal code forbade libeling any class of citizens, the judge said. Beauharnais appealed, challenging the constitutionality of the code.

In upholding the conviction, Associate Justice Felix Frankfurter spoke for the Court with detectable impatience. "Illinois did not have to look far beyond her own borders . . . to conclude that willful purveyors of falsehood concerning racial and religious groups promote strife . . . often [later] flaring into violence and destruction. In many of these outbreaks, utterances of the character here in question, so the Illinois legislature could conclude, played a significant part," he said.

Justice Frankfurter then cited the "Cicero riots" of the year before, in which an all-white apartment house was wrecked by a mob when a Negro bus driver and his family tried to move in. As further proof of his point, he recalled the "race war" in Springfield that shocked the nation in 1908 and led to the establishment of the National Association for the Advancement of Colored People. He recalled, too, the hate-crazed mob that in 1837 murdered the abolitionist printer Elijah Lovejoy, who died defending his presses.

He could have added that similar hate mongers, in 1844, had incited the lynching of Joseph Smith, the leader of the Mormon Church, plunging western Illinois into two years of bloody terror. Nor did he need to limit himself to Illinois. He could have related the tale of the pitched battles in St. Louis in August of 1854 between the Irish and the anti-Catholic "Know-Nothings," who later called themselves "The American Party." Incidents such as these would have added to his argument that group libelers justify group libel laws, even when there is no likelihood of immediate strife.

Justice Black, however, reasoned differently. He wrote a dissenting opinion and read it from the bench. "The motives behind the state law may have been to do good," he conceded. He then claimed the group libel law was, nevertheless, state censorship and was at war with the Bill of Rights. "History," he said, "indicates that urges to do good have led to the burning of books and even to the burning of 'witches.' " Then Black pointed out that the same reasoning under which Beauharnais was fined could be used to send integrationists to jail in other states.

It was obvious that he and Douglas, feeling no sympathy for Illinois's libel law, also felt none for Louisiana's, especially since Jim was convicted for criticizing public officials. Despite the questions raised about the integrity of the judiciary, both these justices put free speech first. They sympathized with the statement made by Associate Justice Arthur Goldberg, a President Kennedy appointee later to leave the Court and represent the United States before the United Nations.

Said Goldberg, "In *New York Times Co. v. Sullivan* . . . I expressed my conviction 'that the Constitution accords citizens and press an unconditional freedom to criticize official conduct.' . . . *New York Times* was a civil case; this is a criminal libel prosecution. In my view, if the rule that libel on government has no place in our Constitution is to have real meaing, then libel [criminal or civil] on the official conduct of the governors likewise can have no place in our Constitution."

Brennan again spoke for the majority. He did not want to go quite as far as Black, Douglas, or Goldberg. He noted, however, that the Louisiana courts had based Jim Garrison's conviction solely on two counts. The state supreme court had found that the evidence supported a finding of ill will, enmity, or wanton desire to injure. In addition, the trial judge had said, "It is inconceivable to me that the Defendant could have had a reasonable belief, which could be defined as an honest belief, that not one but all eight of these Judges of the Criminal District Court were guilty of what he charged them with. . . ."

A reasonable belief, according to the trial judge, was one that "an ordinarily prudent man might be able to assign a just and fair reason for. . . ." Brennan and the majority of the Supreme Court justices ruled that this was not an adequate basis for a conviction. It was not enough that, possibly, reasonable care might have led Jim to think differently. There had to be proof that he knew his statements were false or proof that he made his statements with a high degree of awareness of their probable falsity. Under the standards laid down in *New York Times Co. v. Sullivan,* the Louisiana law was unconstitutional in limiting free criticism of public officials. Thus, criticism was to be protected.

Meanwhile, as we shall see in the next chapter, an even more inflammatory question faced the justices.

"To Err Politically"

DR. Corliss Lamont of New York, a writer and college lecturer on Soviet affairs, had come to the Government's attention on previous occasions. Lamont's history, in fact, was tied up with a number of civil rights issues.

To begin with, Lamont had written a letter to the *New York Times* criticizing the Supreme Court's 1951 decision broadening the application of the clear and present danger test and upholding the conviction of eleven Communists. The case was called *Dennis v. United States.* The eleven were charged with violating a law called the Smith Act. Under the provisions of that act, they were convicted of conspiring to organize the Communist party of the United States as a group to teach and advocate the overthrow of the government by force and violence.

Lamont, among others, insisted the Smith Act was unconstitutional. The men had not been convicted of any act of violence, or even of inflammatory speech, but for what they intended to say and do at a later date. Lamont was aware that those who defended the law and the Court decision claimed that whatever right might exist to advocate revolution against a tyrannical government did not exist in the United States where the right to vote, the right to lobby, and the power to amend the Constitution provided the machinery for orderly change. Lamont agreed that we did have the machinery for peaceful change but said we were surrendering the country's birthright when we denied citizens the liberty to preach otherwise.

In spite of the fact that the objectors were joined by Justices Black and Douglas, the majority of the Court, led by Chief Justice Fred Vinson, stuck to the opinion of the court of appeals judge, Learned Hand. Judge Hand was impressed by the fact that the Communists were a highly disciplined organization adept at masking their purposes and infiltrating into strategic positions. He pointed to Communist aggression in Europe and felt that the defendants "were acting in close concert with this movement." In addition, he reviewed the finding of the jury in the lower court. "The jury has found that the conspirators will strike as soon as success seems possible," he said. Hand feared that any national catastrophe or emergency might give them their chance.

He decided that when agitators posed this much of a threat to society they should be stopped, even if the danger these men sought to bring about was not certain to occur immediately.

Many who agreed with Lamont answered that words likely to bring about a danger in the indefinite future should be met with Brandeis' formula of more speech. They in turn were answered by other citizens, who insisted that advocating was not merely speech or the expression of an idea but was a call to action, now or in the future.

The tumult over the eleven Communists and the Dennis decision had anything but died down when, in September of 1953, Lamont received a subpoena. The subpoena was an order commanding Lamont to appear on the twenty-third of that month, at 2:30 in the afternoon, at the United States Court House on Foley Square in New York City. The order was signed "Joe McCarthy." United States Senator Joseph R. McCarthy was chairman of the Subcommittee on Investigation of the Committee on Government Operations. He was also chairman of the full Committee on Government Operations. Needless to say, Lamont appeared.

Lamont, it seemed, had written a book entitled *The Peoples of the Soviet Union*. He was also the author of one chapter in another book called *U.S.S.R., A Concise Handbook*. McCarthy said that these writings had been purchased by the Army and used to "indoctrinate our troops." The Senator wanted to know more about the political motives of the author of this material used for teaching soldiers. Lamont insisted that "I am a loyal American and I am not now and never have been a member of the Communist Party."

McCarthy then asked him a number of questions: Did he know that the editor of the *Handbook* was a member of the Communist party? Did he know whether various other people were Communists? Had any Communists advised or instructed Mr. Lamont in his writings? How much time had Mr. Lamont spent in Russia?

Lamont did not answer the questions. Instead, he cited the First Amendment and objected to any investigation into his "beliefs" or "any other personal and private affairs" or his "associational activities." Congress had no power to make such an investigation, except for the purpose of planning legislation, he claimed. Therefore, he challenged McCarthy's authority to ask him these questions.

McCarthy reported the incident to the rest of the Senate. The angry lawmakers agreed to have the United States attorney in New

York bring Lamont before a grand jury. There, the attorney was to try to get the jurors to indict Lamont for contempt of the Senate. If indicted, he could be put on trial for the offense.

The indictment was secured but then the lower courts dismissed it. McCarthy's queries were not pertinent to any work that Congress had assigned to his committee. Therefore, said the judge, the Senator could not force Lamont to answer the interrogation.

That ended the prosecution of Lamont, but it did not end the congressional interrogation issue and it did not end Lamont's involvement in the closely related question of a teacher's or author's academic freedom. He was to come back into the story.

The next step in the development of the issue came in May of 1954. Lloyd Barenblatt, a thirty-one-year-old college instructor who was unemployed, was called before members of the House Committee on Un-American Activities. He sat at a wooden table facing six congressmen and refused to answer their question: "Are you now, or have you ever been, a member of the Communist Party?" He was admittedly afraid that having been called before the committee would hurt his chances of getting decent work. Barenblatt, like Lamont, did not claim the Fifth Amendment—he did not claim that answering the questions would incriminate him. He cited, instead, the First, the Ninth, and the Tenth Amendments to the Constitution.

He cited the First because of its guarantee of freedom of speech, which the courts have ruled includes freedom of association—i.e., the right to converse with anyone. He cited the Ninth and Tenth because they reserve for the states and the people all powers not given to the Federal Government.

Under these amendments, the youthful instructor concluded, Congress had no power to investigate except in connection with its power to legislate. It could not legislate against anything anyone had already said or written. By making him come here to testify, the committee was acting like a court. By the harassment of hearings, investigations, reports, and subpoenas the government was holding a club over speech. Subjecting him to all this, he argued, was like passing a bill of attainder.

A bill of attainder is the act of a legislature by which a man is punished without a court trial. Such bills were once a ruthless weapon, used when the King or Parliament wanted to dispose of various unpleasing persons and did not have enough evidence to put before a jury. The Constitution forbids the passing of a bill of attainder by either the states or the Federal Government. The congressmen on the Un-American Activities Committee did not consider that this was what they were doing. They considered that the witness was in contempt for refusing to answer their questions. They asked the Justice Department to get Barenblatt convicted in court.

This time the case went through the lower courts to the Supreme Court. After reading the facts, the justices were deeply divided. Five of them agreed with the sentiments of the investigating congressmen: that the House of Representatives had given its committee the authority to make the investigation; that, in fact, the committee's plan to interrogate educators as to their Communistic activities had been discussed even before Congress gave the committee its money; that Congress already had worked on legislation to protect the nation from subversives; and that for all these reasons the questions asked Barenblatt were pertinent. Therefore, Congress was within its rights to demand that they be answered. The instructor had been convicted in the lower courts and sentenced to six months in jail and a $250 fine. The conviction should stand.

The four dissenting justices, almost half the Court, were outraged. In the first place, three of them said, the House had given the committee the power to compel witnesses to give evidence about "un-American propaganda." The phrase was so vague it was frightening. In the future it could be applied to any unpopular idea. In the second place, Congress had overstepped its bounds by acting like a court. It was, actually, trying Barenblatt and other witnesses and punishing them because they were, or had been, Communists or because they refused to admit or deny Communist affiliations. The punishment was subjecting them to public humiliation. Of course, members of the Communist party who violated the laws should be punished, but *only* through the courts. Government committees should not be engaged in "exposing" people for their past affiliations.

Such practices, the dissenters said, ignore

the interest of the people as a whole in being able to join organizations, advocate causes and make political "mistakes" without later being subject to governmental penalties. . . . It is this right, the right to err politically, which keeps us strong as a Nation. . . . The obloquy which results from investigations such as this not only stifles "mistakes" but prevents all but the most courageous from hazarding any views which might at some later time become disfavored. This result . . . is doubly crucial when it affects the universities, on which we must largely rely for the experimentation and development of new ideas essential to our country's welfare.

In support of their argument, the dissenting justices pointed out that once the followers of Thomas Jefferson had been considered subversives. Later, abolitionists were considered revolutionaries of the most dangerous sort. The dissenters feared for a future where most people, in order to stay out of trouble, would never examine a new idea or look into the proposals of a new group. Such a state of affairs should be avoided no matter how undesirable the Communists were.

Associate Justice Harlan answered the dissenters and announced the Court's official position on June 8, 1959, a day in Washington that was made warm not only by the weather but also by the high temperatures this issue generated. Harlan himself was calm. Considered by many to be a sound conservative, he was the tall, lean, balding grandson of another Supreme Court justice and came from a background of giving legal help to some of the big industries of the country. One wonders how many hours he spent between the tall red-brick walls that hid his tiny Georgetown garden, with its lovely cherry tree and its attractively placed shrubs, while he weighed the problems presented by this case.

"The power of inquiry has been employed by Congress throughout our history," he noted. Obviously the power was limited by the Bill of Rights, he said, but this time its use was justified by the Government's right of self-preservation. This was an investigation of advocacy or preparation to overthrow the government. Certainly, it included the right to identify a witness as a member of a revolutionary party. The Communists were not merely another political group. The record showed testimony concerning their revolutionary purposes and foreign domination. It also showed Congress' intent to legislate in this area. He concluded that "the balance between the individual and the governmental interests here at stake must be struck in favor of the latter. . . ." The conviction was upheld.

Before he finished, Harlan made a promise. Possibly he made it because of the dissenters' concern to protect new ideas coming out of schools and colleges. He said, "When academic teaching-freedom and its corollary learning-freedom, so essential to the well-being of the Nation, are claimed, this Court will always be on the alert against intrusion by Congress. . . ." In other words, the Court was pledged to protect academic freedom.

A year and a half later a different application of that pledge was tested. In November, 1960, the case of the Arkansas schoolteachers came before the justices. The teachers had no tenure. They could find themselves without a job at the end of any school year. On top of this, a law was passed saying that, to be rehired, teachers had to list the names of all organizations to which they had belonged for the last five years. Ernest T. Gephardt, a high school teacher in Little Rock, resisted the order. A college professor named Max Carr also refused to make out the list.

During the court proceedings it was shown that they had nothing to hide. Gephardt was a member of the American Legion and of the Arkansas Educational Association. Both men were willing to swear they were not subversives. They were confident they could answer any question as to their teaching competence. Not making out the list was a matter of conscience and the Bill of Rights. They simply felt that it was not up to the school system to inquire into their private associations. When they were not rehired, they had brought this suit not only for themselves but for others in the same position. One of their colleagues was a member of a civil rights group which was nationally respected but very unpopular in segregation-minded Arkansas. He also resisted the law. Others wondered how teachers across the country would be affected if this type of regulation became widespread. Obviously, the list had to include what church the person attended and, in many instances, would show which major party a teacher had supported at the last election. Job applicants could be chosen accordingly.

Carr and Gephardt must have been pleased when the Supreme Court was firm in support of their position. School boards have the right to examine job applicants, but the Arkansas inquiry into the private affairs of teachers by a government agency was too broad to be constitutional, the majority felt. They said, "The pressure on a teacher to avoid any ties which might displease those who control his professional destiny would be constant and heavy." This was not in keeping with freedom of association and freedom of inquiry, both of which the Court felt were part of freedom of speech. Besides, the Court said, "Scholarship cannot flourish in an atmosphere of suspicion and distrust. Teachers and students must always remain free to inquire, to study and to evaluate." The justices might have added, "in and out of the classroom."

It was several years after the schoolteacher episode when the college lecturer on Soviet affairs, Dr. Corliss Lamont, re-entered the picture. He too had a problem in studying and evaluating. Lamont, who was busy putting out a series of pamphlets on international issues, was incensed because he had received the following notice from the post office: "This office is holding unsealed mail matter addressed to you from a foreign country . . . [and] the Secretary of the Treasury has determined this mail to be Communist political propaganda. It cannot be delivered to you unless you have subscribed to it, or otherwise want it." Lamont was then instructed to mark on an enclosed card that he wanted this mail and return it to the post office.

The Post Office Department, in cooperation with the Bureau of Customs, was acting under a law passed by Congress. The idea was to avoid subsidizing Communist propaganda. The lawmakers felt that using the United States mails to deliver propaganda to people who did not want it was helping the Communists spread their material.

Lamont, however, did not want his name put on a list of people desiring to receive Communist propaganda. He wanted his mail, but he did not mark the enclosed card. Instead, he started suit and took his case to the Supreme Court.

The justices could, of course, remember all the past controversy that had whirled around him. Nevertheless, the Court listened to his arguments. It was easy for the justices to see that the publisher of pamphlets might need Communist periodicals in order to predict, explain, or report on attitudes or events overseas. It was also easy to imagine that political science teachers, news commentators, or others might fear they would invite disaster if they read what the government said contained seeds of treason.

As it happened, Lamont's case was heard at the same time as the case of Leif Heilberg. And Mr. Heilberg's complaint was a good example of what could happen under the post office practice. He had immigrated from Denmark to California and he wanted to become an American citizen. The United States seemed like a proper home for him, a man with both convictions and ideas. As one of his interests, he belonged to the Universal Esperanto Association. Esperanto is an artificial language made up of words from many European tongues. Those who sponsor it believe it could be easily learned by men of many lands and hence promote international communication and understanding.

Leif Heilberg was going ahead with his plans and his interests when he got the same notice from the Post Office Department that Lamont had received. He was frightened. The Universal Esperanto Association has never been listed as an undesirable group by the

Justice Department, but because of it Heilberg received a good deal of mail from Communist countries. He was afraid that indicating he desired to receive this mail would endanger his getting his citizenship. He went to a lawyer. The lawyer took the case into the California federal district court, where the post office practice was declared unconstitutional under the First Amendment. The Government appealed to the Supreme Court.

Justice Douglas delivered the opinion of the Court in May, 1965. In upholding the California court, he quoted Associate Justice Oliver Wendell Holmes that "the use of the mails is almost as much a part of free speech as the right to use our tongues. . . ." Nothing, Douglas insisted, should deter a citizen from receiving his mail. This law was certainly a deterrent, he felt. He said, "The Act sets administrative officials astride the flow of mail to inspect it, appraise it, write the addressee about it, and await a response before dispatching the mail. . . . [Because] any addressee is likely to feel some inhibition in sending for literature which federal officials have condemned . . . this Act is at war with the 'uninhibited, robust, and wide-open' debate and discussion that are contemplated by the First Amendment." Thus he ended by quoting the *New York Times* case.

It is amazing that one lawsuit should have affected so many different kinds of people. It is amazing, too, how many different kinds of "clear and present danger" the Court has to consider—danger to a free press, danger to robust and wide-open debate, danger to academic freedom and new ideas, as well as danger caused by revolutionists threatening national security. As a result of these many cases, millions of people can safely read all the news, receive all their mail, and express their views freely. Most of them paid no attention to the *New York Times* case; they have never heard of the Louisiana district attorney, Jim Garrison, or of the California linguist, Leif Heilberg. They are, therefore, unaware that it takes constant effort and constant vigilance, not only by judges and lawmakers but also by their neighbors—neighbors like the Arkansas schoolteachers—to preserve this kind of a free society and "to secure these rights."

"Constitutionally Intolerable"

Two days after Christmas, in 1963, two state law enforcement officers cruised up the streets of San Antonio, Texas. They were out to search the white frame house at 1118 West Rosewood, where homeowner John W. Stanford, Jr., carried on a mail-order book and pamphlet business under the trade name "All Points of View." Two credible people—so District Attorney James E. Barlow said —had reported that Stanford had in his possession records of the Communist party, including lists and dues payments. The information seemed reasonable, since Stanford had been mailing out material that Barlow and the two officers considered to be Communist propaganda.

The men had reason to feel confident as they walked up to Stanford's door. They carried a search warrant obtained from a county judge.

Stanford was not at home. His wife opened the door. The officers soon found themselves in a maze of books and papers. With the help of several investigators, they searched for hours. Still, they found no record of Communist party or any party lists or dues payments. Their warrant, however, was broadly written. It ordered the men to take possession of "books," "pamphlets," and "other written instruments" relating to the operations of the Communist party in Texas. How broadly it could be interpreted became dramatically clear later when the court learned what the officers packed into fourteen cartons and hauled out of the house. Among other papers they had Stanford's marriage certificate, insurance policies, and private letters. Among the books they took were works by Associate Justice Black and by Pope John XXIII.

Some of this may have been taken by mistake. Most of it was taken on the theory that Stanford's books and documents were the instruments of his operation. Texas officials would have been willing to hand back a few of his private letters. When, however, the magistrate who had issued the warrant refused to quash it or throw it out, Stanford hired a lawyer to take his case to the Supreme Court.

Stanford's lawyer may have counted on the fact that the justices are always wary of searches and seizures that involve books and papers, and he expected that the justices would view Stanford's books differently than they would view a dope addict's needle or a bank robber's gun. He knew that under certain conditions a policeman does not even need a warrant to seize instruments of crime such as these, nor does he always need a warrant to seize stolen goods. The policeman is allowed to decide that a suspect, being legitimately arrested, is likely to commit an assault with a weapon or is likely to destroy evidence of crime. He may then—at the time of the arrest—take the gun or the goods. When he does go out with a warrant, he can be trusted to decide that what he finds is an illicit narcotic or a lethal weapon. But the justices are not willing to let him decide what is an objectionable idea, an obscene or treasonous writing.

The justices are very strict with the police. They feel that a warrant to search a man's papers can be a warrant to invade his privacy; a warrant to seize papers can be a warrant to grab a citizen's most personal possessions. Moreover, this can happen before the citizen has been proved guilty of anything, for, to make police work possible, warrants have to be issued if there is at least "probable cause" for them. Therefore, to protect the privacy of the innocent, the justices require the warrant to state what paper or what book is to be seized.

Equally important to the justices is the age-old relation between "search and seizure" and freedom of speech, press, and religion. "Search and seizure" was one method by which the Tudor and the Stuart kings of England uncovered religious and political dissenters such as Catholics, Puritans, and so-called libelers of the crown. Armed with "general warrants" that did not specify where they were to search or what was to be seized, the King's messengers roamed the countryside, ransacking homes while looking for forbidden religious or political literature.

Since this treatment of subjects was legal in England, it was therefore also legal in England's colonies in the new world—that is, for a while it was. Then things began to happen. They started happening on a February afternoon in 1761.

Court was in session in the council chamber of Boston's Old Town House. James Otis rose from his chair at the attorney's table. Usually his demeanor was that of a round-faced, smiling patriot. That day, a spectator said, he "was a flame of fire."

He was there to speak against those general warrants, the writs of assistance. "A person with this writ," said Otis, "may enter all houses, shops, etc., at will, and command all to assist him." The writs were "the worst instrument of arbitrary power . . . [placing] the liberty of every man in the hands of every petty officer. . . . [In addition,] every man prompted by revenge, ill humor, or wantonness to inspect the inside of his neighbor's house, may get a Writ of Assistance."

Listening to Otis, and enthroned around the hall's fireplace, were the five Colonial judges, wearing robes of scarlet and traditional long wigs. Farther back in the big square chamber, and crowded together, sat the worried merchants of Boston; looking down from the wall, as if still alive, were the full-length portraits of the Stuart kings, Charles II and James II. Yes, Charles II had issued general warrants with a heavy hand, but those days were gone, Otis argued. With every word he uttered Otis showed his conviction that England had left behind the idea that kings had a divine right to rule as they pleased, a concept that still bound subjects in European countries. In 1215, the Magna Carta put the Constitution above the King, and English subjects had again claimed their due during the revolution of 1688, which brought forth the English Bill of Rights. Otis was therefore demanding the rights of an Englishman. "This writ," he said, "is against the fundamental principles of English law." An Englishman, Otis insisted, was entitled to be "as secure in his house as a prince in his castle."

Otis then claimed something more. Man was born with inalienable rights to liberty and justice. No mortal monarch was at liberty to disregard the rule that "an act against natural equity is void." To prove his point, Otis reminded the judges how the exercise of arbitrary power had cost "one King of England [Charles I] his head and another [James II] his throne."

Seated as close to Otis as one could get, and hanging on every word, was a future President of the United States, young John Adams. "Then and there," Adams said years later, "then and there the child independence was born." For many a man left the room ready to take up arms against the writs.

Otis did not win his case, but he did win the ever-growing support of his countrymen. Indirectly, he probably had another effect. Old letters, on paper long since turned brown, reveal that Otis was in correspondence with one John Wilkes, Member of Parliament. Not long after the Boston episode, Wilkes, who was a daredevil, decided to strike a blow at general warrants.

Wilkes put out a publication called the *North Briton*. In April of

1763, No. 45 of the *North Briton* attacked the King's ministers as "tools of despotism." A week later the Secretary of State sent out a general warrant. The King's messengers were to hunt the authors, printers, and publishers of the *North Briton* No. 45 and, "any of them having found, to . . . seize together with their papers." While arresting nearly fifty suspects, they finally heard about Wilkes. He refused to even stand up for the searchers, and the King's men carried him out of his house still seated in his chair. While Wilkes was being thrown into the Tower of London, locksmiths broke open his bureau drawers. The King's messengers carted away his private papers. Wilkes responded by suing the messengers.

Wilkes was lucky. At the time, Britain's chief justice of the Court of Common Pleas was a man named Charles Pratt. He is remembered by grateful jurists on both sides of the ocean as Lord Camden.

A portait of him painted by Sir Joshua Reynolds gives us a record of what Pratt looked like when the King's messengers appeared before him. His shoulders did not reach to the top of his chair. Long curls flowed down from his judge's wig and the messengers saw the long thin face and dark piercing eyes of a sensitive man.

Pratt told the King's messengers that theirs was "a ridiculous warrant against the whole English nation." He considered it outrageous "to enter a man's house by virtue of a nameless warrant, in order to procure evidence. It certainly may affect the person and property of every man in the Kingdom. . . ."

The messengers answered that they were acting under orders.

The great justice replied that they were trespassing. He refused to interfere when the jury allowed Wilkes 4,000 pounds in damages.

The story did not end there. Encouraged by Wilkes' daring, John Entick—an author suspected of criticizing the Crown—brought a similar complaint against another general warrant. And Lord Camden spoke again: The warrant against Entick was illegal. It was of a kind that allowed the messengers to rifle all of a subject's papers. His house could be entered and his most valuable secrets taken before the papers in question had been found to be criminal by any competent court. Courts and not enforcement officers were competent to weigh evidence and find guilt. It was certain, Lord Camden said, that English law called for the protection of the innocent. A man could not be made to "accuse himself," lest the innocent be pressured or tortured into a false confession. For the same reason the King's messengers could not be allowed to seize a man's papers in the hope of finding evidence. "There too the innocent would be confounded with the guilty."

Since no courts in England can overrule an act of Parliament, as the Supreme Court can void an act of Congress, Lord Camden could only affect the lawmakers indirectly. He could not stop the Townshend Act of 1767, which called for general warrants to be used against the American colonists. Eventually, though, his pronouncements did prevail with the English-speaking peoples. The House of Commons did pass resolutions against general warrants, and later, when the time came, Americans wrote the Fourth Amendment into the United States Constitution: "The right of the people to be secure in their persons, houses, papers, and effects, against unreasonable searches and seizures, shall not be violated, and no Warrants shall issue, but upon probable cause, supported by Oath or affirmation, and particularly describing the place to be searched, and the persons or things to be seized."

Time and again in upholding that amendment the Supreme Court justices have turned their attention back to Lord Camden. They quoted him in 1886 in *Boyd v. United States,* when a district attorney in a customs case demanded to see an importer's private papers in the hope of finding evidence against him. This the Court called an unreasonable search.

They quoted Lord Camden again in 1959 in the case of *Frank v. Maryland,* where the justices disagreed among themselves as to whether to uphold the enforcement of a health law. Gentry, a Baltimore Health Department inspector, had paced around Frank's shabby, broken-down home. Frank came around the side of the house and asked the inspector what he was doing. Gentry said he had found evidence of the presence of rats. He had. In the back of the building, mixed into a pile of straw, were rat feces. The inspector demanded to be let into Frank's basement. Frank refused. Gentry did not have a warrant, but nevertheless Frank was fined for his resistance.

Five of the Supreme Court justices noted that the Baltimore code governing health inspections was carefully written. Inspectors had to make their surveys in the daytime; they could not force their way into private premises. The fine for resisting their authority was small, $20. The majority of the Court, therefore, felt that the inconvenience to Frank was small in comparison to the importance of maintaining community health. They ruled to uphold the city code.

They did not rule, however, without hearing strong arguments against their stand from Justices Douglas, Brennan, and Black and Chief Justice Earl Warren. That the fine was small was not the measure of right, said the dissenters. "The right is the guarantee against invasion of the home by officers without a warrant. . . . Health inspections are important," they conceded. "But they are hardly more important than the search for narcotic peddlers, rapists, kidnappers, murderers, and other criminal elements." A policeman on the hunt needs a warrant to invade a private home. The public interest in protecting privacy is equally as great when a health inspector is at work, said Douglas, Brennan, Black, and Warren.

Gentry, they insisted, had abundant evidence of the existence of rats. He could have gone to a magistrate and gotten a warrant. He should have been required to do so. Baltimore's procedures, they claimed, diluted a provision of the Fourth Amendment that every American homeowner had a right to consider part of his heritage.

This dissent, along with its quotes from Lord Camden, went into the record. Even though the law had been upheld, the dissent was a message to future justices. Perhaps they might want to overturn the present ruling. The Court had tightened the application of the Fourth Admendment before.*

For example, starting in 1914, overeager federal prosecutors could be in trouble if they won a case with evidence illegally seized. The opposing lawyer could simply get the Supreme Court to nullify the judgment which they had worked so hard to obtain.

This rule had come out of a case called *Weeks v. United States.* In *Weeks* the justices had explained, "If letters and private documents can thus be seized [illegally] and held and used in evidence against a citizen accused of an offense, the protection of the Fourth Amendment declaring his right to be secure against such searches and seizures is of no value, and . . . might as well be stricken from the Constitution." The Court would throw out any federal conviction so obtained.

At the same time, the Court recognized the frustrated feelings of men like the Texas law enforcement officers trying to do their jobs. Daniel Gutman, the dean of New York Law School, has worded their feelings: "The criminal gets the breaks." The justices gave their answer to this view in *Weeks.*

"The efforts . . . to bring the guilty to punishment, praiseworthy as they are, are not to be aided by the sacrifice of those great principles established by years of endeavor and suffering which have re-

* In June of 1967 the Court did overrule Frank v. Maryland. Now, except in emergencies, an occupant can force an inspector to get a warrant identifying the authority of the searcher and keeping the search within legal bounds.

sulted in their embodiment in the fundamental law of the land." (But the *Weeks* rule only applied to the Federal courts.)

Then in 1961 the Court further decided it would have to apply the *Weeks* rule to the states. The case was called *Mapp v. Ohio.* Dollree Mapp lived in a house in Cleveland. Police officers broke open her back door and searched the rooms. When they uncovered indecent literature, Dollree was convicted for possessing it. At the trial no warrant was exhibited, and the justices had grave doubts that any warrant had ever existed.

A shocked Court decided to "close the only courtroom door remaining open to evidence secured by official lawlessness." Justice Clark, who gave the opinion, explained, "Having once recognized that . . . the right to be secure against rude invasions of privacy by State officers is . . . constitutional in origin, we can no longer permit that right to remain an empty promise."

Under this reasoning it was also necessary to forbid the states to use general warrants. The Kansas City police learned as much in a case called *Marcus v. Search Warrant,* decided in 1961. The police had, as the law required, found "probable cause" for their search. They also had, as was necessary, sworn to this before a magistrate and, as is also required, they named the specific places to be searched—five newsstands and a distributor. The judge issued the warrant and then the police seized all magazines, which they said in our judgment "were obscene." Two hundred and eighty publications were hauled back to the courthouse. Over two months later, only one hundred of these proved to be illegal.

The Supreme Court reversed every conviction the police obtained because the search had been conducted without "any safeguards to protect legitimate expression." As might have been expected, they quoted Lord Camden on the use of general warrants.

All this had taken place before the Stanford question came before the justices. When the day to decide that case arrived, Chief Justice Warren called on Associate Justice Potter Stewart to give the ruling. Stewart had been on the Supreme Court bench since 1958. He was a Republican from Ohio and was considered a cautious man.

Considering all the decisions that had preceded this one, it is not surprising that Stewart figuratively shook his head at the Texas attorney general; "it would be a needless exercise in pedantry to review again the detailed history of the use of general warrants as an instrument of oppression," he said. He referred the Texas lawyer to the earlier cases, from James Otis through *Marcus v. Search Warrant*.

There was no dissent. Stewart was speaking for all the justices. He quoted the Fourth Amendment, emphasizing the requirement for a warrant "particularly describing . . . the things to be seized." He then repeated Justice Douglas' comment in the case of the Baltimore health inspector. As to the First, Fourth, and Fifth Amendments, "These three amendments are indeed clearly related, safeguarding not only privacy and protection against self-incrimination but conscience and human dignity and freedom of expression as well."

Justice Stewart gave a warning. The command to describe "the things to be seized" is to be scrupulously obeyed, he said, especially when the "things" are books and the basis for their seizure is the ideas that they contain. As to what is to be taken, he quoted from an earlier case that "nothing is left to the discretion of the officer executing the warrant," and, as in other cases of search, the police cannot take one thing while searching for another.

Before he finished, Stewart characterized the language of the Texas warrant as "constitutionally intolerable. . . . To hold otherwise," he said, "would be false to the terms of the Fourth Amendment . . . and false to its history." He upset the ruling of the Texas magistrate, and he also paid tribute to Lord Camden. Stewart himself must have grinned as he wondered what Charles Pratt, Lord Camden, would have thought of the Communists. Perhaps he would have considered these men, who seek to bring about the workers' dictatorship, wild radicals. More likely he would have considered them fantastic reactionaries for believing that the governing group should seize and control everything.

In any case, the Fourth and the Fourteenth Amendments shielded John Stanford from having his home ransacked and his papers seized by virtue of a general warrant, partly because our Founding Fathers and the Supreme Court justices who came after them were aware of Lord Camden's wisdom. They knew that what can be applied to one unpopular group today can be applied to another unpopular group in the future. They wanted to protect both human dignity and freedom of expression.

The justices are not the only government officials wanting to preserve this precious heritage of the English-speaking peoples. In the same spirit Congress has outlawed disclosing information gained from intercepting telephone calls. In addition to protecting the public, the lawmaker himself wants to discuss confidential plans and carry on private conversations without having to worry whether someone is listening or how the eavesdropper will exploit or misinterpret some remark which was not carefully phrased because it was intended only for the ears of a friend.

Other forms of electronic eavesdropping have now been developed to a point that shocks both lawmakers and the President. Enforcement officers are already forbidden to intrude into private quarters in order to install these spying devices, and the Court has decided that before the police may electronically eavesdrop on a conversation which the speakers intend to keep private, the officers must have a precisely written court order. The problem is part of the struggle to protect both the effectiveness of government and the rights of all individuals.

Since we live in a world that is growing increasingly more crowded, we can expect that in the years ahead there will be more pressure to protect society. Health codes will grow in importance. As weapons become more dangerous, the fear of subversives and criminals will naturally increase. At the same time, we Americans have decreed that government officials are not to increase their authority by a series of abridgements of our liberties. Our privacy is basic to our free way of life. We do not want to lose our liberties while fighting to keep them from being destroyed by others.

BIBLIOGRAPHY FOR PART I

Principal Sources on Freedom of Speech and the Press

BOOKS

Buranelli, Vincent (ed.). *The Trial of Peter Zenger.* New York, 1957.
Current Biography. Published by the Wilson Co., New York, 1957.
Douglas, William O. *The Right of the People.* Garden City, 1958.
Lasson, Nelson B. *The History and Development of the Fourth Amendment of the United States Constitution.* Baltimore, 1937.
Levy, Leonard W. *Legacy of Suppression.* Massachusetts, 1960.
Locke, John. *Essay Concerning Human Understanding,* 2d ed. London, 1690.
Milton, John. *Areopagitica.* London, 1644.
Smith, James Morton. *Freedom's Fetters.* New York, 1956.
Tudor, William. *Life of James Otis.* Boston, 1823.

UNITED STATES FEDERAL RECORDS

Congressional Records
U.S. Congress, *Hearings Before the Permanent Subcommittee on Investigations of the Committee on Government Operations,* United States Senate, 83rd Congress, 1953.

Supreme Court Records (Transcripts and Records of Briefs)

 Abrams v. United States, 250 U.S. 616 (1919).

 Barenblatt v. United States, 360 U.S. 109 (1959).

 Beauharnais v. Illinois, 343 U.S. 250 (1952).

 Boyd v. United States, 116 U.S. 616 (1886).

 Bridges v. California, 314 U.S. 252 (1941).

 Dennis v. United States, 341 U.S. 494 (1951).

 Frank v. Maryland, 359 U.S. 360 (1959).

 Garrison v. Louisiana, 379 U.S. 64 (1964).

 Lamont v. Postmaster, 381 U.S. 301 (1964).

 Mapp v. Ohio, 367 U.S. 643 (1961).

 Marcus v. Search Warrant, 367 U.S. 717 (1961).

 New York Times Co. v. Sullivan, 376 U.S. 254 (1964).

 Roth v. United States, 354 U.S. 476 (1957).

 Schenck v. United States, 249 U.S. 47 (1919).

 Shelton v. Tucker, 364 U.S. 479 (1960).

 Stanford v. Texas, 379 U.S. 476 (1964).

 Weeks v. United States, 232 U.S. 383 (1914).

 Whitney v. California, 274 U.S. 357 (1927).

MAGAZINE

Kalven, Harry, Jr. "The New York Times Case." *The Supreme Court Review,* 1964.

PART TWO

CITIZENS

WHO ORGANIZE

FOR ACTION

"Congress shall make no law . . . abridging . . . the right of the people peaceably to assemble, and to petition the Government for a redress of grievances."

—First Amendment

". . . the accused shall enjoy the right to a speedy and public trial, by an impartial jury . . . and to have the Assistance of Counsel for his defence."

—Sixth Amendment

THE RIGHTS AND THE ISSUES

Group lobbying, or petitioning the government, has been essential to the American way of life since before the Revolution.

"Our repeated Petitions have been answered only by repeated Injury," said the signers of the Declaration of Independence, in explaining their break with England.

Since freedom of speech and the right to petition would have less political value if citizens could not first gather and meet to exchange ideas and solicit support for their views and complaints, freedom peacefully to assemble as well as freedom of petition are among the most cherished rights of American citizens.

When, in 1836, southerners in the House of Representatives managed to get a "gag" rule passed to have all petitions relating to slavery "laid on the table" (that is, not considered), they did more to strengthen the abolitionist cause than all the firebrands screaming for emancipation. As William Jay, son of the first Chief Justice, wrote, "We commenced the present struggle to obtain the freedom of the slave; we are compelled to continue it to preserve our own."

Ex-President John Quincy Adams was no abolitionist, but he had as violent a reaction. He was serving in Congress, and he fought the "gag" rule on the floor of the House, rallying the northern liberals with all the fire that earned him the name of "Old Man Eloquent."

Since then the issues that have arisen in the course of preserving freedom of assembly and petition have not been easy. Sometimes an outdoor rally looks like the beginning of a riot. Sometimes a street meeting obstructs traffic or disturbs the peace.

The courts, the public, and the Congress have had to cope with the needs of the aggrieved and the needs of society, ever aware that almost all major reformers in the United States, including suffragists, labor organizers, and Negro leaders, have depended as much on the right to assemble and petition as on the right to free speech. Justices and statesmen are mindful, too, that the Founding Fathers, realizing the relationship between these freedoms, purposefully combined them into the same amendment. They knew that not everything would always be well with the Republic, and they expected there would always be some individuals and groups who would want to stand apart from the satisfied and cry out for what they believed was justice.

Here follow three American sagas in which the need of the people to assemble peacefully and petition the Government for a redress of a grievance played a vital role.

"In the Eye of the Law Civilly Dead"

LUCRETIA Coffin, born on the island of Nantucket in 1793, was destined to be one of four ladies who would one day meet and plot to change the course of American history. Their story is one of the most inspiring episodes in the chronicles of freedom of assembly and the right to petition for the redress of a grievance. As dedicated reformers they fought together; but first they separately developed an understanding of the evils of their time, of what rights they had, and of what rights they needed.

Lucretia, the oldest of these ladies, was fortunate—her father saw to it that she got an education. Thomas Coffin was a whaling captain in the East India trade. When he gave up the sea and moved his family to Boston, he discovered that girls were allowed to go to public elementary schools for only two hours a day. Public high schools for girls were a thing of the future. Lucretia's parents were Quakers and, since little public education was available, she was sent to a Quaker school.

Being a Quaker gave Lucretia another advantage: She learned to stand on her feet and speak in church. Nowhere outside of a Quaker meeting house were females given a chance to express themselves in public. To many, the idea that they should address an audience which included men was fantastic and repugnant.

In 1809, at the age of sixteen, Lucretia became a schoolteacher —the only profession open to women at the time. At the Nine Partners School, in spite of the fact that she was expected to do the same work as a male instructor, she was paid only half of a man's salary. Lucretia's soul rebelled. Then and there she took her first psychological step toward becoming a reformer.

In 1811 Lucretia took the next step toward her destiny. She married a tall, flaxen-haired abolitionist named James Mott. Crusading for abolition gave Lucretia ample experience in using the power of assembly to influence public opinion. Though short and frail, she held herself like a queen, and she made an excellent preacher to help James in his work against Negro slavery.

Three years later, and unknown to the Motts, Judge and Mrs. Daniel Cady of Johnstown, New York, announced the birth of their daughter Elizabeth. Since Judge Cady was an affluent attorney who

worked at home, Elizabeth grew up curiously watching women
clients leave the house in tears. Finally she asked why this was, and
her father explained it to her. Simply because these were women, he
said, all their property—what they inherited and what they earned
—belonged to their husbands, even when these husbands were
spendthrifts or drunkards.

American law came from British common law. Blackstone's
words were, therefore, applicable: "By marriage, the very being or
legal existence of a woman is suspended. . . ."

That meant that a woman could not, without her husband's consent, sue if she were injured or enter into a contract. Her husband
was guardian of her children; he could take their custody from his
wife. Almost no professions were open to women, and spinsters
were not only looked down upon but by tradition subject to the
control of the men of the household, so most women hastened to
get married. But marriage, as the future suffrage workers would
put it, made them "in the eye of the law civilly dead."

When Judge Cady showed his little daughter the relevant pages
in the law books, Elizabeth tried to cut away the offensive words
with a pair of scissors. The incident earned her no end of teasing
from her father's law clerks, who gleefully noted that one day the
very clothes on her back would belong to her spouse. They saw
Elizabeth's anger but, of course, could not see that their stinging
words were going to alter their country's future.

Meanwhile, on a rocky Massachusetts farm, young Lucy Stone
was helping her parents with their arduous chores. The cows needed
milking, the laundry, weaving, and sewing had to be done by hand;
the job of picking berries also occupied the girl's time. One day,
when she was sixteen, a simple event changed Lucy's future. She
was attending a regular meeting of the village church sewing circle.
While the ladies sewed they listened to a talk given by a muscular,
redheaded woman named Mary Lyon. Mary had an idea. Though
many people thought it both crazy and sinful, she was going to start
an institution of higher education for women. Lucy deliberately put
down her needle. She would use her spare time from now on to
earn money to go to college. Women's wages in those days were
meager—$16 a month, or even less, for teaching a school. Lucy
was twenty-five before she got to college. Mary had already started
Mount Holyoke but Lucy finally went to Oberlin, founded in 1833
and, since 1841, the first college to give degrees to women.

At Oberlin Lucy had a stormy history. Or course, the college did
not permit women students to speak in public. Nevertheless, Lucy,

with her usual beguiling sweetness, persuaded an indiscreet professor to let her take part in a public debate with men classmates. In addition to that, she spoke from the platform at a meeting organized by Negroes. Oberlin already admitted Negroes, the first college to do so, but that did not mean that a lady could speak from a platform in mixed company with males, white or colored. Worst of all, when called to account, Lucy told the Ladies' Board that she saw nothing out of place in all this shocking conduct. What the Ladies' Board did not know was that Lucy had organized a secret society of girl students, which met off campus to practice public speaking.

By some miracle, and due in large measure to her sweet voice and gentle manners, she was allowed to graduate in 1847 in spite of her infractions. A year after she was out of Oberlin, Lucy joined the Massachusetts Anti-Slavery Society and went out giving public lectures for abolition. Many audiences were polite, but not all. At times she was met by jeers. An egg or even a prayerbook might be hurled at her. Some of the rowdies were against abolition; others were against a woman not keeping her place. The other women in Lucy's family told her that putting herself in this position was a disgrace. Lucy replied that she couldn't give up, or "I would forever despise Lucy Stone."

Before long, Lucy was in trouble even with the advanced thinkers in the antislavery society. At assembly after assembly, Lucy was injecting spirited comments for women's rights. When the men complained, Lucy answered, "I was a woman before I was an abolitionist."

Then she compromised. She spoke against slavery when sponsored by the society, but in addition she went out by herself, at her own expense, to face the hostile crowds and raise her single voice for women. It was a lonely life.

By that time another Quaker, Susan B. Anthony, had, like Lucretia Mott, become a schoolteacher. Susan's background included a better-than-average education. It included, also, the painful memory of having seen her mother's furniture and family silver sold to pay her father's debts. Daniel Anthony had been ruined by the financial panic of 1837. Susan had gone out to teach and, like Lucretia, lived through the humiliation of being paid less than her male colleagues. Besides this, Susan was led into being a reformer by her will to fight the evils of alcohol; in addition to being an abolitionist, she was a temperance worker. Unlike the others, though, she was a shy girl and at first not overeager to speak out in public. She was to force herself to overcome this as she ran into prejudice against her sex in both her teaching and her temperance work. Susan was to decide that she must speak up.

At last the hour struck for these women to meet. In 1840 Lucretia and James were attending an antislavery convention in England. No sooner had they reached their London boardinghouse than an unpleasantness occurred. The Motts were made to understand that, because Lucretia was a woman, the conference was not going to accept her as a bona fide delegate. Also staying at the boardinghouse was a young woman on her honeymoon. Much to the disgust of Judge Cady, Elizabeth had married the abolitionist Henry Stanton. When all Henry Stanton and James Mott could do was to get Lucretia and the other woman delegates admitted to the gallery of the convention hall, without the right to be recognized or heard, Elizabeth and Lucretia set up an alliance. It was an alliance, though, that had to bide its time.

For the next eight years, Elizabeth was busy having and rearing her children and Lucretia was busy fighting for abolition. Then in 1848 they met again in the sleepy little factory town of Seneca Falls, New York. Henry Stanton had moved his family there. The Motts were visiting close by. Things began to happen. Elizabeth and Lucretia sent a notice to the local papers: "WOMEN'S RIGHTS CONVENTION . . . will be held in the Wesleyan Chapel . . . on Wednesday and Thursday the 19 and 20 of July current; commencing at ten o'clock A.M."

Thus finally women were to assemble for the first convention to demand women's rights. They came by wagon. They came on foot. Many of them came because they were poor women who had to work and thought it unjust that their menfolk could not only choose their tasks but also take their wages. Elizabeth Stanton, thanks to the teaching of her father's clerks, knew what state laws needed to be changed to help these people. Lucretia Mott knew how to impress an audience. Neither of them had ever conducted a meeting, and James Mott kindly agreed to preside.

In the discussion, Lucretia was as restrained as her plain bonnet and modest Quaker dress. Elizabeth appeared plump and fashionable and bold. With many emotion-packed words, she told the ladies that it "is the duty of the women of this country to secure to themselves their sacred right to the elective franchise."

Lucretia had warned her against this proposal, saying, "Why, Lizzie, thee will make us ridiculous."

Shocked silence greeted Elizabeth's words, yet she persisted. Doubtless she realized that, to secure their other rights, women would need the right to vote. Following her proposal, the discussion was lively. Might not such a demand hurt the cause? women wondered. Finally Elizabeth convinced the majority. The ladies voted for woman suffrage, and a great campaign had begun. This first convention was soon followed by another at Rochester, New York.

Newspapers reporting on all this called the ladies' demands for rights and a vote "impractical, absurd, and ridiculous!" But the newspapers gave the ladies what they needed—publicity. Susan B. Anthony heard about the conventions from her family. Lucy Stone must have read about them.

In 1850, Lucy and a few friends were the instigators of a women's rights convention, organized by Paulina W. Davis and held at Worcester, Massachusetts. It was no mean achievement. Conventions are expensive, and even those women who wanted their rights had no access to the family funds. Lucy, though, was spurred on by the great abolitionist William Lloyd Garrison, who had already been all but lynched during his own crusade.

"There never was a movement that began so small and so poor as the antislavery movement," Garrison told Lucy, "but it was rich in truth, and because it was . . . it will succeed. Yours is just as true. . . . Never be discouraged."

When the day came and the convention met in Brinley Hall, there were over a thousand people present. There were even participants from far-off California, which had only been a state for a matter of weeks. The famous editor of the New York *Tribune,* Horace Greeley, was there, and so was Lucy's future sister-in-law, Elizabeth Blackwell, the first woman in the United States to hold a medical degree. Lucretia Mott was there and Elizabeth Stanton sent a message of support. Lucy was no longer alone.

Susan Anthony saw an account of the speech that Lucy had delivered in Horace Greeley's *Tribune* and was immediately fascinated. She wanted to meet Lucy and Elizabeth. A temperance friend, Amelia Bloomer, arranged for the meeting in Seneca Falls.

At the time Susan came on the scene, the others were attempting to reform women's fashions. A cousin of Elizabeth's, a Mrs. Miller, had shortened her skirts by a good twelve inches, to a point only a few inches below the knee. Under the skirt she wore frilly leggings pulled tight around her ankles. The effect was sensational. Amelia Bloomer at once recommended, in her temperance newspaper, *The Lily,* that the costume be generally adopted. Women would be able to move faster and more freely. Mrs. Miller's leggings were soon named "bloomers," after Amelia, who publicized them. Susan tried to be cooperative and wear them as Lucy and Elizabeth did, but the hoots and jeers of startled little boys in the streets were too much for this shy woman. Encouraged by Elizabeth's kindness, Susan soon put on her long skirt again.

Susan, nevertheless, was now a full-fledged member of the group. She and Elizabeth set to work to abolish New York's discriminatory laws against women. They decided that Elizabeth with her wit and humor should address the legislature. For the lawmakers to be impressed, however, Susan would have to gather petitions showing that women wanted the reform.

A number of the ladies conducted meetings in various parts of New York to educate the female public. Then Susan set out to travel the length and breadth of the state, gathering petitions. It was a mammoth undertaking. Only at times was a train available to get from one town to another. More often Susan was bounced in a carriage with wooden wheels over muddy, rutted roads. In sleet and snow she got from one community to another in a horse-drawn sleigh, hugging the sleigh blanket over her knees. Once she reached a town, the job got worse. Through snow and mud, in skirts that barely cleared the ground, she trudged from house to house. The prim homemakers who answered their door knockers and saw Susan standing there had been warned against these feminists.

"Fanatical radicals" and "fugitive lunatics," one newspaper article called them. Often a woman's own clergyman had denounced the suffragists as trying to step out of their God-given sphere. Woman's work was at home. She did not belong out voting or entering the professions, and there was no need for her to own her own property or wages. To demand such things was sinful folly.

If a woman believed all this, it was little use for Susan to point out the plight of a mother who couldn't feed her children because her drunken husband seized whatever she could earn.

Despite the opposition she faced, Susan and her workers collected so many names on their petitions that in 1860 the New York legislature changed the law. The lawmakers gave women control over their property and their earnings and joint control, with their husbands, over their children. They gave women the right to sue if injured and the right to make contracts or agreements.

All this was revolutionary progress, even if women still couldn't vote, and it had all been achieved by the power of assembly and petition. No lives had been lost, no blood shed. Moreover, once the legislature acted, the press began to change its attitude and to take the women's demands seriously. From Massachusetts, Lucy too sent messages of progress achieved. Susan and Elizabeth were in a gay mood in 1860. Then tragedy struck and the heartbreaks began.

In December, South Carolina left the Union. Following her example, Mississippi, Florida, Alabama, Georgia, Louisiana, and Texas seceded, one after another. By mid-April of 1861, Fort Sumter had been fired on and the Civil War was under way.

With the country at war, the fight for women's rights was dropped. Everyone turned his attention toward working for victory and a return to peace. Nevertheless, the idea that woman was man's political partner had at least been born.

It was to have its effect even on the conduct of war. Far from staying by their firesides, women flocked to their country's defense. Lucretia, by now an old lady, was opposed to this or any war. But Lucy Stone's sister-in-law, Elizabeth Blackwell—with her medical degree—ran a training program turning women into nurses at her New York infirmary. Dorothea Dix, already famous for her efforts to reform insane asylums, prisons, and poorhouses, became superintendent over women war nurses. One of these nurses in a Washington hospital was the famous author, Louisa May Alcott. Clara Barton not only nursed, she organized a system of getting supplies to the front; she would one day be the organizer of the American Red Cross. Lucy, still a good seamstress, made clothing for the soldiers. Susan worked on the Anthony family farm because her brothers had enlisted in the United States forces. All the work that women did should have helped the women's cause. It didn't.

While the ladies were thus occupied, the New York legislature in April of 1862 repealed most of the hard-won law for women's property rights. It was one more piece of evidence that without the power to vote they would never be sure of keeping what gains they made.

They had hardly recovered from this shock when a new demand was made on their efforts. In September of 1862, Lincoln issued the Emancipation Proclamation, proclaiming freedom for the slaves in the Confederate states.

Susan, Lucy, and Elizabeth formed the Woman's National Loyal League to organize women to gather petitions for a constitutional amendment that would permanently free all slaves.

They gathered 400,000 signatures, and Senator Charles Sumner presented these to the lawmakers in Congress; but when the women demanded their own rights, the abolitionist politicians deserted them. "This," said the men, "is the Negroes' hour."

It was a cruel slap, but the worst blow fell while Susan was visit-

ing in Kansas and the proposed Fourteenth Amendment was announced. The new amendment contained the word "male!" It permitted Congress to decrease the representation of any state which
"denied to any of the male inhabitants of such State, being twenty-
one years of age, and citizens . . ." the right to vote. Here was an
obstacle to woman suffrage that had never been there before. The
Constitution had never before specified sex.

Susan rushed east to gather up her friends to protest. When their
efforts failed, they fought among themselves. Lucy was able to
understand the political difficulties of the Republicans in Congress.
They simply wouldn't jeopardize Negro suffrage for the sake of the
less popular women's cause. Susan and Elizabeth could stand no
more. They came out against the Fifteenth Amendment, which
said, "The right of the citizens of the United States to vote shall not
be denied or abridged by the United States or by any State on account of race, color, or previous condition of servitude"—but did
not add "sex."

They lost that battle. The Fifteenth Amendment was adopted in
1870 without the word "sex." Worst of all, the conflict split the
women's movement into two groups. Lucy ran one segment, Susan
and Elizabeth the other. Twenty years were to come and go before
the two fragments would reunite. Lucy turned her attention to getting women enfranchised by their state legislatures. Susan and Elizabeth were sure that nothing short of changing the United States
Constitution would ever get women the vote. While the friends
were so divided, the postwar period slipped away and with it the
country's urge to reform. Then the dismal years began.

In 1869, Wyoming, which was a territory and not a state, had
enfranchised women, but from then on, for a long time, nothing
more happened to give women the vote. The women struggled on.
Susan for a short time ran a newspaper called *The Revolution,*
which tried to educate women to demand their liberties. Its slogan
was "men, their rights and nothing more; women, their rights and
nothing less."

Lucy also ran a paper. Hers was *The Woman's Journal.* In addition, crusading suffragettes traveled. They slept in cheap hotels and
ate the poor tavern food in order to make speeches for the cause.
In state after state they assembled what people they could in school-
rooms, churches, and stores. A few of them always joined Susan
when she made her regularly unsuccessful trips to Washington to
plead for woman suffrage with each succeeding Congress.

In 1889 Wyoming applied for statehood. Immediately the well-organized southern senators pressured the territory to disfranchise women voters as a prerequisite to joining the Union. The Wyoming legislators replied, "We will remain out of the Union a hundred years rather than come in without woman suffrage." Congress yielded, and the first woman-suffrage state was born, in 1890.

By the turn of the century, however, Susan could count only four states out of forty-five that had enfranchised their women. With the backing of only four states it was impossible to get a constitutional amendment passed. Not all the senators and congressmen were unsympathetic when Susan and her followers appeared again and again, but they recognized that the obstacles to women getting the vote had multiplied. The southern senators had again become powerful and were trying to reassert their doctrine of states' rights. They wanted no more constitutional amendments that would tell their local constituents what to do. With their opposition, it was impossible to get the necessary vote of two-thirds of both the House and the Senate to propose an amendment and send it to the states for ratification.

When a state did enfranchise its women, its elected representatives supported suffrage, but getting more states to do so was difficult.

In 1906, Susan B. Anthony died. Lucretia Mott, Lucy Stone, and Elizabeth Cady Stanton had already passed from the scene. New women took up the fight for the suffrage amendment and for new reasons. By now they had access to an education and the states had given them property rights. They wanted the authority of the ballot in order to demand money for schools, aid to orphans, better sanitation in cities, improved working conditions for factory women, and an end to child labor.

Whereas the large majority of suffrage workers joined the ladylike National American Woman Suffrage Association, others became part of the "militant" Woman's Party. Members picketed the White House with banners and signs directed at President Woodrow Wilson. After the United States declared war on Germany in April of 1917, their presence became obnoxious and they were arrested in June for obstructing traffic.

Senator James Reed of Missouri told the Senate, "No one who will not obey a law has the right to ask to make a law . . . for others to obey." He felt that their acts gave comfort to the enemy in time of war.

He was outraged when forty Woman's Party members gathered in front of a crowd in the park across the street from the White House and there, with a bronze torch, set fire to a Wilson speech to show the "burning indignation of women" who wanted their amendment passed.

Senator John Sharp Williams of Mississippi was quoted as saying that "not even the President could persuade him to support a cause advocated by such outrageous methods." Yet there were others who hailed these women as martyrs who were helping the cause.

Most of the women were guided by their leaders along less sensational lines. Hefty and warm Dr. Anna Howard Shaw—author, minister, doctor of medicine, a colorful speaker and zealous organizer—was one president of the National American Woman Suffrage Association. In the final crucial years, the women turned to Carrie Chapman Catt, a hardheaded widow and ex-school superintendent, not as warm and human as Anna but a masterfully efficient campaigner who made use of every woman willing to work.

Usually Carrie's lieutenants did what their predecessors had done. They opened the doors of halls, lit the lights, made speeches, drew up petitions and gathered signatures, and took up collections, wrote letters to congressmen and state legislators, and got their followers to trudge to Congress or to their state capitols begging for support. To these older methods they added colorful parades—up Pennsylvania Avenue in the Nation's capital, along New York's Fifth Avenue, and, most important, to the convention halls when the major political parties convened. Their exercise of the rights of assembly and petition were weapons that could not be ignored.

On one such occasion—the Republican convention of 1916— over five thousand suffragists defied a cloudburst to march from the Chicago Loop to the Coliseum, where they descended, dripping wet, on a Republican resolutions committee meeting. Watery dye from their colored scarves ran down over their dresses. The once-stiff brims of their straw hats, sagging from the heavy rain, hung down in ripples, but they were just in time to fill the hall and glare defiance at a speaker who claimed women did not want the vote.

Slowly, ever so slowly, the cause gathered support. In 1900 women voted in four states. In 1916 they could vote in twelve.

In November of 1917 New York and two others were added. In January of 1918 President Wilson finally endorsed their amendment campaign. Then in June of 1919 Congress approved the Nineteenth Amendment and sent it to the States. Three-fourths of the states—thirty-six—would have to ratify before it could become part of the supreme law of the land.

By now hundreds of thousands of women had devoted their time and given of their funds to bring the amendment about. Those who were still alive watched it progress as it was considered by one state legislature after another. They watched and they worked. Finally they had thirty-five states and the question was up to Tennessee. Until the last minute Tennessee's vote remained in doubt. Mrs. Catt raced to the state to rally her supporters. Finally, on August 26, the amendment was law.

The long campaign was over. Women could vote, and the suffragists turned their attention to teaching newly enfranchised women to use the vote wisely. For their students and for all Americans their story stands as a monument and as a lesson showing that peaceful methods of petition and assembly in the hands of dedicated citizens can bring about badly needed reform by the orderly processes provided for free people in a free society.

"Labor Must Do Its Best to Maintain Justice"

To live as free men, American factory hands had to have some say as to what wages they would accept and what hours they would work. From the beginning of the industrial era, the workers saw that it was going to take a long hard campaign to get the business world to listen to their demands. Then they found that, even worse, in order to run any campaign they also had to put up a fight for their right to peaceably assemble.

It was not enough that in 1842 Massachusetts Chief Justice Lemuel Shaw reversed an earlier decision and said the men were entitled to carry on trade union activities, with the right to strike to keep nonunion help out of their place of employment, provided the methods and the objectives of the union were legal. Economists went on insisting that workmen who assembled to force their boss to better their working conditions were a menace; they were conducting an outrageous conspiracy against the property owners and interfering with trade. An adult man should steer away from agitators and make his own employment contracts. The most skillful workers would thus rise to the top.

The impatient union men did not believe that mere skill would pull them very far up the economic ladder. That had happened in the old days, they said, when a mechanic could ply his trade in his own handicraft shop. With the coming of expensive machinery, the worker faced a lifetime of being someone else's employee. Unemployed or immigrant job seekers could always be used to replace him if he tried alone to bargain with his boss. He needed an organization.

Earlier, workingmen's organizations had helped win needed reforms. In the 1820s they had helped to get rid of the property qualifications for voters. After that they had helped to get imprisonment for debt abolished, and they had helped in the fight for free public schools.

After the Civil War the workers felt they desperately needed to fight for themselves. They needed to continue their fight against the intolerably long workday, and they needed to fight for a living wage. Before they could hope to have any success, labor's right to conduct an orderly meeting or rally would have to be respected. To win respect, organized labor needed effective leadership.

Since United States citizens take pride in being a nation of immigrants from many lands and of every creed, the background that prepared one of America's first outstanding labor leaders was not surprising.

Samuel Gompers was thirteen in July of 1863, when he and his family first saw the shores of lower Manhattan Island from the deck of a sailing vessel. Mr. and Mrs. Gompers were Dutch Jews, but they were coming from England, where Samuel had been born. From the minute they landed, the travelers faced a city of hot, angry men. Mobs had rioted against the Civil War draft act. In all this turmoil Samuel's parents had to find a place to house their large family.

The apartment they found was typical of the miserable living conditions of working people at the time. Eight—or even more— occupants crowded into four rooms. The running water and the toilet, which they shared with all the other big families in the building, were placed in the back yard. To reach them a tenant fumbled his way along the perpetually dark tenement-house corridors and down the lightless staircase. In bad weather dampness oozed through the walls, and in all weather the building stank from the garbage thrown in the back court and from the slaughterhouse nearby.

Samuel and his father used the family's main room as a workshop, where they sat at a table and rolled cigars from dawn till dusk. After living and working this way for a year and a half, Samuel went out and found a job in a cigar factory, where he joined the union. The future president of the American Federation of Labor had become one of the ranks of organized workers. He saw, he said, in the early labor meetings "passionate feeling . . . but little practical aid." He was stirred even more by the injustice done the workers and was particularly excited by an incident which took place in January of 1874.

A large group of workers were in the process of gathering around an old drill field inside a park. They were there to protest the city's neglect of its hungry families. The financial panic, which had started the year before, caused the number of jobless to increase steadily, and every worker dreaded the day when he might become one of the penniless unemployed. As Gompers recalled it, the gathering crowd was quiet, but to the police this horde of shabby men looked like the beginning of a radical uprising. Down they swooped on the crowd, indiscriminately swinging their clubs at any head they could reach, while mounted officers rode down the bystanders. For the rest of his life Gompers would be able to picture that wild scene and hear the cries of the injured.

He was fully aware of what had caused the police to fear the assembly. Demonstrations by the jobless needy were being exploited by the city's radical elements. At the time German anarchists, Irish Home Rulers, and refugee Marxists used New York as a platform from which to spout their violent doctrines. The press got the idea that radicals were leading all the unrest.

As a result, for a considerable period after the rally, the police invaded private indoor meetings and chased out the audience. Included were meetings called to protest police brutality and demand labor's right of assembly. Gompers, who resented both the police and the radicals, later wrote, "I saw how professions of radicalism . . . concentrated all the forces of organized society against a labor movement and nullified in advance normal, necessary activity."

His thinking took a further step during the events of 1877. More men were out of work. Pay scales were still going down. Gompers was trying to use mass meetings to convince the impoverished men not to economize by leaving the union so as to save their dues for bread money.

In July railroad workers on the Baltimore and Ohio started a strike which spread along the rail lines all the way north to Buffalo and west to St. Louis.

Gompers' sympathies were overwhelmingly with the men, whose wages were being cut 10 per cent for the second time in three years. At mass meetings in New York he expressed his approval of their courage and found it a beacon of hope. Then, as he watched the progress of events, he realized that, though desperate and determined, the railroad men did not have a strong enough organization to run a proper strike. (Nor had the nation established machinery for arbitration, mediation, or any other of the methods for reaching a settlement available today.)

The great strike was doomed to turn into more of a rebellion than an orderly protest. When the resentful idle men milled through the streets, panic gripped many of the local authorities. They sent for state militias. The workers met this show of force with force. They rioted, wrecked roundhouses and freight cars, and started fires. To add to the ugly picture, the police broke up a peaceful meeting of labor delegates in St. Louis who were coming together to decide what to do about the situation. Finally, President Hayes sent federal troops into the affected areas, and the strike was broken.

All this Gompers had in mind when he went to work—attending meetings, making speeches, and editing a paper—to build the national trade union movement. Strikes were risky and expensive. To succeed, they had to be well disciplined and well financed; strikers must eat. If all trade unions belonged to a federation, a union caught in a struggle with employers could get help from other unions. "An alliance for defense" was what he wanted.

One obstacle was the Noble Order of the Knights of Labor. The Knights had a large following and a treasury, and they had won some strikes and had helped persuade Congress to forbid the importation of cheap foreign labor under pre-immigration contracts. But they wanted everyone to belong to a single reforming labor group. They took in employers as well as employees, unskilled men as well as skilled—drawing the line only at bankers, lawyers, and liquor dealers. Gompers said it was a "hodgepodge with no basis for solidarity. . . ." Its conservative members were antiunion. "Not respectable," they said of the unions. Others members were those revolutionary theorists who had already made so much trouble.

Trouble was inevitable when representatives of the Knights tried to dominate the local trade union people without always being in sympathy with the demands of the unionists. Carpet weavers, garment workers, and cigar makers were made furious. Gompers, as part of a committee, sent a message to the Knights at their 1886 assembly in Cleveland telling them to leave the trade unions alone. Trade unions, he felt, had to be run by men with like work problems.

Meanwhile the president of the Knights, Terence V. Powderly, did something which spurred the unionists into calling a December meeting to sever themselves from the Order by forming the American Federation of Labor, with no treasury but with Gompers as president.

The trade union people were organizing a general strike for May 1. Strikers were to demand that the standard work day be cut to eight hours. Powderly, a timid, bespectacled little man, discouraged his members from cooperating. "Neither employer nor employee are educated to the needs and necessities for the short hour plan. . . . It is nonsense to think about it . . . ," Powderly wrote.

Sick and tired of the Order, the trade unionists determined to go ahead without his support and a large number of the Knights joined them. In spite of Powderly, had it not been for an almost coincidental catastrophe, the effort would have been a great success. The big May 1 work stoppage involved 340,000 people, and, although not all of them actually left their jobs, 190,000 gained some concessions from their bosses. The eight-hour day was not established, but a fine beginning had been made in the campaign. In New York that night, workers carried banners and torches to Union Square, bands played, and fireworks went off. Gompers was one of the speakers. He must have been in a wonderful mood. Labor was making progress when it could gather its forces into orderly strikes and parades and get good results. Labor was benefiting from its right to assemble. Gompers would have felt sick had he realized that a setback in the use of that right was already tragically imminent.

In Chicago, too, all had at first gone well. There had been parades, and many people paid little attention to the labor dispute that had been going on for some time at the McCormick farm machinery plant.

Then on May 3 a huge group of strikers gathered near the plant to hear a German anarchist named August Spies speak on the eight-hour day. The plant whistle blew and strikebreakers began leaving the factory to go home. A big segment of the audience deserted the speaker to shower rocks at "those scabs." They found themselves in a fight with the police. According to Spies, six workingmen were shot down. Spies' reaction was to help organize a protest meeting to be held at Haymarket Square at 7:30 the following evening. Unfortunately, he also circulated a description of the McCormick incident headed by the words: "Revenge! Workingmen, To Arms!!"

Nevertheless, the meeting started off peaceably in the shadowy, gaslit square. Three speakers in turn climbed on a wagon and addressed the gathering. The mayor, Carter Harrison, was in the crowd. He testified later that the first speaker, August Spies, was "a little incendiary." The second speaker, Albert R. Parsons, was "not very incendiary." Then at ten o'clock it began to rain. The last speaker, a thin bearded anarchist named Samuel Fielden, had not quite finished. His Honor and many of the spectators left. A few moments later a contingent of police approached the speaker.

"I command you . . . to immediately and peaceably disperse," the captain ordered.

"We are peaceable," Fielden protested and descended from the wagon. At that moment a dynamite bomb exploded. In the dim light nobody saw who threw it, but the blast killed policeman Mathias J. Degan. At the sound of the explosion a riot started and then there were more killings.

Eight anarchists were rounded up to be tried for Degan's murder, and a nationwide attitude of hysterical hatred—fanned by the daily newspapers—invaded the courtroom. An unusual procedure was used. The bailiff, Henry Ryce, went out to pick the jury. An acquaintance of Ryce's swore that he said, "I'm managing this case, and know what I am about. Those fellows are going to be hanged as certain as death."

Typical of the jurors Ryce brought in was one manufacturer who frankly stated, "It would take pretty strong evidence to remove the impression that I now have."

Another juror, a local wholesaler, added, "It would be hard to change my conviction."

Judge Joseph E. Gary made it easy for these jurors to have no scruples in finding the men guilty. As Gary later explained, he reasoned that "they had generally by speech and print advised large classes to commit murder . . . [and] influenced by that advice, somebody, not known, did throw the bomb that caused Degan's death." The men were thus convicted of a crime when even the judge had to admit that the evidence did not prove they had committed it.

When they were about to be hanged, Gompers was in mourning for his eight-hour-day campaign. Dynamite and the eight-hour day were lumped together in people's minds. Gompers and his friends had to wait before reactivating their issue, for the labor movement itself was in jeopardy. It was maddening, but Gompers recognized that "labor must do its best to maintain justice . . . or find itself denied the rights of free men." Gompers got on a Springfield-bound train and went to see Governor John Oglesby of Illinois.

Once inside the governor's chamber, Gompers found that several other civic groups, including women, legislators, and farmers were also petitioning for justice. When Gompers' turn to speak came he explained that he represented the American Federation of Labor, an organization opposed to anarchism but convinced that these men must not be made to look like martyrs in the cause of freedom of speech and assembly.

In spite of the impassioned pleas of the shocked citizens, four of the men went to the gallows (one other committed suicide) and the remaining three were kept in prison. And still the impact of the biased trial had not spent itself. Since one of the condemned men, Parsons, was a Knight, the publicity helped cripple that organization. There are those who say that as the Knights faded from the scene so did the hopes of unskilled laborers for decades to come. They argue that the American Federation of Labor replaced the Knights only in part. Gompers' motto was, "The stronger the union the fewer the strikes." The A.F. of L. was strong not only because it was highly organized but also because the majority of its members were skilled workmen, hard to replace in large numbers.

In addition to all of this, the Haymarket tragedy ruined a promising career. In 1892 the new Illinois governor, John Peter Altgeld, listened to a pardon petition, reviewed the trial record, and saw that the men had been victims of injustice born of public frenzy. Knowingly flouting the public's prejudice, he issued a pardon in 1893 for Fielden and for the two others still in prison. By doing so he committed political suicide.

The fact was that the American people were scared. They thought they felt the winds of revolution. In times of fear the Bill of Rights is likely to suffer.

For the next decades, trade unions had a painfully slow upward climb. The next blow to hit them was the Sherman Antitrust Act; passed by Congress to stop the giant industrial firms from getting together in so-called "conspiracies" to monopolize or restrain the country's trade, it was turned against labor. Once again, many strikes were called conspiracies—they restrained trade. Court orders, called injunctions, were issued against the strikers. Violation of these court orders—whether served under the Sherman Act or some other law—meant a prison sentence, as Eugene V. Debs, head of the American Railway Union, learned after the disastrous Pullman strike of 1894.

In 1906 Gompers and other labor leaders drew up a petition of grievances protesting the use of injunctions and claiming that the Sherman Antitrust Act was being perverted to deny workers their rights. The labor leaders sent copies of the petition to all members of Congress and the President, but Gompers characterized their reaction as "deaf."

Labor then turned to the American people, urging their help in electing men who would not be deaf to labor's demands. In spite of all the speeches labor leaders made during political campaigns, and in spite of all their lobbying, it was 1914 before they managed to get the Clayton Act passed.

Gompers, choked with emotion, watched from the Senate galleries as it was passed. From then on, the legitimate activities of agricultural cooperatives and labor unions were not to be considered conspiracies in restraint of trade. One section of the law limited the use of injunctions to situations where private property or property rights were endangered. Another section was designed to protect peaceable strikes, pickets, and boycotts.

Gompers called the bill labor's Magna Carta, referring to the earliest English charter of a subject's rights, but elated labor leaders were soon to be disappointed. The bill was not tightly drawn and the courts interpreted much of it away. Besides, the Supreme Court justices declared unconstitutional minimum-wage laws, and laws limiting the number of hours a man could work, and laws forbidding "yellow-dog contracts," in which an employer made a job applicant promise to stay out of the union. Said the justices, the legislators were interfering with the rights of the people to make their own contracts and exercising too much control over private matters. This was not the function of government. It would tend to deprive citizens of their independence. Therefore, except for a brief period during World War I, laborers were no better off than before.

Then came the Great Depression of the thirties—the bank failures, the armies of unemployed, the bread lines, the daily spectacles of more and more bankruptcies. Fear gripped not only the workers but all classes of Americans.

Gompers was gone. William Green, the new president of the A.F. of L., addressed the Senate Committee on Education and Labor. He was not a belligerent man. He relied rather on his own powers of persuasion. Part of the blame for the business collapse, he said, was due to the fact that wage earners did not share fully in the benefits of the machine age. They made more goods but did not have the means to buy them. In addition, Green described workers as "discharged, thrown out of work. What for? . . . they had dared to join a labor union. . . ." He urged that Congress guarantee to labor the right to organize, to choose its own representatives freely and unafraid, and to bargain collectively. Led by President Franklin Delano Roosevelt, millions of Americans demanded pro-labor legislation as part of a "New Deal."

Congress had already passed the Norris-La Guardia Act in 1932 to make yellow-dog contracts unenforceable and further limit the use of injunctions against peaceful strikes or pickets. In 1935 it passed the famous bill introduced by Senator Robert F. Wagner, the National Labor Relations Act, which created the National Labor Relations Board.

The board was to prohibit "unfair labor practices." Employees were to be free from coercion by the boss when they wanted to meet, organize, and select a union of their choice to bargain collectively or engage in other concerted activities for the purpose of their mutual aid or protection. Employers were required by law to sit down with the employees' union and bargain over working conditions.

The board set up regional offices. An organizer could write to one of these if the union had lost an election because the management had intimidated the workers or had pressured the workers into accepting a company-dominated union. Workers who were fired for union activities could also file a charge with the regional office; the regional director would then notify the employer of the charge and appoint a board agent to investigate. If in spite of the efforts of the agent no settlement was reached which the regional office could approve, the regional director was to issue a formal complaint and notice of hearing. Trial examiners were selected to hold courtlike hearings and listen to the employer, the Government, and—if he wanted to be there—the complainant or his attorney. A trial examiner's decision that an employee be reinstated or an election declared void stood unless the losing party appealed to the board for review. After that, the trial examiner's decision if upheld by the board was enforceable in the court of appeals, provided the courts found no legal faults with the board's actions. Employers could not fire a man for having filed his charge. They could be made to put up printed notices that they intended to comply with the law and the board's ruling on it.

In a state of intense suspense, people asked each other whether the Supreme Court would uphold this law. Workers and employers alike knew the justices to be equally divided. They waited for their answer until April of 1937. By then the justices themselves were alive to the country's new thinking. They did uphold the Wagner Act because of the relation between labor disputes and interstate commerce.

That decision was only one incident in a fantastic year in the history of labor and of freedom of assembly. On January 4, the Supreme Court justices—in *De Jonge v. Oregon*—ruled on whether even the hated Communists could hold an orderly meeting where no one advocated the overthrow of the government. The meeting had grown out of Oregon's bitter maritime strike and had been broken up by the police. Chief Justice Charles Evans Hughes— looking the part of wisdom itself, with his erect posture and his trim beard and mustache—explained the Court's decision. "If the persons assembling have committed crimes elsewhere, if they . . . are engaged in conspiracies against the public peace . . . they may be prosecuted for their conspiracy [but not for] mere participation in a peaceable assembly. . . ." The meeting was legal. A great battle had been won.

Meanwhile, outside the courtroom the big issue of labor-management relations was heading for a surprising turn.

"Both Sides . . . of the Labor Relation"

DURING the mid-1930s rebels inside the A.F. of L. were challenging Green's leadership. John L. Lewis was a man with big eyebrows and big ambitions, and his belligerent mind bubbled with a sense of drama. In 1936 and again in 1937 he staged the most unusual strikes in American history. First rubber workers and then automobile workers sat down inside their plants, demanding collective bargaining. They did no damage. They only waited—waited out the long weeks. When Governor Frank Murphy of Michigan, though nagged and pressured, refused to use soldiers to evict the auto workers, both strikes were won. Emboldened, and led by Lewis, the Congress of Industrial Organizations split from the A.F. of L. trade unions (to remain a separate organization until 1955). The new C.I.O. was intent on welding the skilled and unskilled into industry-wide organizations.

To this end, Lewis had already decided to organize the steel-workers. He put the staggering task in the hands of a future C.I.O. president, Philip Murray.

"The most difficult thing we were up against was . . . fear," Murray said. "In most steel plants even a kind word about a union meant loss of your job—and probably black-listing besides." Once a man's name was on a company's black list he couldn't find work anywhere in the industry. He was without a livelihood. Obviously, under these conditions, none of the men dared exercise their consti-tutional right to assemble at a labor rally.

Murray's task would have been hopeless had it not been for an-other unusual American. Robert M. La Follette was a crusading idealist with unflagging energy. Starting in 1936, La Follette headed a Senate subcommittee "to investigate violations of the rights of free speech and assembly and interference with the rights of labor to organize. . . ." Said La Follette, "Men cannot meet freely . . . so long as the machinery of espionage pervades their daily life."

Bit by bit, La Follette drew out of the witnesses at his hearings a record that read like a gory crime novel. Antilabor detective agen-cies supplied their operators to a number of employers. Agency spies, using aliases and keeping records in code, joined the union and reported back on which workers were the labor leaders. The union men could then be fired and black-listed on some invented pretext. The right to assemble at a union meeting thus became a trap. As one worker told La Follette, "You get suspicious of every-body."

The record showed that the detective agencies were not beneath bribing union officials to learn union plans, including strike plans. "Forewarned is forearmed," agency operators told the manage-ment. When a strike started, an agency would be ready with phony strikers who entered orderly street meetings and "started slugging." Managers could then call the police or get an injunction, and the legal meeting became an illegal disturbance. As a further service, an agency might supply ex-convicts to serve as deputy police or as strikebreakers. Other companies were set up to sell weapons to employers.

One group of paid spies tried to tell Senator La Follette they were helping the plant owners get rid of Communists. La Follette, by subsequent questioning, put himself in a position to tell his fellow senators that "none of them could define or describe a Communist." After all this exposure, the agencies began a self-reforming program. Besides, the existence of the La Follette committee put an ingenious device at Murray's disposal in his struggles for the frightened steelworkers.

Speeding into one steel town after another went Murray's organizers, often accompanied by a car draped with a banner bearing the words:

CAR OF THE UNITED STATES SENATE
LA FOLLETTE CIVIL LIBERTIES COMMITTEE.

In the car were special investigators from Washington. To them no abuse could be offered. Plant managers and antiunion sheriffs took a long look, and some say they sighed.

Antiunion employers were to have more to sigh about in the years ahead. The steelworkers were not the only ones to be organized. With all their newly won protection, unions skyrocketed in size and number. Earlier, the birth of the industrial era had concentrated control over the men's lives and the nation's welfare into the hands of the plant owners and managers. In the closing years of the 1930s some of that power began to shift to the great union bosses. With this shift, new problems lay ahead.

In 1943, in the midst of World War II, with the country's survival in danger, John L. Lewis—then president of the United Mine Workers—called a work stoppage. Without coal the steel mills supplying the defense plants could not stoke their blast furnaces, and the railroads could not run. Harping on the misery of being a miner, Lewis stubbornly defied the anger of both government and public, and he got concessions. People began to worry about the power of big strikes to cripple business and endanger the public safety.

After the war another group had reason to petition the Government. From all over the country, employers—some of whom had never before had trouble with their help—complained to Congress that, if they had to sit down and bargain in good faith, labor should have to keep its contracts.

Tall, slow-speaking Senator Ball of Minnesota agreed with them. "Far too many unions today seem to regard collective bargaining contracts as entirely one-way agreements," he told a Senate committee. Ball added a warning: "It is one of the axioms of a free society that special privilege, legal immunities, and irresponsible power corrupt even the best of men, and union leaders are quite human in this regard."

After Ball finished speaking, Congress heard more complaints. A New Englander told Congress that union bosses were so mighty they could dictate to a contractor what suppliers to patronize or put him out of business by withdrawing his labor. Other employers complained that the N.L.R.B. considered their slightest comment as an unfair labor practice. "How could words like 'We don't want an outside union to come and run our business for us' be coercive?" they asked.

The board answered that most of their "propaganda, even when it contains no direct or even indirect threat, is aimed at the worker's fear of losing his job." Each case required examination of the circumstances in which the words were uttered.

The employers did not go only to Congress, they went also to court. Judge Learned Hand upheld the board. Said Hand, "What to an outsider will be no more than vigorous presentation of a conviction, to an employee may be the manifestation of a determination which it is unsafe to thwart."

In 1945, the Supreme Court justices got into the argument. The occasion was the case of *Thomas v. Collins*. It started out as a simple case of freedom of assembly. Thomas, who was a C.I.O. organizer, went to Houston, Texas. On Thursday, September 23, 1943, he intended to address a mass meeting and urge employees of the Humble Oil Refinery Company to join the union. Six hours before he was to speak he was served with a restraining order because Texas law required him to register and get a paid organizer's card.

Thomas decided that the order was a restraint on freedom of speech and assembly and went ahead with the meeting. He was arrested, and a Texas judge fixed the penalty at $100 fine and three days in prison.

Thomas appealed his case to the United States Supreme Court. Justice Wiley B. Rutledge spoke for the majority. "It is . . . in our tradition to allow the widest room for discussion, the narrowest range for its restriction, particularly when this right is exercised in conjunction with peaceable assembly. It is not by accident or coincidence that the rights to freedom in speech and press were coupled in a single guaranty with the rights of the people peaceably to assemble and to petition for redress of grievances. All these . . . are inseparable."

Before ruling on whether these precious rights had been violated in the Thomas case, Justice Rutledge referred to the Court's ruling in a 1939 New Jersey dispute, called *Hague v. Committee for Industrial Organization*. The justices there had thrown out a Jersey City ordinance because it gave the director of public safety the power to forbid any outdoor rally which in his opinion might end in a disturbance. Since Mayor Frank Hague wanted to lure big industries into Jersey City, his subordinates used the ordinance to forbid C.I.O. meetings.

In the Hague case Justice Owen J. Roberts had said, "The *privilege* . . . to use the streets and parks for [assemblies] may be regulated . . . in subordination to the general comfort and convenience, and in consonance with peace and good order; but it must not, in the guise of regulation, be abridged or denied." This ordinance was void on its face.

As ordinances governing the time, place, and manner of parades and assemblies vary from city to city, Roberts undoubtedly realized that the justices would have to rule on this question again (and they are ruling still). They are determined that all such regulations be proper and reasonable, leaving no unfettered discretion in the hands of enforcement officials to use against unpopular groups.

With these principles in mind, the justices had decided the Thomas case. In soliciting people to join a union, Thomas had not threatened public health, safety, or morality or any other substantial community interest. Thomas had not, for example, wanted to lead a parade and tie up traffic in the rush hour. If Thomas had wanted to collect funds it might have been reasonable to make him register and identify himself, but this also was not involved. Thomas merely wanted to get members for the union. "If one who solicits support for the cause of labor may be required to register . . . so may he who seeks to rally support for any social, business, religious, or political cause," said Rutledge. Such a situation was "quite incompatible with the requirements of the First Amendment." The Texas law, like the Jersey City ordinance, was invalid. It abridged the right of freedom of assembly and by so doing limited the right of freedom of speech.

Justice Robert H. Jackson was delighted with the decision but pointed out, "We are applying to Thomas a rule the benefit of which in all its breadth and vigor this Court denies to employers in

National Labor Relations Board cases. Free . . . both sides . . . of the labor relation . . . ," he said. The employer "should be free to answer, and to turn publicity on the records of the leaders or the unions which seek the confidence of his men."

Justice Douglas still insisted that an employer's voice could carry a threat, but the Eightieth Congress shared Jackson's frame of mind. Senator Robert A. Taft of Ohio—called Mr. Republican—led Congress in a five-month debate over possible changes in the National Labor Relations Act. The result was the Taft-Hartley Act of 1947. Unions were to be fair to employers. Unions as well as employers were to bargain in good faith. Refusal by either side to sign a contract once an agreement was reached was an unfair labor practice. If as a part of the bargain a union agreed not to strike for the duration of the contract and then broke its word, the employer under the Taft-Hartley Act had access to the courts. A union which knew it did not represent a majority of employees was not to picket for employer recognition, and unions were to give up secondary boycotts such as refusing to handle the goods of anyone who did business with one of their adversaries in a dispute. (Secondary boycotts also include refusing to handle goods made in a particular plant to help punish someone else's employer.) Along with these and other changes, the bill provided that an expression of opinion by an employer "shall not constitute or be evidence of an unfair labor practice . . . if such expression contains no threat of reprisal or force or promise of benefit."

Later Congress found it needed to give more protection (than it already had) to another group of people who were having trouble with certain overbearing union bosses—the workers. For some time the evidence had been coming in little by little. In California a determined individual in the entertainment field was expelled from a union for refusing to pay a one-dollar assessment to help the union petition against a state law. Thus for conscience a man could lose his livelihood. Similarly, in New York two rather idealistic deck officers in the merchant marine were also expelled when they held an "unauthorized meeting" and put together a slate to oppose the union officers running for re-election. The deck officers then faced the fact that the union controlled the employment practices of every merchant ship in New York harbor. Although later they fought their way back into the union, they first paid dearly in loss of income for insisting that their local respect their right to call meetings or assemblies and express their views.

In another case a man lost his union card when he insisted on

campaigning for a Republican candidate for public office whom the
union opposed. Other workers were ousted from their brotherhoods
on various charges without even a fair hearing. The courts did what
they could for these desperate people, but the fact is that unions are
private organizations—not fully subject to the Bill of Rights unless
the lawmakers so decree.

By 1959 a congressional investigation was unraveling even more
sensational stories. Lean, proper, but inquisitive Senator John L.
McClellan of Arkansas, aided by his staff, turned the spotlight on
those union leaders who pilfered union funds in order to finance
their own homes, cars, or outside money-making schemes. Some
leaders also exacted large presents or other improper benefits from
employers, at times by picketing. The Teamsters Union, partly because of its size and strength, was of particular interest. Robert
Kennedy—later Attorney General and senator from New York—
said of it, "The Teamsters Union is the most powerful institution
in this country—aside from the United States Government itself. In
many metropolitan areas the Teamsters control all transportation."

The public therefore was duly concerned when Senator Mc-
Clellan questioned chunky "Jimmy" Hoffa, renowned as the
shrewd, cocky, and fast-moving executive of the Teamsters. "Mr.
Hoffa," the Senator asked, "from this testimony do you know any
other conclusion that fair-minded men, impartial, can draw other
than the fact that you surround yourself with criminals in the
course of the administration of the affairs of the Teamsters Union,
that you keep them there, and intend to keep them there if you have
your way about it?"

Hoffa answered, "The situation will clear up. . . . I am sure of
that."

If more was needed to frighten the public it was supplied when
James Elkins, a gambler and ex-pinball king, testified that a Team-
ster boss in Seattle had bragged to him, "I make mayors and I break
mayors, and I make chiefs of police. . . . If you bother my two
boys, if you embarrass my two boys, you will find yourself wading
across Lake Washington with a pair of concrete boots."

Less sensational, but equally important, was the evidence on
what was happening to workers' civil rights. Letters cascaded into
McClellan's office from wine sellers, plumbers, painters, meat-
cutters, truck drivers, textile workers, and others. Some praised
their unions but others complained about unfair union assessments,
rigged elections, or racial discrimination. Still others complained

that they lived in fear—fear of losing their jobs or of being physically beaten.

"They poured in by the thousands," McClellan wrote, "reports of bestiality that made a man shudder with horror and revulsion as he read them."

On April 22, the Senator told his colleagues what could happen at certain union meetings. "Union officers send to other places and bring in thugs and hoodlums. If a union member undertakes to speak, or to try to gain the floor, they move over toward him and suggest, 'Be quiet, bud. You're out of order.' " An autocratic union, it seemed, could block freedom of assembly as easily as could a tyrannical boss or local official.

All this led to the Labor-Management Reporting and Disclosure Act of 1959, called the Landrum-Griffin Act. Among other things, it prohibited using picketing to get improper favors from employers. It protected union funds by making union leaders keep financial records and send annual reports to the Secretary of Labor. Above all it provided workers with a "Bill of Rights."

All members were to have equal rights at union gatherings, to take part in discussions, to nominate candidates, and to vote. In addition, every member had the right to meet with other members and express any views. Members, or their delegates, were to vote on dues and assessments, and voting procedures were regulated by law. Members could no longer be expelled from the union without first being served with written charges and given a fair hearing. Nor could any members be forbidden by the union from exercising their rights to petition the legislature or from testifying in court.

Although obviously most employers and most labor leaders were never guilty of these many abuses, the legislation was still essential. Otherwise, as one worker wrote to McClellan, "We don't live under the Constitution of the United States." She meant the spirit and the principles of liberty and justice expressed in that great charter.

The Constitution as interpreted by the courts forbids either the states or the Federal Government from depriving Americans of their rights. In the spirit of the great bill, Congress has had to act to keep those of us who acquire too much authority from depriving others of their rights. Ultimately, it has had to protect all sides of the labor relation.

"In this Case, the Wrongs
Are Enormous"

————◆◆————

THE newspapers carried ugly reports of brutality. The radio and
TV gave out more shattering details. Groups of Negroes demanding their voting rights were clashing with southern white supremacists. By March of 1965 a shocked public realized that not only
voting rights but also the freedom to assemble and petition was involved. Not all of the public knew how the situation had developed
before they tuned in.

Prior to 1944, many southern Negroes showed slight interest in
trying to vote. In 1944 that changed. A Negro attorney represent-
ing the National Association for the Advancement of Colored People (N.A.A.C.P.) went before the Supreme Court justices in a case
called *Smith v. Allwright* and argued away the all-white primary.
The attorney's name was Thurgood Marshall. Physically, he was a
tall, sturdy man. Professionally he came to be known as "Mr. Civil
Rights," and he was a future United States Solicitor General. Then
another Supreme Court decision tightened the rules laid down in
Smith v. Allwright. More Negroes gave thought to fighting for their
future place in the community. One battle led to another.

Spurred on by victory, Marshall was again before the justices in
1953–1954, asking for school desegregation. The justices were glad
to see that the N.A.A.C.P. had picked Marshall to do the argument.
He knew his subject and he was not rattled by questions from the
bench.

When Marshall won the school case, called *Brown v. Board of
Education,* the number of Negroes who looked hopefully forward
reached an all-time high. The executive director of the N.A.A.C.P.,
Roy Wilkins, later called this victory the "second emancipation." It
smashed the old legal doctrine that so-called "separate-but-equal"
facilities were good enough. It changed the attitude of many Negroes. They began to feel that they could and should demand their
rights.

As a result many a startled southern registrar saw dark-skinned
people struggling to reach the polls. White supremacists had en-

joyed local political control ever since the Reconstruction period after the close of the Civil War. They had no intention of letting the size of the Negro vote skyrocket; nor did they. In describing their conduct a Justice Department official used two verbs: "obstructing" and "intimidating."

Negroes looked to Washington, hoping the Federal Government would take the next step and help them. They had reason to hope. Back in 1947 President Harry S. Truman had created a special committee to find ways to safeguard the rights of the people; "we are not making progress fast enough," Truman told the committee members. They recommended the establishment of a permanent Commission on Civil Rights.

It was 1957 before Congress brought the Civil Rights Commission into existence. Congress gave the commission the power to investigate denials of the franchise. At the same time Congress gave the Attorney General the authority to go into court to enforce voting rights.

Negroes in Alabama were impressed. They began petitioning the new agency. It was more than a year later before their insistent complaints persuaded the six commissioners to come to Montgomery and hold a hearing.

When these distinguished gentlemen finally arrived, it was December, 1958. Among them were two ex-governors, a former assistant secretary of labor, and two university presidents. One of the university heads was the chairman, John A. Hannah.

Chosen by both Presidents Truman and Eisenhower to hold positions of public trust, Hannah was destined to be called on again by Presidents Kennedy and Johnson. The smooth and gracious vice-chairman was Robert G. Storey, a former president of the American Bar Association.

The commissioners took over the court of appeals chamber in the Montgomery post office building and lined themselves up in judges' chairs. Storey, because he was both vice-chairman and a lawyer, did most of the questioning of the flood of witnesses. They came by car and by bus from all the surrounding counties. They packed the obviously too-small room.

After hearing several statements, Storey called a rural Negro named Aaron Sellers to the witness stand. In cheerful, clipped sentences, Sellers described his life as a citizen of Bullock County as he answered Storey's questions.

"Do you own your own farm?"

"I do."

"Are you married?"

"I am."

"Do you have any children?"

"I do have."

"Are you a registered voter?"

"I am not."

Before going any further with this dialogue, Storey inquired about Aaron Sellers' education. He had finished high school and beyond that he spent two summers taking agricultural courses at Tuskegee Institute.

Had he ever tried to register to vote?

"I have applied to register on six occasions," he said.

As Sellers told it, he was not easily discouraged. He and five friends had gone down to the courthouse to get their names on the voter rolls. A registrar said he was quite busy and asked that "you all come back tomorrow." Also, the Negroes understood that someone who was already a voter would have to vouch for them. In a community where few Negroes voted this was a problem, but they found a sponsor and returned the next day.

They were left sitting for an hour. At last a white man who was not the registrar approached them and suggested that "if I were you all, I would go on back home."

When the Negroes continued to sit in the registration room for another half hour, the same white man returned and said, "I thought I told you all to get the hell out of here." A few of the Negroes became anxious, and the group left.

"Did you go back after that?" Storey asked.

"We did," Sellers said.

Sellers gathered up some more friends, and two weeks later eleven of them went back to the courthouse with him. This time the registration board had moved. Sellers stayed in town and kept watching. Around noon he saw the chief board worker returning from lunch, and the little crowd followed the white official back to his quarters.

Again the registrar refused to enroll the Negroes, saying that he was alone and that it took two people to approve a registration.

After that, Sellers and three others hired a lawyer. Their attorney won a court order for them. The court said they were to be enrolled. Then, before they could get back to the board, the registrars had resigned.

"For a year and a half," Sellers said, "we didn't have a board."

At the time he testified, Sellers was still not registered, but "I'm determined to register," he said.

The picture differed slightly from county to county. From Macon County, Dr. William Andrew Hunter, an acting dean and associate professor at Tuskegee with a Ph.D. in science education, took the stand. He had wasted about three days standing in the long line waiting to get into the registration room at the courthouse.

At last, after getting inside, "I was given the application form, which I filled out, and it took me about two hours to do so," Hunter said. "After this time, I was asked to indicate what person would vouch for me and I was given the oath. . . . I self-addressed an envelope and was told I would hear from the board if I passed, and, of course, I didn't hear from the board." He sounded disgusted. "I waited six months before I tried again," Hunter added. In answer to the commissioners' questions, he stated that he never did hear from the board. Undoubtedly, there were people behind him in line who never so much as got into the registration room.

As the six commissioners realized, all of this was happening at a time when most would-be new voters were Negroes. Since Alabama had permanent registration, almost any white adult who had ever wanted to vote was already on the rolls.

More of the picture came from Mrs. Amelia Boynton, a poised, middle-aged Negro matron and businesswoman. Mrs. Boynton, being the local manager for an insurance company, traveled about the surrounding counties. At the same time she was civil liberties chairman of one group and political action chairman of another.

She spoke to Negroes everywhere and brought up the subject of registration. Many of her race were fearful, she reported. They thought they would be criticized or unpopular if they showed up at the polls.

Her testimony came close to indicating another fact. As the Negroes heightened their efforts, the segregationists increased their resistance. Vice-Chairman Robert G. Storey was soon to see this for himself. As he had encouraged the Negroes, so this courteous gentleman made every effort to make the southern registrars feel at ease.

"My grandfathers were Confederate soldiers," he said, and added that "history moves on. We are one nation now."

Then he asked a registrar, ". . . can you tell us how many you have refused to certify or to register . . . ?"

All the answer he got was "I refuse to answer. . . ." Storey

thought he got the picture, but it would be several years more before the stamina and courage needed by civil rights workers like
Mrs. Boynton would become fully apparent. Meanwhile, other tales
of Negroes denied the vote came from other states.

The Negroes and the fact finders in the Civil Rights Commission
got impatient. The men working under the Attorney General at the
Department of Justice found trying to deal with the situation utterly
frustrating. Records they needed were closed to them. A registrar
facing suit resigned, so that the legal action fell by the wayside,
while the evil continued.

In 1960 Congress tried again. It amended the Civil Rights Act.
The Attorney General's men were given the authority to go into
local courthouses and inspect voter registration records. New rules
made it easier for the "Federals" to bring a law suit. Energetic and
able attorneys from the Civil Rights Division of the Department of
Justice pitched into the drudgery of gathering evidence. John Doar,
the Division's first assistant, guided the work.

Doar, tall, handsome, and well-respected, would later be Assistant Attorney General. Under his leadership the men photographed
voting records, interviewed more witnesses, and spent as much as
6,000 man-hours checking out the voting practices in a single
county. What they uncovered in Louisiana and Mississippi as well
as Alabama was almost unbelievable.

Louisiana had an "interpretation test." The rules required that a
voter be able to interpret any section of the complicated state constitution or the federal one. In some parishes (counties) the test
was given orally. Negroes with advanced academic degrees complained that they had been rejected on the basis of this test, while
whites with less than a sixth-grade education had been registered
without even taking it. Deciding whether an applicant met the requirement seemed to be left to the whim of the registrars.

The registrars, it turned out, had been forced to attend a program set up by a state legislative committee on how to promote
white political control. In 21 parishes out of 64, the registrars were
using the test to discriminate. "This is not a test but a trap," objected one federal official. Almost 70 per cent of Louisiana's Negroes were not registered.

How a test could become a trap was again graphically illustrated
by an incident the investigators brought to light in Mississippi.
Again, Negro college graduates were rejected as unqualified to
vote. A white applicant satisfied the registrar when he wrote that

the duties and obligations of citizenship were "under Standing of pepper & Government ship blessing."

In Dallas County, Alabama, the Justice Department needed a handwriting expert. The attorneys, as usual, pulled out a sampling of the registration forms of the white residents. Surprisingly, almost half of them had been made out, at least in part, by someone other than the applicant. One question called for listing some of the duties of a citizen. On over a thousand forms it had been filled in by someone who always used the same wording. Evidently, a cautious registrar did not trust all of his white neighbors to answer that one themselves.

Meanwhile, a Negro dressmaker with one year of college claimed she had filled in these same forms by herself nine times without getting registered. A Negro elementary school teacher said she had filled them in five times with no result. A dentist had made them out three times. None of these people heard from the board, and without a rejection slip they had nothing to take to court.

After hearing their stories, John Doar decided that the Justice Department should bring one of its lawsuits against Dallas County. He thought the relevant statistics would interest Judge Daniel H. Thomas of the United States District Court. Dallas County, with Selma as its capital, had 15,115 voting-age Negroes. Exactly 156 of them, or 1.03 per cent, were registered. Exactly 18 of these people had registered in the past seven years.

The department filed its charges on April 13, 1961. The case finally came to trial thirteen months later. It was six months before His Honor gave his ruling: Yes, the old registrar had discriminated but there were new registrars now and he refused to enjoin them. He felt they were not discriminating. Some Negroes were getting registered.

Doar said that the new registrars had indeed changed procedures. They were using the application form as a test and rejecting Negroes for minor errors or omissions. They were, at the same time, overlooking the mistakes made by whites. Also, they were asking Negroes oral questions they didn't ask all whites. The department took the case to appeal.

Two and a half years after the case had started, the court of appeals made its ruling. It did order the lower court to issue an injunction against future discrimination. But that was not enough help.

The Justice Department's lawyers reminded the judges that most whites were now permanently registered. The three appeals judges still refused to require the registrars to apply the same lenient standards to Negroes that had been applied to whites during the long discrimination period. Such a ruling, the judges felt, would condone the help given to the whites by a former registrar.

Nicholas de B. Katzenbach, later Attorney General, voiced the discouragement of both Negroes and attorneys when he said, "Thus, after two and a half years, the first round of litigation against discrimination in Selma ended, substantially in failure."

Time after time, that October, sixty or more persons waited in line at the registration board but little more than half of them got to fill out forms. Katzenbach said that "the registrars . . . were using one of their most effective indirect methods—delay." The next February the situation became still worse. Alabama adopted a complicated literacy and knowledge-of-government test. In March, 1964, the Government went back to court.

This time Judge Thomas forbade the use of the complicated test and on February 4, 1965, he gave orders against the delay tactics. Four years had been spent in litigation, and still less than 400 Negroes were registered to vote in Dallas County.

Meanwhile, many Negroes, including Mrs. Boynton, were trying to help themselves. They were conducting a nonviolent campaign. The young people walked around town carrying "get registered to vote" picket signs. According to subsequent court records, they were subjected to "mass arrests without just cause."

Then groups of Negroes tried mounting mass demonstrations. Sheriff James Clark's deputies and possemen herded off the demonstrators with night sticks and electric-shock cattle prods.

The rising tension reached its climax in Selma on Sunday, March 7, 1965. About 650 Negroes started from a church and filed over a bridge at the south end of the city. They lined the grassy edge of the highway and headed for Montgomery. There they were going to petition Governor George C. Wallace for a redress of their grievances.

Instead, they were intercepted by state troopers, Sheriff Clark and his deputies, and possemen riding on horseback. The officer in charge of the troopers gave the petitioners two minutes to disperse. Then—in less than one minute, some say—his masked and helmeted soldiers moved in. Tear and nausea gas filled the air. Mounted possemen chased and clubbed fleeing civilians.

Headlines of the violence capped the pages of the nation's papers. Sympathetic whites, including nuns in their habits and clergymen of every faith, headed for Selma. On March 15, a white southern official, Selma's dedicated director of public safety, Wilson Baker, helped an integrated group of 3,500 Negroes, civil rights workers, and clergymen to get the protection of a court order to walk seven blocks.

This solemn procession through the streets at twilight was a memorial to a non-Negro martyr, the Reverend James J. Reeb. Reeb was a Unitarian minister who was born in Boston thirty-eight years before. He was both loved and respected in the North. While in Alabama, Reeb took part in an unsuccessful voter demonstration. He ate dinner in a Negro restaurant. After that he was clubbed to death by five white men.

By now, white and Negro civil rights leaders felt they would have to do something big and dramatic to get any results. They planned a huge 54-mile, five-day march from Selma to the state capitol in Montgomery. Their idea was to have a great crowd confront the governor and demand votes for all the state's Negroes. Spokesmen for Reverend Martin Luther King's Southern Christian Leadership Conference said that this mass demonstration was attracting five to ten thousand marchers from all over the country. Governor Wallace firmly banned this planned deluge of protestors.

Admittedly, the power to vote and the power to assemble and petition are all fundamental parts of a citizen's right to make his views known to the government. Also, admittedly, legal officials have not only the right but also the duty to keep highways open for regular users. Obviously, then, freedom of assembly is subject to local regulations for the convenience and safety of all.

United States District Judge Frank M. Johnson, Jr., had no easy task when N.A.A.C.P. lawyers, backed by the Justice Department, brought a complaint before him. Their clients, Hosea Williams, John Lewis, and Amelia Boynton, demanded the right of freedom of assembly and petition, not only for their own groups but also for their supporters. The lawyers cited the First and the Fourteenth Amendments. They also cited the Fifteenth Amendment because the marchers were petitioning for the Negroes' right to vote. The Fifteenth says, "The right of citizens of the United States to vote shall not be denied or abridged by the United States or by any State on account of race, color, or previous condition of servitude."

Judge Johnson later said he kept in mind that "local and national organizations, have conducted voter registration drives in recent years . . ." and he added that "the demonstrations have been peaceful." While considering this case he took a critical look at

what earlier smaller and less spectacular demonstrations had accomplished in this section of Alabama. In Dallas County he saw
that now 2.2 per cent of the Negroes were registered; in Perry
County, 7 per cent; in Wilcox County, none!

Meanwhile, civil rights workers who were awaiting his decision
and hoping to make the Selma march gigantic, to attract national
attention, were thinking that it was equally imperative to remember
another small-size and tragically unsuccessful voter registration
drive in a neighboring state. These people had in mind the image of
a twenty-four-year-old white social worker with a beard, whose
name was Mickey Schwerner. To the civil rights worker Mickey's
story contributed to the necessity for the Selma demonstration.

Mickey had left New York in January, 1964, and moved to
Mississippi to work under the auspices of the Congress of Racial
Equality. A little congregation of farming Negroes had lent him the
use of their church for his voter education program, and the church
was burned down by terrorists—an assault on freedom of assembly
as well as on voting rights, but it did not stop with the burning of a
church.

Then, while Mickey and his wife, Rita, were working, Congress
passed the 1964 Civil Rights Act. The act desegregated restaurants,
public parks, public housing, and other accommodations. It called
for an end to job discrimination and it strengthened the voting
rights section of the previous bill. Henceforth, registration cases
were to go right to a three-judge court and then to the Supreme
Court.

The bill, written by statesmen in Washington, was another red
flag in the face of white supremacists. The next day, Sunday, June
21, Mickey was riding through Neshoba County in his blue station
wagon with a young aide, a college boy on vacation named Andrew
Goodman, and a twenty-one-year-old Negro helper, James E.
Chaney. By nightfall they were missing. It took the F.B.I. over a
month to find their bodies in the red earth at the bottom of a water
dam. The brutality of the crime revolted newspaper readers across
the country. The number of people involved in the deed made it
worse.

The Justice Department brought charges against eighteen defendants. The county's elected sheriff and his deputy sheriff and a
patrolman were among the accused. A murder trial is a state matter, not a federal one. Many people felt that, even if guilty, the men
would never be convicted by a local jury.

Attorney David Robert Owen from the Justice Department refused to speculate on how much trouble the state might have in calling witnesses and running a trial. Sheriff Rainey, unless proven guilty, could continue exercising his authority. He and Deputy Price could continue making arrests and temporarily jailing their prisoners. All Owen would tell inquirers was, "We thought we had a case and we could win it so we went into Federal Court."

Other attorneys had their doubts about what the department was trying to do. It was relying on two enforcement acts, passed after the Civil War, to protect the rights that Congress wanted to give freedmen.

The first, an act of 1866, would let the Government fine the men $1,000 or imprison them for a year if it could be proved that under color of law they had deprived anyone of the rights secured by the Constitution or the laws of the United States. The other, an act of 1870, carried a much larger fine—$5,000—or a ten-year penalty. It was aimed at any two persons who conspired to injure or intimidate any citizen in order to prevent that citizen from enjoying rights granted by the United States Government—including voting rights. The key sentence in both statutes called for enforcing only federally secured rights.

The Department of Justice lawyers hopefully went before the federal grand jury in Meridian, Mississippi. There they claimed that the defendants had acted to punish the civil rights workers. Since the civil rights workers had not been taken to court for any offense, this punishment violated their right to due process of law, as called for by the Fourteenth Amendment.

The listening jurors were a much larger cross-section of the state's citizens than would have been called for a local murder trial. Judge Harold Cox said it was "a very intelligent and a very fine grand jury." Then he dismissed, or threw out, part of the findings the jurors made when they indicted—that is, said the men were to be put on trial.

The judge did not feel that the nonofficials could be tried for acting under color of law to deny anyone due process, since they were not state officials.

As Mickey's murder was attracting marchers to Alabama, John Doar was arranging to take the question of the legality of the grand jury's indictment to the Supreme Court.

In Alabama, Judge Johnson, while keeping his mind on the case before him, was fully aware of the total picture, conceding in his decision that "the right to petition one's government for the redress of grievances may be exercised in large groups. Indeed," he added, "where, as here, minorities have been harrassed, coerced and intimidated, group association may be the only realistic way of exercising such rights." In support of his position, he cited earlier cases where the Supreme Court had struck down convictions against large groups for breach of the peace.

Breach of the peace because a group was large! There must have been Negroes who were itching to point out that, in the summer of 1963, not five or ten thousand but two hundred thousand civil rights agitators had descended on Washington, D.C., demanding that Congress pass what became the Civil Rights Act of 1964. The day had passed without incident. Visitors were impressed with the courteousness of the marchers. Congress, too, was impressed with the vast numbers wanting the legislation, and the bill passed. Clearly, a nonviolent march, however large, need not end in bloodshed or injury.

As if to answer their thoughts and point out the difference between Washington, D.C., and Alabama, lawyers for the state were urging that there was local hostility to the march. Earlier that week Governor Wallace, nervously pacing the floor in his paneled office and lighting and relighting his cigar, had answered reporters' inquiries on his use of troops against the March 7 demonstration. "We saved their lives by stopping that march," he said. He gave the impression that he was afraid hostility would erupt into public disorder.

Judge Johnson said his court was faced with finding the boundary line between the competing interests of society: "the extent of the right to assemble, demonstrate and march peaceably along the highways and streets in an orderly manner should be commensurate with the enormity of the wrongs that are being protested and petitioned against. In this case, the wrongs are enormous," he said.

On March 18, newspaper readers opened their papers to see the headline COURT PERMITS ALABAMA MARCH; HITS OFFICIALS, ORDERS PROTECTION (for marchers). If they read carefully, the citizens could see with what anguish Judge Johnson had strained over his decision. "It is recognized," he said, "that the plan [here] allowed reaches . . . to the outer limits of what is constitutionally allowed. However, the wrongs and injustices inflicted upon these plaintiffs . . . have clearly exceeded—and continue to exceed— the outer limits of what is constitutionally permissible."

Other white officials in Alabama also saw the need for justice. The state attorney general, Richmond M. Flowers, redheaded and over six feet tall, had been urging his fellow citizens since he took office to forget massive resistance and obey the law. He reminded loyal Alabamans that he was the grandson of a Confederate soldier, but he urged them now to live under the Star-Spangled Banner.

Flowers minced no words when he condemned private racist groups. The average Ku Klux Klanner "is a fifth-grade dropout," he said. "Because he cannot qualify for the future, he fights it. . . . When a pitiable misfit puts on his $15 sheet, society can no longer ignore him." At the same time Flowers reminded his northern readers that Klan membership was only 0.2 per cent of the state's white population.

Besides Flowers, there was hefty Safety Director Wilson Baker. Mr. Baker, although bleary-eyed from overwork—and no integrationist—was doing his best to stay good-natured in the face of repeated demonstrations. There was also Sheriff Mac S. Butler in Montgomery. During the night of March 16, Butler had been meeting with the Negro minister, Reverend Martin Luther King, and King's committee while other Negro and white petitioners waited outside the courthouse in the rain to hear the results of their negotiations. Near midnight Dr. King and the sheriff made a statement that only "well-trained, uniformed law enforcement officers" would be called in to handle demonstrators hereafter. That, at least, eliminated the possibility of action like that of the possemen in Montgomery.

Finally on Sunday the great march started, and by the following Thursday 25,000 protestors of every color and denomination, singing and carrying American flags, faced the steps that led up to the white-columned entrance of Alabama's domed capitol. It was not a complete victory. Besides Reeb, two more marchers had been killed. Nor did Governor Wallace come out to receive their petition of grievances.

In spite of this, no one went home wondering what good he had done. The population had stood up for its rights to assemble and petition against a grievance. Nor was this all the great march had achieved. The marchers turned their eyes toward Washington.

In the Nation's capital, the aftereffects of the great petition had already begun. What these effects were, what clashes they brought about, and what results they achieved makes up the story in the next chapter.

"After Enduring Nearly a Century"

ON Thursday, March 18, 1965, Congressman Emanuel Celler called the House Judiciary Committee to order. It was a fine committee. After much work by this committee, Congress and the states had ratified the Twenty-fourth Amendment in 1964. It said a citizen could not lose his vote—in a federal election—for having failed to pay his poll tax. (The use of the hated tax in state elections would be outlawed in 1966 by the Supreme Court.) Now the committee faced the problem of getting voting rights enforced. President Lyndon Johnson was calling for a strong bill. "The integrity of our Federal system is in contest," he said.

Before hearing witnesses on the bill proposed by the President, Congressman Celler made a few brief remarks. "Recent events in Alabama . . . have so aroused the Nation as to make action by this Congress necessary and speedy," he said. "Freedom to vote must be made meaningful. The legalisms, stratagems, trickery, and coercion that now stand in the path of the Southern Negro when he seeks to vote must be smashed. . . ." Then he added, "The climate of public opinion throughout the Nation has so changed, because of the Alabama outrages, as to make assured passage of . . . a bill that would have been inconceivable a year ago. . . ." The newspaper readers were petitioning their congressmen. Once the public was aroused, the Negro had a powerful ally to outnumber southern officials.

Celler was right. The passage of the 1965 Voting Rights Bill would have been unthinkable at an earlier date. Traditionally, the states had set the literacy and other qualifications for their voters. Nevertheless, the act of 1965 hits at tests. The law has a "trigger provision" which takes effect if the Attorney General and Director of the Census find that, in any state or part of a state, less than 50 per cent of the residents of voting age were registered or cast a ballot in November, 1964.

Once this finding has been made, all test devices are suspended for five years without further review. There is no relief unless the state, county, or parish can go into court and prove its voter qualification tests were not used for discriminatory purposes. During the suspension period no new test may go into effect without the permission of federal authorities. Besides this, federal examiners can go into any affected area if twenty or more people complain of voter discrimination. An examiner can then determine who should be qualified to vote and require their names to be put on the voting rolls.

No one was surprised when a southern state challenged the constitutionality of this law. It was fine that the power of assembly and petition could convince Congress and the public that America needed a stronger law. The law still had to be constitutional. South Carolina sued Attorney General Katzenbach, and the Supreme Court granted a prompt hearing.

Recognizing the urgency of the question, the Court invited all of the other states to participate as friends of the Court. A majority responded. They sent either attorneys or written statements (briefs) to the Court. Five states supported South Carolina, twenty supported the Attorney General, and the argument was on.

First to appear before the justices, in behalf of South Carolina, was David W. Robinson, II, a well-spoken, slim, pleasant-looking man in an olive-green suit. His argument was calm and reasonable. "A literacy requirement, after all, is not a bad thing," he said. He argued, quite rightly, that the Fifteenth Amendment did not give Congress the power to suspend reasonable state restrictions on voting. Besides, Robinson added, "The Act applies to us because we had a small vote. This is no evidence of discrimination." Congress could legislate, but in judging a state discriminatory it was taking over the function of the courts.

There were more arguments but everybody had expected these. All the Fifteenth Amendment says is that people may not be denied their right to vote because of race or color or previous condition of servitude, and this is what Congress may enforce.

To answer South Carolina, it would not be enough to show that individual registrars had used the existing test to discriminate. Congress and the President had exercised authority even against tests not yet enacted by the states and called this enforcing the Fifteenth Amendment. To justify this the Attorney General must prove to the Court that the most innocently worded tests were, in fact, instruments of discrimination. It was not enough for the justices to realize as much. It must be clear on the record if the law was to be upheld.

Katzenbach put into play the same approach that scholarly Circuit Court Judge John Minor Wisdom had used in writing a decision to throw out the Louisiana interpretation test. Wisdom's ruling had been upheld by the Supreme Court justices Katzenbach now faced.

Wisdom had said the purpose of the law was part of its content and to find the purpose one must review the history surrounding the legislation. The justices of the Supreme Court, too, looked back to find the true intentions of the men who had written the legislation.

At times it was also imperative, the justices felt, to see what had happened to a law or an amendment since it had been passed. Otherwise they had no way of deciding the necessity or the validity of new ways of applying it.

At the moment the justices had two reasons for using this historical approach. While listening to the arguments in the voting rights case, the Court was also faced with announcing its evaluation of the Mississippi indictment involving the use of the Fourteenth Amendment and the old enforcement acts.

It was a time then to relive the past. Lawyers and justices must see the events experienced by the men who wrote the Civil War amendments and the enforcement acts. Everyone's attention must be riveted on the happenings that had made necessary the actions of the lawmakers. Above all it was a time to ask: How much had the post-Civil War Congress hoped to accomplish?

The attorneys and the justices also reviewed the memories and wishes of the southerners who wrote the voter qualification laws. They studied what had happened after the Civil War amendments and the qualification laws had been put on the books. Without so doing they could not tell whether Congress was justified in resorting to the steps it had taken. They could not tell whether Judge Cox in Mississippi was justified or whether the draftsman for the grand jury had indeed written the indictment within the meaning of the law. Thus the clocks in the courthouse seemed to be turning backwards, letting each man, through his own eyes, see the United States of a century ago and the developments which brought about the present problems.

It was one week before Christmas, 1865. Abolitionists gathered around their hearths had reason to be cheerful. Finally all the forces at work had managed to impel the adoption of the Thirteenth Amendment. Slavery was abolished. If some raised their glasses in song, others stared thoughtfully into the fire contemplating what lay ahead.

Four million people who had once been in bondage were now completely left to their own resources. The freedman who left his former master—often stealing his master's horse to get away—had nowhere to go. According to one Tennessee Negro, it was like being a "bunch of stray dogs, no homes, no clothes, no nothing . . . and sometimes we went three days without a bite to eat."

Looking for work they wandered through communities where, only recently, the civic leaders had echoed the sentiments mouthed by Chief Justice Taney in 1857: Negroes "had no rights which the white man was bound to respect." In many southern states it had been illegal to educate a slave, and most of these homeless, destitute people were illiterate.

Lincoln had been deeply troubled by the problems their future presented when he signed the Emancipation Proclamation in 1863 and freed the slaves in the rebel states. As part of his postwar plans he wanted the Confederate states to "recognize and declare [the Negroes'] permanent freedom [and] provide for their education."

Instead, even before the Thirteenth Amendment was ratified, southern states began passing "black codes." These laws substituted the words "master and servant" for the words "master and slave." Jobless Negroes were fined for being vagrants. Penniless vagrants were turned over to a white master who paid the fine and recouped the money through the enforced labor of the captive freedman.

When northern abolitionists moved South to become school-teachers and help with the other relief work of the Freedmen's Bureau, they were called "nigger-loving meddlers." The still resistant elements, who for the most part had not enjoyed the benefit of free schools for their own children, were shocked at the prospect of educated ex-slaves. They set fire to the schoolhouses.

The abler colored people did what they could. In Charleston, Mobile, Nashville, Raleigh, and in parts of Mississippi, Negroes congregated in conventions. They demanded that Congress outlaw discriminatory codes, enfranchise colored people, and, above all, provide protection for basic rights.

Northern abolitionists also wrote to members of Congress, and 1866 found the congressmen and the senators in Washington debating the problem. Legislation was introduced which declared the Negroes citizens. As Senator Jacob Howard put it, the legislation "simply gives to persons who are of different races or colors the same rights."

A problem immediately arose as to whether the Federal Government had any power to tell the states who was a citizen and what rights they should have. Senator Howard was quick to point out why the bill was urgent. "We will not say to the emancipated slave,

'We set you free, but beyond this we give you no protection; we allow you again to be reduced to slavery by your old masters. . . .' "

Everyone in the chamber, of course, foresaw difficulty. The bill would have to be submitted for the President's signature. Lincoln was gone, shot down in 1865 by an assassin's bullet. Now the man in the White House was Andrew Johnson, an ex-slaveholder and fervent believer in states' rights.

Johnson would not consider the bill legal or even desirable. The new President was more concerned with gluing back together the pieces of the Union than in pushing the Negro forward. This he felt was his duty. Johnson no doubt remembered how Lincoln during the war had scolded the abolitionist editor Horace Greeley, saying "My paramount objective in this struggle is to save the Union, and not either to save or destroy slavery."

To restore the Union, Johnson had wanted the southern states readmitted to Congress in December, 1865. A caustic, radical Republican congressman named Thaddeus Stevens would have none of it. Stevens had the ear of the House. The deeply resentful southern states were not readmitted.

Congress then further infuriated the President. It extended the life of the Freedmen's Bureau. Johnson's veto message rang with his disapproval. "The Congress of the United States has never . . . founded schools for any class . . . ," he said, and ". . . it was never intended that they [the Negroes] should thenceforth be fed, clothed, educated, and sheltered by the United States." The President did not believe that Congress had any authority to spend the public's money for such things.

Congress would eventually override the President's veto, but first it presented Andrew Johnson with the Civil Rights Bill of 1866. Not surprisingly, he vetoed this measure too. He was well able to see its implications. If Congress could declare who was a citizen, entitled to own land, to testify in court, and to have other rights mentioned in the bill, then Congress could say who could vote. "In all our history, in all our experience as a people," the President said, ". . . no such system as that contemplated by the details of this bill has ever been proposed or adopted. . . . It is another step, or rather stride, toward centralization and the concentration of all legislative powers in the National Government. The tendency of the bill must be to resuscitate the spirit of rebellion. . . ."

The lawmakers passed the bill over the President's veto, but not everyone in Congress was happy about it. Congressman John Bingham, in spite of his sympathy for the freedmen and their need to have their rights protected, recognized that the constitutionality of the Civil Rights Bill could indeed be challenged. As a member of the joint committee of senators and congressmen appointed to deal with the problems of reconstruction, Bingham had set himself the task of laboring over the wording of what became the Fourteenth Amendment.

"All persons born or naturalized in the United States, and subject to the jurisdiction thereof, are citizens of the United States and of the State wherein they reside. No State shall make or enforce any law which shall abridge the privileges or immunities of citizens of the United States; nor shall any State deprive any person of life, liberty, or property, without due process of law; nor deny to any person within its jurisdiction the equal protection of the laws." The congressman ended his amendment with a punch. "The Congress shall have power to enforce, by appropriate legislation, the provisions of this article."

Bingham made what he had in mind very clear when he told his colleagues, "Gentlemen who oppose this amendment oppose the grant of power to enforce the Bill of Rights." Here, then, in the record was the purpose of the Fourteenth Amendment as expressed by its author. Not everyone liked it. Not everyone does today.

Congressman Rogers of New Jersey was very much opposed. The amendment would let the Federal Government "exercise an absolute, despotic, uncontrolled power. . . ." He went on—and on. It gave Congress too much power. No wonder he was excited; they were changing the nature of the Union. They were moving the apex of power from the states to the Federal Government. After much debate, Congress sent the new amendment to the states in June. Ratification took two years.

Meanwhile, the liberty-loving congressmen knew they were in trouble. Mob violence broke out against the freedmen in Memphis in May; in New Orleans in July. Congress sent a committee to both cities to investigate.

In Memphis the committee members questioned a long list of witnesses. What caused the riot? Some said the Negro soldiers, discharged but hanging around with nothing to do but wait for their back pay, had quarreled with the police. Major General George Stoneman refuted the explanation. To be sure, that had happened, but "the Negro had nothing to do with it after the first day, except to be killed and abused," he said.

Mrs. Ellen Dilts, a local housewife, testified. She heard the shouts of the white men passing her door. "They said something about the Negroes having done them harm in the war by fighting against them, and they wanted to kill all the Negroes," she reported.

The committee members, wondering what to do about the South, asked a local criminal judge, William Hunter, "Do you think there is any civil remedy for the existing evils short of a military force?"

His answer was almost a prophecy of Congress' thinking at the next session. The judge replied, "I think there is none. . . ."

By now the 1866 Enforcement Act was on the books. No one was to act under color of law to deprive others of their rights. It was not very effective in New Orleans.

There, at the end of July, 1866, Negroes and whites were conducting a peaceful meeting inside the Mechanics Institute. They were discussing possible changes in the state constitution. Rioters, who included police and Confederate veterans, broke into the building. More rioters murdered the people as they tried to leave the hall. General Philip Sheridan called it "an absolute massacre."

Following these episodes the country was plunged into the election campaign of 1866. The President did not hurt the cause of the radical Republicans in Congress when he referred to them as "the traitors of the North." They were destroying states' rights. All the radicals had to do in reply was point to Memphis and New Orleans and the voters were aroused.

The next Congress divided the Old South into military districts to be run under the eyes of the Army. Only Tennessee, which had already ratified the Fourteenth Amendment, was spared this punishment. To get back home rule, the ten occupied states must not only ratify the Fourteenth Amendment but also give the franchise to all "of whatever race, color, or previous condition . . . except such as may be disfranchised for participation in the rebellion. . . ."

There followed a series of episodes that would shape southern attitudes for generations to come. Union soldiers 20,000 strong, armed with bayonets and advice from Washington, invaded the capitulated South. With them came northern adventurers called "carpetbaggers." According to southern tradition, they came bringing their few miserable possessions in satchels made of carpet, and they came eager to get rich quick. They saw the whipped and devastated Confederacy as a green pasture for their greedy hopes.

These characters, plus the antisecession southerners called "scalawags" and, to a lesser extent, the Negroes, controlled local governments for a short time. The carpetbaggers and the scalawags are often remembered for colorful corruption. They bought gold watches and china spittoons with state funds. They channeled money from public works into their own pockets. They caused taxes and public debt to skyrocket and they manipulated the newly enfranchised Negroes, particularly the illiterate ones. As one disappointed Negro put it, "I believe, my friends and fellow citizens, we are not prepared for this suffrage. . . ."

Contrary to southern tradition, some good was done. Reconstruction governments did repeal black codes, repair war-damaged roads and bridges, establish public school systems, and, in South Carolina, abolish imprisonment for debt. Men with black faces were elected to the legislatures, and they pored over their states' problems seeking progress, not revenge. But even if these governments had been a lot better, they would have been loathed.

The southern veteran, a hero to his neighbors, was disfranchised for his part in the rebellion. He stayed voteless until he was pardoned. His ex-slave could vote and hold office. To many, Congress seemed to be acting in a spirit of revenge. Hot-passioned veterans bent on resistance formed themselves into secret societies: the Knights of the White Camellia, the Ku Klux Klan. Night-riding comrades, disguised in sheets and hoods, made hideous the hours after dark. They carried torches, guns, and whips to drive out the leaders of the reconstruction, both white and Negro. They burned homes and flogged, hanged, or shot their victims.

In 1868 the Klan's Grand Imperial Wizard announced what everyone already knew—his men were against Negro suffrage under any and all circumstances. The Wizard's announcement only served to remind the Republicans in Congress that no easily repealable law was going to protect Negro voting rights. Naturally, the Republicans were astute enough to see that few white southerners would be voting for the party of Reconstruction fame for generations to come. They pinned their future hopes on the Negroes. The ex-slave, now freed, would henceforth be fully counted in determining the number of congressmen to which the South was entitled. The worst thing that could happen to the Republican crowd was to have the Negro first counted and then chased from the polls. The southern whites would then enjoy not only their own but also the Negroes' share of representation in the halls of government.

Politics and conviction flowed together, and in 1869 Congress sent the Fifteenth Amendment to the states. It was ratified a year later. Two months thereafter the lawmakers passed the Act of 1870, saying they intended to enforce the new amendment, to protect citizens' other rights, and to discourage terrorists. At the same time Congress re-enacted that part of the Enforcement Act of 1866 which is now on the books.

Resistance mounted. The Klan spread. Reconstruction governments teetered on the verge of collapse. Frightened legislators resorted to extreme measures, making it legal to hunt and shoot the disguised men. Congress also resorted to an extreme measure: It gave President Grant the power to suspend the writ of habeas corpus!

That meant that federal officials could keep a man in jail awaiting a trial and refuse to bring him in front of a judge to see if he was being held improperly. The right protected by this writ, the right of a prisoner to have a judge examine his detention, is one of the most powerful guardians of freedom. It is one of the main differences between a free society and a police state. Knowing its worth from their British history, and knowing too that without it innocent men had rotted in dungeons, the Founding Fathers put into the Constitution, "The privilege of the writ of habeas corpus shall not be suspended, unless when in cases of rebellion or invasion the public safety may require it." This time Congress considered that parts of the South were again in rebellion.

In October of 1871, the President reluctantly suspended the writ in nine South Carolina counties. How serious a step he had taken became evident three months later when Attorney General Kerman submitted the first annual report of the newly created Department of Justice. "With the exception of a few mistakes . . . which were soon corrected, I am satisfied that no innocent person was arrested," Kerman wrote. The South Carolinians who were arrested were probably not as satisfied as Kerman. On the other hand, the rest of Kerman's report shed a terrifying light on the prevailing chaos. Terrorism was annihilating both reconstruction and justice.

In the November term the Justice Department managed to get 420 people indicted in Columbia, South Carolina. The less heinous cases had to be postponed. The grand jury did not have time to investigate all the charges. Besides, it took the court over a month to try five cases. Kerman said that "many hundreds more . . . deserve to be indicted." The incidents of lawlessness, he concluded, "exceed the present capacity of the courts of the United States. . . ."

The congressmen went on for a while, passing civil rights bills, but the temper of their constituents changed. Up North people grumbled; the war was over, wasn't it? When were they going to stop rushing troops down South?

When in 1875 Mississippi demanded more soldiers, President Grant explained to his Attorney General, Edwards Pierrepont that "the whole public are tired out . . . and the great majority are ready now to condemn any interference on the part of the Government." In other words: No troops for Mississippi.

The next president, Rutherford B. Hayes, withdrew the last federal troops from the South. The Reconstruction era was over, and Congress began repealing some of its own Reconstruction legislation.

Time passed and southerners, back in control of their own state governments, rewrote their state constitutions. At South Carolina's constitutional convention of 1895, "Pitchfork" Benjamin Tillman, a senator and former governor, damned the reconstruction rulers and told the other delegates why they were there. "The Negroes put the little pieces of paper in the [ballot] box that gave the commission to these white scoundrels . . . [and] we are met in Convention . . . to put such safeguards around this ballot in future, to so restrict the suffrage and circumscribe it, that this infamy can never come about again."

Later, when Virginia's constitutional convention met, Carter Glass summed up the purpose of other old Confederate states. "Discrimination: Why that is precisely what we propose . . . with a view to the elimination of every Negro voter who can be gotten rid of, legally. . . ."

Here, then, in the records of the constitutional conventions was the evidence. Here was the purpose of the innocently worded voting laws that Katzenbach must expose. Beyond that there was the wonder that time had not disposed of these relics of post-Reconstruction reaction. Instead, like a plant they had grown new roots.

Among the roots was a speech given by a Negro leader and educator. In September of 1895, Booker T. Washington stood on the platform at the Atlanta exposition, surrounded by the exhibits of the great "new south"—machinery and prize animals. "It is at the bottom of life we must begin, and not at the top," he said. "The opportunity to earn a dollar in a factory just now is worth infinitely more than the opportunity to spend a dollar in an opera house."

Negroes needed jobs and schools more than equality in order to get started up from slavery. When many Negroes accepted this as their temporary fate, Washington's words "begin" and "just now" were forgotten. The South settled down to a long tradition of expecting the Negro to be forever content with second-class citizenship. The voices raised in dissent, including the cold, aloof voice of the Negro writer, W. E. B. DuBois, were hardly heard. The Fourteenth Amendment was equally ignored. The country was not ready for it and so it became like a forgotten letter, dusted off occasionally to impede the states in regulating railroads. The American people returned to their long-cherished tradition of letting each locality govern itself. Further complicating the later legal problem, the justices of the Supreme Court, being human, reflected the general attitude of the times and the people.

As far as civil rights were concerned, Justice Joseph P. Bradley, who was not a southerner but from New Jersey, expressed the feelings of the Court. He said that "When a man has emerged from slavery . . . there must be some state in the progress of his elevation when he takes the rank of a mere citizen, and ceases to be the special favorite of the laws, and when his rights as a citizen, or a man, are to be protected in the ordinary modes by which other men's rights are protected." By "ordinary modes" Bradley meant state laws. Mere discrimination at inns and amusement places and in public conveyances was no affair of the Federal Government.

Justice Harlan, the grandfather of the present justice, dissented vigorously. For the moment, he was overruled. For the time being, Bradley's voice was the voice of the law. It was, moreover, the tradition of law in which southerners—the southern attorney and the southern office seeker—were reared. The states' rights issue was joined to the belief that if the Negro was not stirred up by white scoundrels from the north he would remain satisfied. In addition southerners nurtured dreadful memories of Reconstruction days. Good people throughout the rest of the nation hoped that race relations would improve themselves gradually. Not everybody thought they would.

In January, 1909, a "call" went out, drafted by the highly respected journalist Oswald Garrison Villard of the New York *Evening Post*. It summoned "all the believers in democracy" to a national conference on the Negro question. The conference, at its second meeting in New York in May, 1910, formed the National Association for the Advancement of Colored People. Americans were again resorting to their right to assemble and to associate to voice their protest effectively.

The new association quickly put together its now-famous legal committee. By 1915, N.A.A.C.P. lawyers had won their first major victory before the Supreme Court. The case was *Guinn v. United States*. In it the court outlawed the all too obvious device of having different rules for people whose grandfathers had been voting before 1866.

Startled southerners still believed that the association's lawyers could never make the court reverse its other decisions. Not expecting any dramatic change in states' rights, they failed to speed up education and opportunity and prepare the Negro for privileges he would one day no longer ask for but demand. They resented the N.A.A.C.P. as a trouble-making organization, but most white supremacists did not foresee its getting very far. Southerners could not guess that a horrendous financial crisis in the thirties would make multitudes of Americans eagerly forget state sovereignty and look to the Federal Government for relief from hunger and panic.

Meanwhile, they did not notice something else fraught with changes and already on the way. At first it was not very noticeable, it was like distant thunder on a hot afternoon. Only the attentive could foresee that a welcome shower would eventually reach Negroes as well as other pleaders. A single raindrop fell in 1897 in the area of private property rights, and another drop fell in 1925 on the First Amendment's territory. Both times the Supreme Court justices imposed articles from the federal Bill of Rights on the states.

To so rule, the justices quoted a clause from the Fourteenth Amendment: ". . . nor shall any State deprive any person of life, liberty, or property, without due process of law. . . ."

"Due process of law" is an elusive phrase. The justices had to decide how much more of the Bill of Rights is so basic to decent government that it can be ruled to be due process and therefore binding on the states by virtue of the Fourteenth Amendment. They moved cautiously, examining each Fourteenth Amendment case brought before them. Only little by little was the Bill of Rights made binding on the states.

Justice Black became impatient, so much so that he copied into a Court opinion a whole section of the 1866 debates in Congress. These words, he hoped, would show the legal world how the authors of the Fourteenth Amendment meant it to extend all of the federal Bill of Rights to the states. Three justices before Black's time had thought the same. Three more agreed in 1947 when Black took his stand in the case called *Adamson v. California.*

What Black had accomplished was to make it necessary for every interested writer, editor, judge, or lawyer to go back and read the *Congressional Globe* (now the *Congressional Record*), which reported Congress' debates in full. The impact on the nation's thinking was tremendous.

With all this study behind them, the justices settled themselves on November 9, 1965, to hear the arguments about the Mississippi indictment. As was expected, the justices took a careful look at how the United States attorney had worded the charges for the grand jury. Had he successfully claimed the violation of a federal right? The attorney charged that the defendants did willfully assault, shoot, and kill Schwerner, Chaney, and Goodman for the purpose and with the intent of punishing the three. The defendants did thereby deprive each of rights and privileges secured by the Constitution of the United States—namely, the due process of a trial. Free men who had not been put on trial for any offense could not thus be summarily punished.

It made no difference to the Justice Department attorneys why the Mississippi people wanted to punish the civil rights workers. The attorney's thinking in this case could apply to any police brutality.

It was irrelevant that many local people considered the civil rights workers a motley crew of invaders, subverting southern tradition.

One of the justices listening to the argument was a new member of the Court. Justice Abe Fortas was appointed by President Johnson in 1965. Before that, Fortas, legally resourceful, bold, thorough, and a political liberal, was in private practice. His opponents called him a "tough lawyer to beat." He came to fame in 1963 when he successfully argued before the Supreme Court that a Florida convict named Clarence Gideon had not had a fair trial because he had had no lawyer to defend him. Gideon was denied advice of counsel in a criminal case in a Florida state court. In a federal case, he would have been granted a lawyer's help with his defense under the Sixth Amendment. Fortas insisted that a state court should provide the accused with the same help for the sake of due process. He convinced the Court. Thus Fortas, even before he became a justice, had taken part in extending to the states the guarantees of liberty in the Bill of Rights.

The Mississippi case was clear to Fortas. "If the Fourteenth Amendment forbids denial of counsel, it clearly denounces denial of any trial at all," he said. Fortas remembered that the Court had said once before that "where the police take matters in their own hands, seize victims, beat and pound them until they confess, there cannot be the slightest doubt that the police have deprived the victim of a right under the Constitution. It is the right of the accused to be tried by a legally constituted court. . . ."

Fortas disagreed with the ruling made by Judge Cox in Mississippi. Fortas considered that even nonofficial persons could be tried for acting under color of law to deny due process. "It was a joint activity, from start to finish . . . if the allegations are true . . . ," he said. For the same reason, he felt, all the defendants could be tried together for "conspiring" to break the Fourteenth Amendment. According to the claim in the indictment, state officers and private persons had planned and collaborated so that the victims were not charged and tried, as required by law. Instead they were intercepted on the highway, shot, and killed.*

Chief Justice Warren appointed Fortas to write the Court's opinion. "It would be strange, indeed, were this Court to revert to a construction of the Fourteenth Amendment which would once again narrow its historical purpose . . . [for] its objective was the protection of civil rights," Fortas said.

He took the same view of the Enforcement Act of 1870 "particularly since the violent denial of legal process was one of the reasons motivating enactment. . . ." Fortas had been reading the *Congressional Globe*. There, in the anguished words of the men who watched their dreams of reconstruction falter and fail, and not in the subsequent statements of the men who came later, Fortas sought the meaning and purpose of both the amendment and the law.

While Fortas was busy preparing all this, the Chief Justice announced the Court's decision in the voting rights case. He answered South Carolina's argument as to her sovereign right to be free of federal interference when she set reasonable voter qualifications. The gist of the matter is, Warren said, "When a state exercises power wholly within the domain of state interest, it is insulated (free) from federal . . . review. But such insulation is not carried over when the state power is used as an instrument for circumventing a federally protected right."

South Carolina had said that only the courts could find the states guilty of discrimination and therefore strike down their laws. Warren disagreed.

"On the contrary, the Fifteenth Amendment expressly declares that 'Congress shall have the power to enforce this article by appropriate legislation.' By adding this authorization, the Framers indicated that Congress was to be chiefly responsible for implementing the rights created. It is the power of Congress which has been enlarged."

This, Warren said, was true in describing each of the Civil War amendments. This is what Bingham and the others who had worked on those amendments had wanted. The Court had echoed their desires before, in *ex Parte Virginia*. "Whatever legislation . . . tends

* In October of 1967, a Mississippi jury did convict Deputy Sheriff Price and six other defendants. Sheriff Rainey was among those acquitted.

to . . . secure to all persons the enjoyment of perfect equality of civil rights and the equal protection of the laws against State denial or invasion, if not prohibited, is brought within the domain of congressional power."

Warren especially pointed to the history of the Fifteenth Amendment and the attempts to enforce it. "Congress," he said, "felt itself confronted by an insidious and pervasive evil. . . . Congress concluded that the unsuccessful remedies which it had prescribed in the past would have to be replaced by sterner and more elaborate measures in order to satisfy the clear commands of the Fifteenth Amendment."

The Chief Justice also paid tribute to the assembled petitioners in Alabama. He cited the statistics used by Katzenbach. After four years of litigation only 383 Negroes out of 15,000 were registered to vote in Dallas County. Said Warren, "Any possibility that these figures were attributable to political apathy was dispelled by the protest demonstrations in Selma in the early months of 1965." The great marches had impressed not only the public and the lawmakers but also the Court.

Warren then ended his approval of the voting rights act on a hopeful note. "After enduring nearly a century of widespread resistance to the Fifteenth Amendment, Congress has marshalled an array of potent weapons against the evil, with authority in the Attorney General to employ them effectively. . . ."

Thus ended the Court battle.

The voting act machinery went into gear. Under the eyes of federal observers, hundreds of Alabama Negroes flocked to the polls to vote in the May primary. The atmosphere was tense. A Confederate flag fluttered from a firehouse. A parked car carried a Confederate emblem and the words "Forget, Hell." There was no violence.

In the November elections of 1966, Wilson Baker became sheriff of Dallas County, replacing Jim Clark. In Macon County a Negro veteran of the Korean War captured the post of sheriff, and Negroes won a few other local offices in Alabama.

The hard-fought-for Voting Enforcement Act was beginning to work. Most Negroes believed it could never have been written without all the assembled efforts. Constituents influence their legislators. The proper exercise of this influence is an integral part of the responsibility that goes with the right peaceably to assemble and petition for a redress of grievances.

Pouring into the streets is an extreme measure and not always justified, as Judge Johnson told the Alabama marchers. The Supreme Court thinks so too. When civil rights workers blocked the entrance to a store and the merchant collected damages from a Georgia jury, the Supreme Court refused to hear an appeal. In November of 1966 the Court upheld a Florida jury's finding of trespassing against student demonstrators. Negro leaders themselves are worried about the damage that rioters or extremists may do to the movement.

Experienced petitioners know that radicalism can chase away support and, worse, make enemies who also petition their congressmen. The lawmakers watch the trends in public opinion. Herein lies the power that goes with freedom of assembly and petition. It is a power that all who speak and all who write share with the petitioner. They not only indicate a trend, they can help make it.

Influencing public opinion, persuading fellow citizens to one's frame of mind and then holding their support, must usually precede influencing Congress. The process can be slow. Aggrieved groups grow impatient. The reformers of the future may also grow impatient. They may forget. This very slowness to embrace change until enough people want it is an essential part of the self-governing process. Without the process all freedom is lost, and we would have no say whatever over our destinies; rather, we would become pawns in the hands of whatever group could seize power, the noisiest or the most violent. To prevent this, the Founding Fathers set up, as part of the elaborate machinery of the Bill of Rights, the guarantees of the right of assembly and petition embodied in the First Amendment.

BIBLIOGRAPHY FOR PART II

Principal Sources on Woman Suffrage

BOOKS

Anthony, Katharine. *Susan B. Anthony*. New York, 1954.

Anthony, Susan B., Elizabeth Stanton, and Matilda Gage. *History of Woman Suffrage*. New York, 1881.

Burnett, Constance B. *Five for Freedom*. New York, 1953.

Hays, Elinor R. *Morning Star: a Biography of Lucy Stone*. New York, 1961.

Leedham, Charles. *Our Changing Constitution*. New York, 1964.

Morrisson, Mary Foulke. *A Crusade and Some Crusaders* (Speech given at Connecticut College). New London, Conn., 1961.

National American Suffrage Association. *Victory, How Women Won It*. New York, 1940.

Park, Maud W. *Front Door Lobby*. Boston, 1960.
Sinclair, Andrew. *The Better Half*. New York, 1965.

UNITED STATES FEDERAL RECORDS

Congressional Record, September, 1918.

Principal Sources on Labor Relations

BOOKS

David, Henry. *The History of the Haymarket Affair*. New York, 1958.
Gompers, Samuel. *Seventy Years of Life and Labor: an Autobiography*. Rev.
    and ed. by Philip Taft and John A. Sessions. New York, 1957.
Kogan, Bernard R. (ed.). *The Chicago Haymarket Riot: Anarchy on Trial*
    (a collection of documents). Boston, 1959.
Mandel, Bernard. *Samuel Gompers*. Yellow Springs, Ohio, 1963.
Pelling, Henry. *American Labor*. Chicago, 1960.
Powderly, Terence V. *Thirty Years of Labor*. Ohio, 1890.
Shister, Joseph, Benjamin Aaron, and Clyde W. Summers. *Public Policy and
    Collective Bargaining*. New York, 1962.

UNITED STATES FEDERAL RECORDS

Congressional Records
    Congressional Record, April, 1959.
    U.S. Congress, *Hearings Before the Senate Committee on Education
    and Labor,* 73rd Congress, 2nd Session, March, 1934.
    U.S. Congress, *Hearings Before the Senate Committee on Labor and
    Public Welfare,* 80th Congress, 1st Session, 1947.
    U.S. Congress, Senate Report No. 46, *Preliminary Report on Violations
    of Free Speech and the Rights of Labor,* 75th Congress, 1st Session,
    1937.
    U.S. Congress, Senate Report No. 621, *Second Interim Report of the
    Committee on Improper Activities in the Labor Management Field,*
    86th Congress, August, 1959.

Supreme Court Records (Transcripts and Records of Briefs)
    DeJong v. Oregon, 299 U.S. 353 (1937).
    Hague v. Committee for Industrial Organization, 307 U.S. 496 (1939).
    N.L.R.B. v. Federbush Co., 121 F. 2d 954 (1941).
    Madden v. Atkins, 4 N.Y. 2d 283, 151 N.E. 2d 73 (1958).
    Thomas v. Collins, 323 U.S. 516 (1945).

MAGAZINES

Aaron, Benjamin. "Employer Free Speech." *Institute of Industrial Relations
    Report,* University of California, 1962.
Cox, Archibald. "The Role of Law in Preserving Union Democracy." *Har-
    vard Law Review,* Vol. 72 (1959), p. 609.
Summers, Clyde W. "Legal Limitations on Union Discipline." *Harvard Law
    Review,* Vol. 64 (1951), page 1049.

Principal Sources on the Negro

BOOKS

Aptheker, Herbert. *A Documentary History of the Negro People in the United States,* 2 vols. New York, 1962, 1964.

Botkin, Benjamin A. (ed.). *Lay My Burden Down: A Folk History of Slavery.* Chicago, 1945.

Brant, Irving. *The Bill of Rights.* New York, 1965.

Cahn, Edmund N. (ed.). *The Great Rights* (a collection of lectures written by Justices Earl Warren, Hugo L. Black, William O. Douglas, and William J. Brennan, Jr.). New York, 1963.

Douglass, Frederick. *Life and Times of Frederick Douglass.* Boston, 1893.

Franklin, John Hope. *Civil Rights in the United States* (unpublished manuscript in the U.S. Commission on Civil Rights Library). 1962.

Morison, Samuel Eliot. *The Oxford History of the American People.* New York, 1965.

Nevins, Allan. *The Emergence of Modern America.* New York, 1927.

Richardson, James. *A Compilation of the Messages and Papers of the Presidents.* Washington, D.C., 1897.

Sandburg, Carl. *Abraham Lincoln.* New York, 1939.

UNITED STATES FEDERAL RECORDS

Attorney General's Annual Reports
House of Representatives Executive Document No. 55, 42nd Congress, 2nd Session, January, 1872, Congressional Serial Set Vol. 1510.

Commission on Civil Rights, Staff Reports
Freedom to the Free, 1863–1963 (A Report to the President). U.S. Government Printing Office, 1963.
Hearings in Montgomery, Alabama, 1958.

Congressional Records
Congressional Globe, 39th Congress, 1st Session, 1866.
House of Representatives Report No. 101, 39th Congress, 1st Session, 1866, Congressional Serial Set Vol. 1274.
House of Representatives Report No. 439, 89th Congress, 1st Session, June, 1965.
Senate Report No. 162, part 3, 89th Congress, 1st Session, April, 1965.

Supreme Court Records (Transcripts and Records of Briefs)
Adamson v. California, 332 U.S. 46 (1947).
Ex Parte Virginia, 100 U.S. 339 (1880).
Louisiana v. United States, 380 U.S. 145 (1965).
Smith v. Allwright, 321 U.S. 649 (1944).
State of South Carolina v. Katzenbach, No. 22, March 7 (1966).
United States v. Atkins, 210 F. Supp. 441 (1962).
United States v. Atkins, 323 F. 2d 733 (1963).
United States v. Clark, Vol. 10 of Race Relations Report, page 236 (1965).

United States v. Louisiana, 225 F. Supp. 353 (1963).
United States v. Price, No. 59 and 60 (March, 1966).
Williams v. United States, 341 U.S. 97 (April, 1951).
Williams v. Wallace, 240 F. Supp. 100 (March, 1965).

NEWSPAPERS AND MAGAZINES

Chicago Journal, August 30, 1866.
New York Times, September 17, 1875, and March 9–25, 1965.
Washington Post, October 23, 1883, and March 15–23, 1965.

PART THREE

THE

WORSHIPERS

"Congress shall make no law respecting an establishment of religion, or prohibiting the free exercise thereof . . ."

—First Amendment

". . . the accused shall enjoy the right to a speedy and public trial, by an impartial jury . . ."

—Sixth Amendment

THE RIGHTS AND THE ISSUES

Probably freedom of religion in the United States seems completely established and utterly secure to most people, but no freedom is ever that safe from assault or controversy. True, the federal Constitution guarantees that "Congress shall make no law respecting an establishment of religion, or prohibiting the free exercise thereof." It also says that "no religious test shall ever be required as a qualification to any office or public trust under the United States." In every one of the fifty state constitutions there is some sort of guarantee of religious freedom. The wordings differ, but over and over again we find this right described as "natural and unalienable," "self-evident," "forever guaranteed." In addition, it is now recognized that the Fourteenth Amendment makes the religious liberty clause in the federal Constitution binding on the states. After that the quarrels begin.

Many states forbid the use of tax funds—collected from all the citizens—to support sectarian schools. After hearing the arguments, however, the Supreme Court refused to stop the states from providing bus service for pupils going to parochial schools. The buses were for the safety of the children and not primarily to aid religious instruction, the Court decided. Another furor arose when Marylanders excluded atheists from the religious liberty principle by requiring every applicant for a commission as notary public to sign a statement that he believed in a Supreme Being. The Supreme Court outlawed the practice in 1961.

What happened in 1964 was more surprising, considering how many states have said in their constitutions that no person shall be compelled to attend any place of worship or support any sect or denomination. The United States Supreme Court had declared unconstitutional the practice of having prayers and ceremonial Bible reading in the public schools, which are run under compulsory attendance laws. Parents had complained that doctrines contrary to their faith were being offered. A hectic and excited campaign, which even threatened to change the First Amendment, followed the announcement of the Court's ruling. Here follows the story of many of the people who became involved in that campaign and the reasons for their actions.

"Make No Law Respecting an Establishment of Religion"

IN 1962 the court fight over government-prescribed religion came out of New York State. The case was called *Engel v. Vitale* and it started a controversy that eventually involved the whole nation.

People working for the New York Board of Regents had written a "nondenominational" prayer for all school children to recite. The angry parents of ten young children started a lawsuit, charging that the use of official prayers in public schools violated the United States Constitution. They quoted the First Amendment to the Constitution: "Congress shall make no law respecting an establishment of religion." They cited the Fourteenth Amendment, which extends this command and forbids state authorities to establish religious practices.

Justice Black, speaking for the Supreme Court, upheld the parents.

> There can be no doubt that New York's state prayer program officially establishes the religious beliefs embodied in the Regents' prayer.
>
> . . . in this country [the Court reminded the Board of Regents] it is no part of the business of government to compose official prayers for any group of the American people to recite. . . .
>
> . . . this very practice of establishing governmentally composed prayers for religious services . . . caused many of our early colonists to leave England and seek religious freedom in America.

Black referred to the persecuted English Puritans, English Quakers, Baptists, and Catholics. He also mentioned the European practice of having each monarch dictate the religious beliefs of his subjects—trampling on the dissenters. Along with English dissenters, persecuted Protestants from France and Germany and Jews from various parts of Europe had sought asylum in the rugged new world.

Black then pointed to the reasons that had compelled the Founding Fathers to make the religious liberty clause a rigid one. "It is an unfortunate fact of history that when some of the very groups which had most strenuously opposed the established Church of England found themselves sufficiently in control of colonial governments in this country to write their own prayers into law, they passed laws making their own religion the official religion of their respective colonies."

In Colonial days, zealots might strip a heretic to the waist and make him feel the sting of thirty lashes with a knotted whip. They jailed or banished the nonconformist or, if he resisted banishment, finished him on the gallows.

Only due to the courage of pioneers did the Colonial population move toward religious liberty. In 1634, Massachusetts was shaken by the "ravings" of the outspoken young son of a merchant tailor. His name was Roger Williams. Reverend Williams declared from his pulpit that the civil authority had no power over a man's spiritual conscience. He not only called for religious freedom for Christians, Jews, and Turks, he also insisted that for all anyone knew the Indian religion might be as acceptable to God as Christianity. To all this he added that "forced worship stinks in God's nostrils."

Horrified, Massachusetts Puritans debated how to handle this "devilish preacher." First they put him on trial in Massachusetts General Court. Then they ordered him banished. In January of 1636 they made a plan to seize him and ship him back to England. Forewarned, Williams fled into the howling winter storms of the New England wilderness. There he passed the bitter winter "without knowing what bread or bed did mean." In the spring, with the help of four companions, Williams founded his settlement in Rhode Island—the first to proclaim the separation of church and state. In 1644 Williams obtained papers of incorporation from Parliament letting the colony (then called Providence Plantations) govern itself, under England.

Historians have marveled ever since that King Charles II of England in 1663 granted Williams and his friends a charter for Rhode Island that included full religious liberty. One historian, Sanford Cobb, has even hinted that the monarch must have acted in an inattentive moment.

In any case the struggle for freedom of conscience continued to make only slow, hard-won progress. In 1733 Georgia gave religious toleration to Jews and Protestants, and by the end of the Colonial period in several colonies all the Christian sects were treated nearly equally, although Catholics were discriminated against in some respects.

After the Revolution of 1776, those colonies which had obediently accepted the Church of England realized that they must henceforth make their own decisions. The issue came to a climax in Virginia. There, even when dissenters were not jailed, it had been the practice to tax them to support the ministers of the established creed, and the ministers—so supported—then preached against the dissenters. With England's authority gone, Virginians debated what to do about public faith. Eventually a tax bill was proposed entitled "A Bill Establishing a Provision for Teachers of the Christian Religion." The money was to be given by the government to the Christian church designated by each taxpayer.

The bill was read and considered in the assembly. It might have passed had not the opponents of the measure been represented in the assembly by James Madison. Madison at once recognized the bill as a return to the earlier abuses of political power. Astutely he maneuvered to have it postponed. Then he wondered how to arouse the citizenry against this dangerous proposal. How could he convince them that religion must not be allowed to depend on the police power of the state—not even the state's power to collect taxes?

To alarm the Virginians, Madison wrote the "Memorial and Remonstrance against Religious Assessments." This document was a masterpiece of legal logic. Because it was Madison who, four years later, wrote the First Amendment to the United States Constitution, justices of the Supreme Court refer to the "Memorial" in their explanation of the meaning of the religious liberty clause in our Bill of Rights. (Black referred to it in *Engel v. Vitale*, as other justices had done before.) Said Madison: "The Religion . . . of every man must be left to the conviction and conscience of every man. . . . This right is in its nature an unalienable right . . . because the opinions of men, depending only on the evidence contemplated by their own minds, cannot follow the dictates of other men. . . ."

Madison then argued that since a man's right to believe as he pleased was unalienable, it followed that it had to be *wholly exempt from the cognizance of the civil powers*. Neither the majority nor the legislature could have any authority to trespass on a minority's right to personal religious opinion. Society could not tell people what to think. The proper separation of those powers that guide men's lives had to be maintained or else men would not remain free. The influences of government and religion, therefore, had to be kept separate.

Madison then sounded a call of alarm. "Who does not see that the same authority which can establish Christianity, in exclusion of all other Religions, may establish with the same ease any particular sect of Christians, in exclusion of all other sects? That the same authority which can force a citizen to contribute three pence only of his property for the support of any one [Religious] establishment, may force him to conform to any other establishment in all cases whatsoever?" If the government had any right to establish Christianity, it had just as much right to establish a particularly favored denomination of Christianity and to decide in what manner a faith must be practiced.

The bill also violated that equality which ought to be the basis of every law. Since all men were equally entitled to be free, they were equally entitled, above all else, to make whatever arrangements conscience dictated for the exercise of their religion.

Finally Madison hit his hardest blow. "[T]he bill," he said, "implies either that the Civil Magistrate is a competent Judge of Religious truth; or that he may employ Religion as an engine of Civil policy. The first is arrogant pretension. . . . The second an unhallowed perversion of the means of salvation." (When Black quoted the "unhallowed perversion" part, it seemed as if Madison were glaring through time, straight at the members of the New York Board of Regents, and asking: What kind of American history is taught in New York?) Madison wanted the men of the future, as well as those of his own day, to safeguard a man's personal religious rights with as much vigor as society uses to protect a man's personal property rights.

The "Memorial" was printed. It was circulated. Madison waited. As the days passed, Baptists, Quakers, Presbyterians, Methodists, the few Roman Catholics in Virginia, and even some members of the once-established Church rallied to its support. At last, just before Christmas of 1785, the Assessment Bill was defeated. Later, Madison was helped by Thomas Jefferson, who believed that any invasion of a man's religious rights was an invasion of natural right. Together Madison and Jefferson managed to get the principle of complete religious freedom incorporated in the Virginia constitution. Similar laws were also considered and at last passed in other states, and by the time the United States Constitution was adopted, most Americans considered any union between church and state disastrous.

Justice Black said Americans knew from bitter personal experience what happened when zealous groups struggled to get the stamp of government approval for their particular brand of worship. Strife and persecution were the result.

The Regents argued that their government-sponsored prayer favored no group but was nonsectarian. It was designed so that it would offend no one. These men forgot, or did not realize, that some churchmen object to having this kind of neutralized religion taught in schools. Those ministers who were offended described the prayer program as offering all children the same meaningless, tasteless, watered-down pablum. The Regents also argued that the program did not require all pupils to recite. It excused those who wished to be excused. In other words, it was voluntary.

Black was not impressed. The Court had faced the "voluntary" argument before. Justice Felix Frankfurter had tackled it in the case of *Illinois ex rel. McCollum v. Board of Education* in 1948. School children in Champaign, Illinois, were being divided up according to their denominations and then sent to separate classrooms for a once-a-week religious instruction period. The whole program involved the use of tax-financed public school property and compulsory school attendance laws to aid religious instruction. The school, of course, could accommodate only a few instructors. As there are in the United States some eighty-three large religious groups and many small ones, what happened next was inevitable. Parents started complaining that "certain Protestant groups have obtained an overshadowing advantage in the propagation of their faiths over other Protestant sects."

It was no answer to this to say that the program was voluntary and that dissenters could continue their secular studies. However, the question was not taken to court until a sensitive ten-year-old boy ended up the only dissenter in his room. His mother, Vashti McCollum, a slim, quiet, intellectual woman, insisted that this situation constituted subtle pressure on him to participate.

The Supreme Court of the United States heartily agreed. Small and restless Justice Felix Frankfurter felt compelled to add his own explanation to that of the Court. "That a child is offered an alternative . . . does not eliminate the operation of influence by the school in matters . . . outside the school's domain. The law of imitation operates, and nonconformity is not an outstanding characteristic of children. The result is an obvious pressure upon children to attend." Frankfurter added, "The children belonging to these non-participating sects will thus have inculcated in them a feeling of separatism when the school should be the training ground for habits of community. . . ." Frankfurter felt strongly that the school had the obligation to teach that in this country we all have the right to go to our own house of worship and to worship in our different ways. In school we live together as a solid group of Americans, leaving our religious differences outside.

Earlier, United States Presidents had seen this need. President Grant and President Theodore Roosevelt had both made strong statements urging that religion be kept out of the public schools.

In 1962 a handsome young President who was much beloved added his sentiment. At his Wednesday afternoon press conference on June 27, President John F. Kennedy faced an auditorium full of inquiring reporters who were keenly aware of how many people were upset by Black's ruling against the Regents' prayer. The President told them that there was an easy remedy for not being allowed to pray in schools.

"We can pray a great deal more at home, we can attend our churches with a good deal more fidelity. . . .

"That power is very much open to us. And I would hope that as a result of this decision, that all American parents will intensify their efforts at home. And that the rest of us will support the Constitution and the responsibility of the Supreme Court in interpreting it. . . ."

The Court had no intention of neglecting its responsibility. A year later another chapter was written in the Court's battle against school-directed prayer. This time the case was *Abington Township v. Schempp.*

Ellory Schempp—a well-liked high school senior and church-going Unitarian—had objected to the literal presentation of certain Bible passages used again and again in the daily devotional in his Pennsylvania public school. His parents understood. He was part of a captive audience at services that included tenets contrary to his beliefs. Pennsylvania decided to have dissenters excused, but Ellory's younger sister Donna emphatically did not want to be excused from school prayers and Bible reading. She was not going to be thought an "oddball."

The story sounded familiar. It reminded Justice Brennan of another episode seventy years before in Wisconsin. There offended Catholic parents objected to Protestant prayers. There, too, it had been argued that dissenters could be excused.

The Wisconsin State Supreme Court had answered that "the practice in question tends to destroy the equality of the pupils which the constitution seeks to establish . . ." and the practice was prohibited. Then, twenty years after the Wisconsin episode, the Louisiana supreme court found that "excusing such children [dissenters] on religious grounds . . . would be a distinct preference in favor of the religious beliefs of the majority. . . ."

It was therefore obvious to Brennan that the fact that children could be excused was constitutionally irrelevant. Governments in the United States could not favor any set of believers, even the majority. The problem was how to help the people, who were already fuming over last year's decision, to accept this one. Brennan sat down at his desk among his lawbooks, his pencils, and his big yellow pads of paper. While he was thinking, some past events came to mind and gave him an idea.

He remembered that in 1961 the Supreme Court had upheld the right of a community to make all businesses close on Sunday. Brennan granted that this had once been a religious law. Now it served a secular purpose—to give everyone a day of rest. Much earlier, in 1879, the Court had upheld the right of a state to forbid a man to have more than one wife. This again was a general, nonreligious law limiting actions, not beliefs, and was enacted to promote peace and order in the community.

This parade of Court decisions had left behind, in some people's minds, a serious misunderstanding. Brennan thought he grasped what this misunderstanding was.

The justice picked up his pencil and wrote that "Nothing in the text of the Establishment clause supports the view that the prevention of the setting up of an official church was meant to be the full extent of the [Amendment's] prohibitions." Nor, he added, was "protection of unpopular creeds . . . the full extent of the Amendment's guarantee. . . ." If it had been, the framers would have said so; the Supreme Court had explained before, in *McGowan v. Maryland*. ". . . what Madison, Jefferson and the others fought to end, was the extension of civil government's support to religion . . . which made the two in some degree interdependent, and thus threatened the freedom of each."

While Brennan was working on his concurring opinion, Justice Tom Clark of Texas worked on the majority opinion, reflecting the conclusions of eight of the nine justices. Justice Stewart was going to dissent. Clark's main problem was that the Schempp case was being heard along with a complaint against school prayers brought by an atheist family, the Murrays. He searched for words to put across what had already been decided in a 1947 case, *Everson v.*

Board of Education, that "the Amendment requires the state to be a neutral in its relations with groups of religious believers and non-believers." James Madison had thought the same, and Madison had added that "it is proper to take alarm at the first experiment on our liberties."

Clark also had to tackle another inflammatory question brought up by Justice Stewart: What about the religious freedom of the people who wanted their children exposed to religious influences at school and could not afford private school? Freedom of speech and religion should be available to all, not merely to those who could pay their own way. Closely tied to Stewart's position was the question: What if the majority wanted to pray?

They still could not use the public schools as a place to have their chosen prayers recited out loud. They had to learn that in public school other people have equal rights. Justice Douglas had said they could not make everybody else pay school taxes to support their religious preference. Clark added a quote from Justice Robert H. Jackson. "The very purpose of the Bill of Rights was to withdraw certain subjects from . . . political controversy, to place them beyond the reach of majorities. . . ." And again quoting Jackson, Clark said, "There is no answer to the proposition . . . that the effect of the religious freedom Amendment to our Constitution was to take every form of propagation of religion out of the realm of things which could directly or indirectly to be made public business. . . ."

The Court had patiently reviewed all this before, but this time the public reacted differently. Magazines and newspapers spotlighted the sensational atheist family, whose case was heard along with the Schempps'. The public read the publicity and not always the Court's careful opinion. As a result people made outrageous statements.

The Court was expelling God from the schools! The Court was part of a deliberate design to subordinate the American people to a godless state!

They ignored the fact that the Court had made it very clear that its decision did not prevent the schools from having the children sing patriotic songs or read patriotic passages that included mention of the deity. The prohibition was limited to religious services or exercises, selected by governmental school authorities. In fact, Justice Brennan had suggested inspiring good discipline by reading passages from the speeches and messages of great Americans. Many of these contain a reference to God. Clark, in addition, had said that the Bible could be read in connection with the study of history or literature. But neither this nor anything else stopped the barrage of emotionally charged remarks.

Eventually the excited people triggered what some writers called public hysteria and other writers called a national stampede. "Stampeders" were bent on overruling the justices. They wanted to amend the Constitution to permit school-selected prayers. Trouble was in the air.

"A Pandora's Box"

ONE indication of all that was brewing reached a Baptist pastor, Dr. Wayne Dehoney, at his church in Jackson, Tennessee. It was a letter from two young people, afraid that "our nation will become atheist. Do you think anything can be done?" they wrote. Pastor Dehoney took the letter seriously. It was a subject close to his heart. He had a historically rooted abhorrence to government-established religion. Baptist preachers had been jailed in colonial Virginia for preaching without a license from the state church, and Baptists had helped put the First Amendment into the Constitution. Dehoney thought the way to avoid atheism was to belong to your church and really know your religion. It upset Dehoney that multitudes shared these young people's feelings.

Among these multitudes there were some toward whom Dehoney felt particularly critical. Carl J. McIntire, a radio preacher with a western twang and a hearty hello, told the young people sitting by their sets to go through the streets collecting petitions to amend the Constitution. McIntire's own son headed this project. Dehoney knew that the Presbyterian Church had deposed Carl J. McIntire from his ministry in 1936. Later, in 1965, the church's office of information said he "has made a career of maligning the leadership and programs of major church bodies. . . ." Besides the McIntires, another group whipped up support for the "youth petition drive." These people hailed the constitutional amendment as a "body blow to the morale of all the pro-Communists."

Dehoney did not consider himself a pro-Communist, nor did he think that the other ministers of the other denominations, who either agreed with the Supreme Court or who opposed changing the Constitution, were pro-Communists.

Even before the Court had handed down the Schempp decision, the General Assembly of the United Presbyterian Church had come out and said, "Religious observances (should) never be . . . introduced into the public school as part of its program. . . . Bible reading and prayers as devotional acts tend toward indoctrination or meaningless ritual and should be omitted for both reasons." Later John Wesley Lord, a bishop of the Methodist Church, had said, "We need not a new amendment, but greater respect for the First Amendment in its present form."

From all over the land, ministers of the major denominations agreed. Pastor Dehoney was proud that the editors of Baptist periodicals opposed the proposed amendment. In addition they had taken great pains to explain to their readers that the Court decision did not prohibit individuals from praying in silence at school. It did not eliminate chaplains from the Army, where the ministers were there as a service to the men and not as part of a program of state indoctrination. It did not take "In God We Trust" off the coins. Dehoney, like many of his brethren, tried to explain all this to his congregation. Since they were Baptists, he wondered how they would feel if they saw their children in Honolulu offered a Buddhist prayer—or in Utah the Book of Mormon, or elsewhere Hail Marys —as the sanctioned worship of the community.

For the time being the church-paper editors, the ministers, and the constitutional lawyers who were against amending the Constitution were not as numerous as the "stampeders" who, as one Methodist minister in California put it, seemed to have nine lives. Frustrated by the Court, they flooded Congress with mail. They expressed their fears that the country would go atheist. They told their congressmen that this country would never have achieved its present greatness if it had not been a "Nation under God" and its leaders religious men, a fact the Court did not refute; "we are a religious people . . . ," the Court had said. The angry petitioners could then not see how the Court could forbid school prayers when it started its own session with "God save the United States and this Honorable Court." They pointed to all the American Presidents who had said public prayers and to the reference to the Creator in the Declaration of Independence. They seemed unaware that the Court had also mentioned these things, adding that "religious freedom is . . . likewise as strongly imbedded in our public life. . . ." Schools, the justices remembered, were run under compulsory attendance laws for the purpose of providing state-directed instruction. Whatever went on carried the state's endorsement that this was *the right* way to do things.

The petitioners then pointed a finger at the statistics on juvenile delinquency and said the delinquency rate proved the need for prayer—the children needed reverence to inspire good conduct—none of which answered the contention of the justices and the concurring churchmen that this spiritual quality had to come from the home and the church and not be fettered and regimented by the efforts of school authorities trying to deal with America's myriads of different sects. For the most part these petitioners were sincere. Some of them were so outraged they asked the lawmakers to teach the Supreme Court a lesson and amend the Constitution.

They certainly had an effect on their representatives in Washington. One after another, a hundred and fifty resolutions to amend the Constitution were written by congressmen in their offices. Time after time when the session bell rang a congressman could be seen coming in the House of Representatives chamber carrying one of these. Its author would hand it to one of the neat young blue-suited boy pages. The pages edged through the aisles and dropped the proposals into a box near the door called the "hopper." From there the proposals were sent for consideration to the House Judiciary Committee.

Congressman Emanuel Celler of New York, chairman of the Judiciary Committee, was deeply troubled. For over a hundred and seventy years the Bill of Rights had been considered to be virtually unamendable. As Celler saw it, once it became politically feasible to make exceptions to the prohibition in the Great Bill, every American freedom was in jeopardy. That 223 constitutional lawyers thought the same did Celler very little good. As yet, their joint statement had not reached the congressman, nor did he know it was coming.

A host of ministers, law professors, and the president of the American Bar Association, Walter E. Craig, also saw the danger, but mostly they too were still unheard from. Meanwhile it looked as if some decision would have to be made at any moment.

Celler had to be grateful when at last he heard from Erwin N. Griswold, Dean of Harvard Law School. Griswold had been against the Supreme Court decision forbidding religious services in public schools, but now he warned Celler that "once amendments are adopted to any part of the Bill of Rights, the flood gates may be opened." His words painted a picture of future panicky citizens urging restrictions on freedom of speech and the press and demanding the elimination of those safeguards provided for possibly innocent people who had been accused of a crime.

Griswold, however, expressed himself in general terms, saying that "we . . . will eventually wake up to find that we have lost the essential safeguards . . . [which are] our greatest heritage . . . the center and core of our governmental system, the most distinctly American contribution to the art and science of self-government. . . . our generation are trustees of these provisions, for generations yet to come."

Celler, too, could foresee that every time an unpopular court ruling was handed down, every time a national problem arose, large segments of the public could be counted on to be impatient with other people's rights. The present situation was certainly a case in point.

Celler's first reaction was to wait for the excitement to die down. When it didn't, he hoped that outraged lawyers and anxious ministers would rally enough citizens to offset the stampeders.

Justice Brennan had said, "It is not only the nonbeliever who fears the injection of sectarian doctrines and controversies into the civil polity, but in as high degree it is the devout believer who fears. . . ."

There was one big trouble with that. As Celler knew, many church groups send delegates to general conventions or assemblies only once every two or three years. Leaders of these organizations could not commit their groups to opposing the amendment until a discussion had been held at a convention and a resolution voted and passed. Therefore, Celler was waiting for men like Pastor Wayne Dehoney to work out their carefully worded sermons and reach thoughtful individuals in the population. The Congressman hoped more people would be against the proposed constitutional amendment if they understood all its implications.

While Celler waited, he faced a lot of abuse. Pro-amendment forces referred to Celler's "one-man blockade."

Spurred on by the zeal in these remarks, Congressman Frank J. Becker of New York had written a proposed draft for the amendment. He started gathering signatures on a "discharge petition." If a majority of the congressmen signed it, Becker's resolution could bypass Celler's Judiciary Committee and be taken to the floor of the House. There, the idea could be voted on without the benefit of any study by the Judiciary Committee, possibly after only a few hours of debate. This meant that congressmen would be voting under a barrage of claims that either they wanted this amendment or they were godless and, in addition, were ignoring their constituents. Becker, pointing to the mail, insisted that "who can deny that there exists an overwhelming sentiment favorable to this proposition?"

In addition, Becker gleefully pointed out that two eminent religious leaders, evangelist Billy Graham and His Eminence Francis Cardinal Spellman, supported his proposal to legalize school prayers. Graham suggested that the Ten Commandments could be read and said every day in school; Protestants, Catholics, and Jews all agree on the Ten Commandments. Cardinal Spellman, while agreeing that there should be no state religion, felt that there should also be no irreligion either.

Celler thought anxiously of the words of Justice Jackson. "The day this country ceases to be free for irreligion it will cease to be free for religion—except for the sect that can win political power." Becker with equal concern was utterly convinced his cause was right. He pointed to the atheist Madalyn Murray and to Professor Corliss Lamont, who were fighting his bill. "I do not question the sincerity of good people opposed to this amendment, but I think . . . they might be shocked to find what strange and obnoxious company they are keeping," he said.

That statement was too much for Congressman Jacob H. Gilbert of New York, who said that "there is vast opposition to your amendment by responsible and respected religious organizations and groups."

Celler—famous for his ability to ask devastating questions—immediately confronted Becker with, "Isn't it true, Mr. Becker, that the important Catholic organs of the mass media of communication, like *Commonweal* and *America,* have expressed themselves in opposition to this amendment?"

Becker answered Celler that "we, as Catholics, are occasionally in disagreement. . . ." He answered Gilbert that he knew that the Public Affairs Committee of the Baptist Church and the Board of the National Council of Churches did oppose his amendment, but he said, "Let me say this in all honesty. I think the opposition comes from the leadership of these groups but not from the mass of the people."

One hundred and sixty-seven congressman must have agreed. They signed Becker's discharge petition. Faced with this, Celler moved.

He arranged to have his committee hold hearings and listen to testimony on the amendment. On Wednesday, April 22, 1964, at 10

A.M. in Room 346 of the old Cannon Office Building, twenty-six congressmen from states as far apart as California and Connecticut moved into the leather-backed seats placed for their use on a semi-circular mahogany dais.

In spite of the sparkling cut-glass chandelier, the gay light green walls, the red carpeting, and the informal little chairs that had been set out in neat rows for spectators, the atmosphere in the chamber had the austerity of a courtroom. Possibly this was due to the way some of the men on the dais felt about the proposal before them.

Tinkering with the First Amendment was a serious matter. Thwarting the public will was equally serious.

Celler hoped that here in the Committee room people opposed to the amendment would be given a chance to put their reasons on the record. He hoped much could be said to arouse the complacent public. Millions of people were wondering what all the fuss was about. What difference did it make if children said a few words of prayer in school? Perhaps if they had passages from Celler's hearings pointed out or repeated to them, they would understand the magnitude of the question.

As Cellar saw it, words like those in the Becker amendment were very like an iceberg. You see the words, but the mass of meaning is submerged. The Becker amendment did not even use the words "nondenominational prayer." In that regard it merely said, "Nothing in this Constitution shall be deemed to prohibit the offering, reading from, or listening to prayers or biblical Scriptures, if participation therein is on a voluntary basis, in any governmental or public school, institution or place. . . ." At least in committee the wording of the amendment could be adequately studied.

For example, Section 2 of the Becker amendment said, "Nothing in this Constitution shall be deemed to prohibit making reference to belief in, reliance upon, or invoking the aid of God or a Supreme Being in any governmental or public document, proceeding, activity, ceremony, school, institution. . . ."

For how many minutes or hours were these invocations to go on in school? Wasn't it conceivable under this wording to convert a public school into a parochial school? That this was not likely at the moment was no answer. An amendment to the Constitution must be planned for posterity—for an unforeseeable future.

Charles H. Tuttle, attorney and general counsel for the National Council of Churches of Christ—whose board members had officially supported the wisdom of the Supreme Court decision—pointed out another difficulty. Tuttle pointed to Article VI, Paragraph 3, of the Constitution that "no religious test shall ever be required as a qualification to any office or public trust under the United States." Under the wording of the Becker amendment a religious test could be considered a public document or proceeding. Conceivably a religious test could then be required. "Conceivably," is a vastly important word when a constitutional amendment is under consideration.

Celler's big problem was to make these difficulties clear to the American people. As most people never see the record of a congressional hearing, the Congressman knew he would need the help of the public press. Getting this help was another problem.

When the hearings were called they did have publicity, but not all of it was helpful. A pro-amendment periodical called *Liberty Letter* immediately announced that "arch-secularist Celler will pull out all the stops to tie the Becker Amendment into endless knots of procedural red tape until Congress adjourns. . . ."

Congressman Celler recognized their right to push for their opinion, but he wondered what was wrong with some of the big papers from his own state. What were they thinking? Why weren't they also moving to shape public opinion on the Becker amendment? To surmount this disturbing obstacle in his fight to inform the public, Celler again relied on his talent for shaping a revealing question. He discussed the problem with a friendly lobbyist named Seymour Graubard, who came before the committee.

The Chairman to Mr. Graubard: "I would like to ask you this, if I may. The First Amendment is a bundle of liberties. It refers to freedom of religion, press, free speech, and so forth. Is that correct?"

Graubard: "Yes, sir."

Chairman: "Would you say that any change in that First Amendment is likely to open the door to changes in all these other liberties?"

Graubard: ". . . yes, I think you face a whole procession of amendments. . . . You are going to open a Pandora's box. . . ."

Chairman: "The reason I ask the question is this. Quite a number of the newpapers are rather discreetly silent editorially in our home town of New York on this very subject. It is rather strange, because it strikes me that any change in this First Amendment is bound to have some sort of effect upon freedom of speech and freedom of press and so forth because of the inherent dangers of tinkering with the First Amendment. . . ."

Graubard: "I think that if the editors sat here and heard some of the testimony that you hear, they would feel impelled to take a position."

Celler hoped so too. As a first blow in line with this hope, Celler had committee members arrange themselves on their dais to listen to, and then question, Congressman Becker.

They listened carefully to all Becker had to say. His principal idea was that many people subscribe to no religion. Without school services their children would never know there was a God. He also stated that he had met with five other people and together they had agreed on his proposed amendment. He was questioned about this by Congressman Byron G. Rogers, a Protestant Democrat from Denver, Colorado.

Rogers: "At these meetings, did you discuss the question of what form the prayer should be?"

Becker: "No. . . . It was left up to . . . the various schools."

Rogers: "Did you discuss the question of what Biblical Scripture should be read?"

Becker: ". . . that, again, had been left up to the local jurisdiction and we did not discuss it."

Rogers: "And if it is in a Mormon community, then they could read from the Mormon Bible?"

Becker: ". . . the school, whether it be the superintendent, the principal, the teacher, the board of education, whoever decides that prayer or Bible reading can be said in school, should decide . . . what prayer they say, what Bible they read from. . . ."

Rogers: "If they prescribed the prayer of one religion, then the pupils must sit back and abide by that decision?"

Becker: "I think you are belaboring a point."

Becker may have thought so, but the committee did not. They went on discussing the problem after he left.

Congressman William Cahill, a Republican attorney from New Jersey who had held a succession of public offices, had once taught school. He knew school boards, and he wondered out loud what would happen if the members of the school board, selecting the prayer, could not agree among themselves as to what to use.

He was answered by Congressman William (Bill) Cramer, another Republican. Cramer came from Florida. A popular man, he had held elective office all the way back to his school days. He sympathized with Becker. His answer was that "the voters . . . make the final decisions themselves, if they don't like what the school board does, they can turn them out."

With that Celler quickly interrupted. "Just a minute," he said.

"Then you are putting the question of what prayer or what Bible reading there shall be in politics."

Mr. Cramer evidently felt the need to be emphatic. "Mr. Chairman," he said, "so far as I am concerned, the determination of whether prayer should be permitted is logically in the hands of the local school board. It is obvious, further, that the electorate has a right to decide whether they like what the school board does. . . . That has been the view for years and years. . . . What has been wrong with it up to the decision of the Supreme Court?"

Celler answered, "Just because nobody had the courage to test it, doesn't mean that it was right."

While all this was going on, one member of the committee, Congressman George F. Senner, Jr., of Arizona, was keeping many things in mind. He had gone to school, grown up, and practiced law with his father in Miami, Arizona. According to the laws of Arizona, "A teacher who . . . teach[es] any sectarian doctrine or conduct[s] any religious exercises in school [is] guilty of unprofessional conduct and his certificate shall be revoked."

Senner knew that Arizona was not the only state where people felt that way. Prior to the Supreme Court ruling, only twelve states had required devotional Bible readings. In the other states, regulations varied all the way from forbidding morning devotionals to taking no stand. Even in those states where prayer and Bible reading services were not forbidden, local community leaders had reported that in their school (or school system) they did not have such a program.

Those who spoke of going back to things as they were before the Supreme Court ruled were asking Senner and multitudes like him to tread a path where they had never been. Something else worried Senner even more. A question formed itself in his mind, but he held it back while listening to the unusually gripping testimony of Dr. Edwin Bronner.

Dr. Bronner was a history professor and the curator of the Quaker collection at Haverford College. He wanted to encourage the committee members to model themselves after the great statesmen of old and stand firm both for religious liberty and the other essential freedoms with which it was so closely entwined. To bolster his testimony, the curator had brought with him an old but relevant tale of courage and liberty, and he was a good storyteller.

The scene was England. The time was 1670. Quakers, members of the Religious Society of Friends, were being hauled to jail by the hundreds, for they refused to let the rulers of the realm pick their form of worship for them. William Penn was twenty-six. He was the son of a respected admiral, but young Penn was saucy and obstinate, and he insisted on being a Friend. Finally the day came in mid-August when the authorities locked the Quaker meeting house on Gracechurch Street in London. Thereupon, along with a companion, the defiant young man conducted a religious meeting in the street in front of the closed building. He preached to three hundred of the faithful and the curious and was promptly arrested for causing a tumult.

At the trial, besides the city judge—called the Court Recorder —there sat the Lord Mayor of London. It was customary for the Lord Mayor to appear at the opening of a court session, and on those occasions attendants scattered herbs sprinkled with water, to hide the stench that rose from the airless prison cells below in this, the Old Bailey, criminal court building.

Both the judge and Lord Mayor thought they knew how to make fast work of the business before them. After the facts had been attested to, the Lord Mayor pointedly asked the jury, "Was it not an unlawful Assembly?"

The jurors did not at once agree.

Led by one Edward Bushel, the twelve stouthearted men refused to so define a prayer meeting. The timeworn records show that the judge then used many unworthy threats. The jury was sent back to chambers to reconsider. They returned at last and said they had already given their verdict and could give no other. Penn was guilty of speaking in Gracechurch Street but not of unlawful assembly.

Said the judge: "You had as good say nothing, Gentlemen." He then told the jurors, "You shall not be dismissed till we have a Verdict that the Court will accept."

And still the jury did not yield.

The judge next ordered all twelve men locked up for the night without meat, drink, fire, or tobacco, and without a chamber pot for their use. Said he, "we will have a Verdict, by the help of God, or you shall starve for it."

At seven the next morning the court reassembled. The scene of the day before was then repeated. The jury would not declare a prayer meeting tumultuous. That night the judge had the sheriff lock up the twelve jurors in Newgate Prison. At seven the following morning they were again brought to court and again asked, "Are you agreed of your Verdict?" This time they answered, "Not guilty." The trial was over, but the infuriated judge fined the jurors and ordered them held in prison until the fine could be paid.

What happened next changed history. Bushel was a man of means. He was also a man of knowledge and conviction. Although he was able to do so, he did not pay the fine. Instead, he asked for a writ of habeas corpus. This great writ was issued by a justice, and it ordered the jailer to bring Bushel before the court to see if he was being held illegally. The very existence of the writ assured people of the English-speaking countries that they could not be jailed indefinitely without a hearing. Thus, Bushel was taken before Lord Chief Justice Sir John Vaughan and was freed.

The happy ending to this part of the story is reflected in the annals of the New World. Over a century and a half later, when Andrew Hamilton agreed to take the case of Peter Zenger, on trial for libeling the royal governor, he was in a position to tell the jury that, since the case of Mr. Bushel, a principle had been established: "Judges, how great soever they be, have no right to Fine, imprison, or punish a Jury, for not finding a Verdict according to the Direction of the Court." Thus closely is freedom of religion tied up with all the other liberties of free men. Freedom of religion is part of freedom of opinion and a threat to all tyrants. As such it has had to be won inch by inch, by such courageous men as Penn, Zenger, Andrew Hamilton, and Edward Bushel.

The Friends who had been persecuted for their opinions in England were also persecuted in the New World. They would neither attend nor pay taxes to an established church, nor would they recognize the superiority of its ministers, for they believed that all men and women were equal and that divine guidance came from an "inward light." Massachusetts Puritans jailed them, beat them, mutilated them, and even put them to death on the scaffold.

Freed by his courageous jurors, Penn later determined to start his own colony as a "holy experiment." In 1681 King Charles II got rid of his zealous proselytizer without making him a martyr. In any case, in recognition of a debt he owed to William Penn's father, he granted the young firebrand a charter. In 1682 Pennsylvania was founded, and the first law enacted in the colony guaranteed religious liberty. No person inhabiting the province—who believed in God—was to be molested in his person or estate because of his conscientious persuasion, nor was he to be made to frequent or help maintain any religious worship place or ministry contrary to his mind. Penn did not go so far as to have anyone of any religion hold office. Nevertheless, his granting of religious protection to men of all faiths was a tremendous step forward for his day. Later he rewrote the constitution of Pennsylvania and guaranteed that the article which protected the rights of religious conscience "be kept and remain, without any Alteration, inviolable forever."

Dr. Bronner suggested to the Congress that they emulate William Penn and pledge not to amend, not to weaken, the First Amendment but to keep it without any alteration inviolable forever.

It was a moving presentation. Congressman Senner was impressed, but he thought it was time to bring the conversation back to practical everyday politics. In his soft midwestern tone, he asked Dr. Bronner, ". . . could you see the possibility of school board elections reducing themselves down to a fight on what the school prayer will be, in preference to the educational curriculum of the school or the finances of the school?"

Dr. Bronner said, "I think this is a possibility . . . this could create . . . a bad situation."

Congressman Senner persisted, in a questioning tone, "And would, in fact, pit one religion against another?"

Dr. Bronner assured him, "It is possible, yes."

Senner asked the same question of Father William J. Kenealy, a law professor and a Catholic priest of the Jesuit order, who evidently had a sense of humor; he came before the committee in his black cloth and turned collar and announced that he was not an atheist.

Senner asked him in all seriousness whether permitting school boards to select prayers would "pit one religion against another religion for the election of school board officials. . . ."

Father Kenealy answered, "I think this is very likely."

Dr. Bronner and Father Kenealy were not alone in this opinion. A few days later Senner's colleague, Congressman Morris K. Udall, sent out a newsletter to Arizona constituents with the deliberately startling title, "Do We Want Another Bible War?"

Udall documented his alarming question with ugly incidents from America's past. In the 1850s, in Maine, a Catholic priest had been tarred and feathered during a controversy over school prayer and Bible reading. In Boston a small Catholic schoolboy had been whipped for refusing to say the Lord's Prayer and the Ten Commandments from the Protestant Bible. Later, in Cincinnati, Catholics were angrily called atheist when they objected to the same voluntary Bible reading rule now being debated before Celler's committee. Udall and the others could have noted that tempers became so inflamed there, and elsewhere across the country, that one prominent churchman was quoted as saying, "Let the public school system go where it came from—the devil."

Of course Udall and others recognized what had happened at the time to cause all this turmoil. Free public schools in the 1850s were still not universally available. Many people still depended on church schools where a teacher was expected to indoctrinate the pupils in his own faith. Strife among the sects had heightened the demand for tax-supported schools free from clerical control. Nevertheless, as more schools were built, neither the teachers nor the practices changed all at once. When new religious groups moved into an area, trouble was inevitable. In some areas this—and a respect for the principles of the First Amendment—led state courts and state legislatures and some school authorities to outlaw religious services in public schools, long before the Supreme Court took jurisdiction.

Dr. Franklin H. Littell, professor of church history at Chicago Theological Seminary, gave the committee a surprising reassurance that nothing had been lost. He noted that for two centuries the American colonists had a formally established religion. Yet five years after Cornwallis surrendered at Yorktown, according to Dr. Littell's research, church membership across the country had dropped to less than 10 per cent of the population.

Littell did not think much of government-pressured religion. At the time he spoke, after over one hundred and fifty years of freedom, voluntary church membership had risen to 70 per cent of the population. Later, in answer to the argument that dissenters could be excused, he said, "This is not the atmosphere of liberty, but rather the style of toleration."

His voice must have seemed like an echo of the Nation's first President. George Washington had told a welcoming committee at Rhode Island's Jewish Touro Synagogue in 1790: "It is now no more that toleration is spoken of as if it were by the indulgence of one class of people that another enjoyed the exercise of their inherent natural rights. . . . All possess alike liberty of conscience and immunities of citizenship."

Celler welcomed Littell but he listened equally graciously to the long parade of witnesses who wanted the amendment and who pointed to the one Supreme Court justice, Stewart, who had disagreed with the findings of the Court. Sometimes Celler merely thanked them for coming. Sometimes members of the committee asked questions, then patiently listened on. Two thousand seven hundred and twenty-four pages of testimony were to pile up before the hearings were over. Witness after witness repeated what had been said before. To all this the gentlemen on the dais gave their attention. At the same time they wondered what impact all they were hearing and all they were putting into the record was having outside the committee room.

The first indication of how things were going came on a Friday. As soon as the committee returned from the luncheon recess, the chairman announced the appearance of Congressman B. F. Sisk of California.

Sisk said he was amazed by statements in the press indicating that Congress was going to be stampeded. He wanted to express his vigorous opposition to the proposed amendment.

The chairman likened him to a breath of cool air in the heat of summer and also said: "There are attempts being made to stampede Congress . . . [but] I am happy to note that those who are now on the other side of the fence are taking note and are now commencing to realize that their apathy or their indifference has been a bit dangerous . . . [and] the views that are coming in by mail are indicative. . . . Many of the communications that I have received have been in opposition to these amendments."

Celler's patience was at last beginning to be rewarded; the trend in the mail was changing. The opposition was finally beginning to come in.

Sisk reported that his own council of churches, in Fresno, California, had only the week before unanimously adopted a resolution in opposition to amending the Constitution. At one time, he said, his mail had favored the amendment and attacked the Supreme Court, but in the last two weeks he had begun to hear from Methodist, Baptist, and Episcopalian groups, all in opposition to the Becker amendment.

It was not entirely by coincidence that Sisk had picked this day to come before the committee. There were many Armenians among his constituents, he said. "A very wonderful group of people," he called them. For them, he explained, today, April 24, was Martyr Day. On this day Armenians remembered what happened to them in the Turkish massacre in 1915, when the Turkish Government tried to force Armenians to accept the Islamic religion. Sisk thought it was a good day to give fervent thanks and gratitude for the founders of this nation whose hopes to maintain our freedom are embodied in the First Amendment.

He wanted to compliment the committee for taking a great deal of time on this matter and to assure them again that given more time the public would express itself in opposition to this constitutional change. And so it came to pass.

Before the month was out the big New York papers were carrying articles against the amendment, as Celler had hoped they would. In this they joined papers printed in all the big cities, from Washington, D.C., to Honolulu. From Boston the *Christian Science Monitor* carried a series of articles against amending the Constitution, one of them entitled, "Don't Touch the First." In Ohio the *Cleveland Plain Dealer* came out with an editorial, "Prayer Amendment Should Die." What the Supreme Court was actually doing was protecting religion, said the *Chicago Sun Times.* That paper then added a report from one clergyman, who said that probably 90 per cent of the people in his congregation had at first supported the amendment, but now after deeper study, about 80 per cent of them were opposed to it. The *St. Louis Post Dispatch* commended the Congressmen and the Judiciary Committee for resisting rash action. From the *Criterion* in Indianapolis, the *Arkansas Gazette, The Kansas City Star, The Wichita Eagle, The Denver Post,* the *Dayton News,* and *The Detroit Free Press,* voices were raised to preserve the Constitution and religious liberty. From the *Baltimore Morning Sun,* the *Miami News,* the *Memphis Press Scimitar,* and all the way across the land, including the *San Francisco Chronicle* and the *Los Angeles Times,* came the cry to stop the mischief.

People read all about it and began to understand a little better. The Baptists finally had their convention; so did the Seventh-day Adventists and smaller bodies like the American Ethical Union. Now they were ready to oppose the amendment in groups. The Jewish War Veterans sent their national commander, Neal Heller, to Washington to speak before the committee and express their disapproval of proposals to amend the Bill of Rights. The student Y.M.C.A.s and the Y.W.C.A.s from the states of Ohio, Indiana, Michigan, Illinois, Wisconsin, Iowa, Minnesota, North Dakota, and South Dakota sent representatives to their annual Geneva Conference. The conference passed a resolution affirming its belief that the Supreme Court had spoken wisely and expressing its disapproval of the Becker amendment.

Opposition to the amendment also came from the Committee on the Bill of Rights of the Federal Bar Association of New York, New Jersey, and Connecticut. Other letters of opposition came from organizations like The National Council of Jewish Women, the Kansas Annual Conference of Methodist Churches, the Newark Annual Conference of Methodist Churches, the Pittsburgh meeting of The Religious Society of Friends, and the Catholic Council of Civil Liberties in Buffalo, New York. In Philadelphia, a committee was formed of Lutherans, Presbyterians, Baptists, Jews, and members of the United Churches of Christ. Another such group was formed in Maryland, and all of these people wanted to oppose the amendment. Dr. Fredrik Schiotz, president of the American Lutheran Church, put an article against the amendment in the official church paper. Four Episcopalian bishops wrote a joint letter to Congress, expressing their opposition. All these things had their effect.

At last, in addition to the innumerable lawyers, college professors, and clergymen, the man in the pew of every conceivable denomination began writing his congressman or the committee. Finally, early in June, the committee's counsel advised the committee that the trend in the mail was now definitely against the amendment. The constitutional crisis was over. The committee adjourned.

Since then the House Judiciary Committee has been moved into more elaborate quarters in the new marble-halled Rayburn Building. An oil portrait of Congressman Celler hangs on the wall in the spacious new hearing room. The Judiciary Committee still meets, but on other matters. When the meetings are open, anyone who wishes can go in, take a seat, and see at work the patient, dedicated, patriotic men who stopped a stampede.

BIBLIOGRAPHY FOR PART III

Principal Sources on Freedom of Religion

BOOKS

Cobb, Sanford H. *The Rise of Religious Liberty in America.* New York, 1902.

Madison, James. *The Complete Madison.* New York, 1953.

Pfeffer, Leo. *Church State and Freedom.* Boston, 1953.

Seitz, Don C. *The Trial of William Penn and William Mead for Causing a Tumult.* Boston, 1919.

Slosson, Edwin. *The American Spirit in Education.* New Haven, 1921.

Stokes, Anson Phelps, and Leo Pfeffer. *Church and State in the United States,* rev. ed. New York, 1964.

Sweet, William Warren. *The Story of Religion in America.* New York, 1950.

UNITED STATES FEDERAL RECORDS

Congressional Records

U.S. Congress, *Hearings Before the House of Representatives Committee on the Judiciary, Proposed Amendments to the Constitution Relating To Prayer and Bible Reading in Public Schools,* 88th Congress, 2nd Session, 1964.

Supreme Court Records (Transcripts and Records of Briefs)

Engel v. Vitale, 370 U.S. 421 (1962).
Everson v. Board of Education, 330 U.S. 1 (1947).
Illinois ex rel. McCollum, 333 U.S. 203 (1948).
McGowan v. Maryland, 366 U.S. 420 (1961).
Reynolds v. United States, 98 U.S. 145 (1879).
School District of Abington Township v. Schempp, 374 U.S. 203 (1963).
Torcaso v. Watkins, 367 U.S. 488 (1961).
West Virginia Board of Education v. Barnette, 319 U.S. 624 (1943).

NEWSPAPERS

New York Times, June 28, 1962 (and others mentioned in text).

MISCELLANEOUS

"Facts about McIntire," Presbyterian Office of Information, January, 1965.
"Impact of the Supreme Court Prayer Decision on the Public Schools," National Education Association, June, 1963.

PART FOUR

THE

PROPERTY OWNERS

"No person shall be . . . deprived, of life, liberty, or property, without due process of law; nor shall private property be taken for public use, without just compensation."

—FIFTH AMENDMENT

"Life, liberty, and property and the equal protection of law, grouped together in the Constitution, are so related that deprivation of any one of these separate and independent rights may lessen or extinguish the value of the other three."

—ASSOCIATE JUSTICE JOSEPH R. LAMAR, 1914

"The right of the people to be secure in their persons, houses, papers, and effects . . . shall not be violated . . ."

—FOURTH AMENDMENT

"No soldier shall, in time of peace, be quartered in any house, without the consent of the Owner, nor in time of war, but in a manner to be prescribed by law."

—THIRD AMENDMENT

"Congress shall make no law . . . abridging the freedom of speech, or of the press, or the right of the people peaceably to assemble, and to petition the Government for a redress of grievances."

—FIRST AMENDMENT

THE RIGHTS AND THE ISSUES

In a sense, the word "property" refers to all the freedoms we possess. They are ours, guaranteed by our Government and subject to no man's courtesy. Property thus defined is the most important right of all.

John Adams, Benjamin Franklin, Thomas Jefferson, and the other founders of our way of life certainly never got this idea of property from Professor William Blackstone. As Blackstone taught, "The right of property is that sole and despotic domain which one man claims and exercises over the external things of the world, in total exclusion of the right of any other individual in the universe."

Our Founding Fathers obediently read the words of this authoritative Englishman and then, in the privacy of their Colonial homes, steeped themselves in the writings of another Britisher, philosoher John Locke. Locke claimed that one's property included one's life, one's liberties, and one's estate. Furthermore, it was in order to protect this property that man had entered into society. Man, Locke reasoned, had complete freedom in his savage state. He could use his labor to turn the raw materials of the earth into whatever suited his fancy. Thus, while keeping his liberties, he made his own estate. But he had no way to defend life, liberty, and estate. Man, therefore, accepted the authority of rules and rulers to secure his rights. Here was an implied contract between a man and his sovereign. Should the ruler not do his part, he forfeited the loyalty of his subjects. Out of this idea of man and property came the ideas embodied in the Declaration of Independence.

"We hold these Truths to be self-evident, that all Men are created equal, that they are endowed by their Creator with certain unalienable Rights, that among these are Life, Liberty, and the Pursuit of Happiness —That to secure these Rights, Governments are instituted among Men. . . ."

Man allowed himself to be governed in order to secure what was rightfully his. His estate was his private property and included everything from gold mines to pets. When the Bill of Rights was written, it was intended to secure both the personal freedoms man possessed and his private property rights. To the Founding Fathers they went together like interwoven threads in the same fabric. A despotic government which would break one thread would soon break another. And practically everything in the Bill of Rights has an application to the private property owner.

The First Amendment's guarantee of freedom of expression allows man to speak up in behalf of his interests.

The Second Amendment protects the rights of the people to organize a "well regulated Militia," and "to keep and bear Arms" to defend their homes and their local communities.

The Third Amendment assures everyone that in time of peace no soldier shall be quartered in any house without the consent of the owner, "nor in time of war, but in a manner to be prescribed by law." The Fourth Amendment guards the "right of the people to be secure in their persons, houses, papers, and effects. . . ." The justices, in *Stanford v. Texas,* said it was closely aligned with freedom of expression. It is equally closely tied to private property rights. A man has a right to be left alone in his own domicile, be it mansion or hut. He has a right to expect society to leave him and his things alone—unless a warrant has been issued, "upon probable cause, . . . describing the place to be searched, and the persons or things to be seized."

The Founding Fathers went on. In the Fifth Amendment they said that no man was to lose his private property, any more than his liberty, without a fair trial—one that followed those laws of the land called "due process." The Fifth, Sixth, and Seventh, and in a way the Eighth, are concerned with the proper procedures for such a fair trial. Besides the Ninth and Tenth Amendments, which secure to the people and the states all rights not delegated to the Federal Government, the Founders provided another momentous guarantee of private property rights. They placed it in the middle of all these ten amendments, in the Fifth, declaring: "nor shall private property be taken for public use, without just compensation."

Obvious though the command is, how to apply it in this noisy, crowded mechanized world is sometimes a puzzle. Neighbors objecting to the endless clatter, foul smells, or filthy soot of a nearby industry storm the legislature demanding zoning regulations; to protect their own homes, they tell the factory owner what *not to do* with his land. New groups, such as organized laborers or segregated minorities, come along demanding enforcement of what they consider to be their rights. To the paymaster at the mill or the manager of the public lunch counter, these same rights seem to conflict with his traditional liberties.

Besides this, the plunder and waste of our natural resources made the anxious people call for novel regulations that the courts were forced to uphold. After the turn of the century, state laws would not let the prospector, who was only interested in oil, waste the gas from his own well—letting it escape uncaptured into the atmosphere. The age of rapid transportation spawned other new problems. Railroads were required by law to finance and put up gates and maintain gatemen at grade crossings, even when the city had laid a street across their tracks. Later, during a financial crisis, lawmakers trying to deal with the emergency told creditors they would have to temporarily postpone foreclosing mortgages and seizing their legal due. The debtors meanwhile were required to pay them the reasonable rental value of the property. Again and again the courts acquiesced. They saw all this as the legitimate use of the police power of the community in an evolving world forever facing increasingly novel situations.

In addition to government's police power over property, and its tax power, there is its power of eminent domain. Congress or a state legislature can decide under what conditions private property may be taken for the public good—with just compensation, of course. At times the private property owner is more upset when the government does not condemn or acquire his land but authorizes a nearby activity which devalues his holding. He feels he has suffered a loss; the officials feel they have not made "a taking."

In this country, men can contest the action of a government agency. Lawyers and judges can question whether the agency, in its eagerness to promote the general welfare, has acted unfairly or arbitrarily and hence illegally. Otherwise private property and many of the rest of our rights would disappear with a wave of the flag and a cry of the needs of the majority. As it is, the lawmakers and the courts face a series of problems as the facts in a succession of situations are contested.

Was the police power of the state misused? Was a man actually deprived of the uses of his property? What was the property in question really worth? Volumes have been written on these and related questions of property rights. Here follow only a few examples of the puzzles faced.

"Projected into Unexpected Abysses"

THE law passed by the Pennsylvania legislature in 1921 seemed eminently reasonable. It said that "it shall be unlawful for any owner . . . so to mine anthracite coal or so to conduct the operation of mining anthracite coal as to cause the cave-in, collapse, subsidence [sinking] of . . . [any] public building or any structure customarily used by the public . . . including, but not being limited to, churches, schools, hospitals, theaters . . . [and any] dwelling. . . ."

Margaret Craig Mahon had reason to be grateful. She lived in a two-story frame house on the east side of Prospect Place in the city of Pittston. Each room had a familiar feeling, as if the walls and windows had absorbed the scenes of family living for which they had provided the setting during her growing up. Her father, Alexander Craig, had spent his last days in the house and his personality had left its impression. He had been a master mechanic for the Pennsylvania Coal Company, and it was he who had accepted the deed from the coal company for the lot on which this dwelling rested. Affectionately, Craig had intended the house for himself and for his slight and gentle daughter. His will passed the home on to Margaret. She shared it with her husband, Harold J. Mahon.

The Mahons could count on living here indefinitely, in peace and undisturbed, if it were not for one haunting obstacle. Craig had bought only the surface rights to the little footage he called "my place." The deed allowed the Pennsylvania Coal Company to take the coal from under his holding. In 1878, when Craig made this agreement, mining practices were not as thorough as they later became. The diggers in those days left much of the black treasure still in place when they pulled up their car tracks and moved on. Now many of the companies were running out of real estate and were forced to dig out more coal from their old holdings. Besides, new methods enabled them to do this.

State legislators were shocked when streets in nearby Scranton sagged and buildings collapsed as the support below their foundations gave way under the relentless hacking of the ever-busy picks.

Possibly Margaret's father, having lived out much of his life in an

earlier era, had originally expected that only a serious mine accident could endanger his house, but that was not what the deed said.

According to the deed, Craig—and Margaret, as his heir—gave
up any claim against the company if the place were damaged by
mining activities. The new law, called the Kohler Act, had been
passed because deeds like Margaret's were numerous in this anthracite area. The act was passed none too soon for the Mahons. Six
days after it went into effect they got a letter from the president of
the coal company.

September 1, 1921

Dear Sir and Madam:
 You are hereby notified that the mining operation of the Pennsylvania Coal Co. beneath your premises will, by September 15,
have reached a point which will then or shortly thereafter cause
subsidence and disturbance to the surface of your lot. . . .

The shocking words conjured up a picture in Margaret's mind of
the house caving in. She and her husband called on an attorney,
W. L. Pace. The two men, Margaret's husband and Pace, drew up
papers and hastily went to court, asking the judge for an injunction
(a court order to stop the company).

It was granted, but not for long. The trial judge did not even
want to hear oral argument. A deed was a contract, he said. A contract was the property of the people who made it. This deed, or contract, gave the company the right to mine. The Constitution of the
United States stopped the states from making laws impairing the obligations of contracts. Besides, since under the deed the coal company owned the ore beneath their house, what the Mahons were
asking the court to do was give them the company's property.

What about the new law?

The Kohler Act, as the judge saw it, was invalid. It violated the
rights of contract.

Pace helped the Mahons appeal their case to the Supreme Court
of Pennsylvania.

The justices there considered the problem. They decided that the
Kohler Act was a proper use of the police power of the state to protect the public safety. The Mahons, it was true, were suing for
themselves and not for the community, but they were taking legal
action against a public nuisance and they had the right to do this.

What happened next was inevitable. The company appealed to
the Supreme Court of the United States. Obviously, what worried
its managers most was not merely the Mahons' property but the

Kohler Act itself. The company had to fight the act. The management had to protect the organization's investment. The coal was
worthless to them unless they could take it out of the ground. They
had commitments to the hard-working people who had risked their
money in the mining venture, in the trusting belief that everything
would be done to mine the coal. The management figured that, in
order to obey the Kohler law and support surface buildings, they
would have to leave about a third of the coal in place.

The Pennsylvania Coal Company secured the best attorney they
could get. They hired John W. Davis. Lawyers now working in
Washington still remember Davis. By the time they knew him he
was a stooped but courtly old gentleman who, they say, expected to
lose a high percentage of his cases. The big companies went looking
for Davis when they were in a "tough fight." At the time of *Pennsylvania Coal Co. v. Mahon,* Davis was forty-nine. He had already
been a West Virginia congressman, Solicitor General, and ambassador to England, but his greatest hopes and disappointments
still lay ahead. The day would come in 1924 when, as the Democratic presidential candidate opposing Calvin Coolidge, Davis
would have to concede his biggest defeat. Meanwhile, his New
York law office was his newest venture and winning this case was
important to him. To attract clients he wanted a big victory. It
would add to the other advantages he had to offer: his legal knowledge, his public service record, his charming appearance, and his
gracious manner. Above all this, his principal weapon was his
mind. It was brilliant, and so was his argument and his brief. Numbered headings in thick black type told the justices the gist of each
succeeding passage.

1. The Kohler Act was a violation of the rights of contract.

Under this heading, Davis reviewed the terms of the deed. It was,
he pointed out, a solemn and binding agreement.

II. The act violated due process of law.

Davis said the act deprived the coal companies of their property
as much as if the land itself had been appropriated—and this without compensation. This was not legislation but robbery under the
forms of law: "the druggist could not be required to dispense his
medicines for nothing, or a baker his bread. . . ." Why should the
legislature reassign the company's property to a favored few? The
Mahons should move out temporarily while the mining was being
done. They should then use the money they had saved by buying
only the surface rights to fix the cracks in their lawn or sidewalk.
The same was true of the city fathers. Instead of buying the prop-

erty on which to build their schools, they had obtained their space at bargain prices by buying only surface rights. As a governing body they had the power to condemn property—to demand that the owners give it up in return for compensation. This was called the right of eminent domain and they should have exercised it instead of legislating away the company's assets.

III. The Kohler Act was a misuse of the police power of the state.

Public-spirited men were impatient to bring about the reforms they advocated, Davis cautioned. They were unwilling to wait or spend money in order to use the proper constitutional methods. Worse, insistent minorities organized for their own benefit to confiscate the rights of the producers of property. The Court had the duty to hold these people back.

The Kohler Act was written to sound like a police regulation. Davis made fun of this: "it would appear that a considerable part of the population of Pennsylvania is in immediate danger of the loss of life and limb by being . . . projected into unexpected abysses. . . ." Davis did not think the public was so threatened: "damage to date is confined to a small portion of the city of Scranton," he said.

Lined up against this formidable pleader were not only Pace and Mahon but the attorney general of Pennsylvania, the city solicitor of Scranton, and another attorney for a Scranton civic group.

The Pennsylvania lawyers counterattacked by quoting their governor. "Lives have been lost, homes, churches and schools destroyed. . . ." In addition, whole communities had grown up over the anthracite fields. Viewed in this context, they felt the Act "regulates the mining of coal in a manner reasonably required for the protection of life, health and safety of the public." You could not use your private property to injure others. The state could use its police power to stop you. All property within the state was subject to the police power of the state.

The justices did not think the coal case was this simple. They puzzled over it for some weeks. Surprisingly, the two great friends on the bench at the time, Holmes and Brandeis, were in disagreement. Normally, Holmes would make every effort to sustain the act of a legislature even if he personally was repelled by what the lawmakers had done. He plunged into the work of being a justice with deep humility, strict New England self-discipline, and the conviction that the Constitution of the United States was intended to be flexible. If the lawmakers wanted to try something new, and this something new was not obviously forbidden by the Constitution, his attitude was, "Let them."

Brandeis went even further in championing new ideas. He came to the bench steeped in the industrial problems of the newly mechanized world. He anxiously believed that if solutions were not found and adjustments made to relieve the cruel inequities of the machine age, the problems willed to posterity might become insurmountable.

From their formal written opinions, we know what ideas the two friends exchanged over the anthracite situation. Possibly this thinking went on during one of their long rides together into the surrounding countryside, or over a snack in Holmes' book-lined parlor.

In any case Brandeis was insistent: "the right of the owner to use his land is not absolute," he reminded Holmes, and then elaborated. "He may not so use it as to create a public nuisance, and use, once harmless, may, owing to changed conditions, seriously threaten the public welfare."

Brandeis thought this was what had happened in the mining industry. The coal was being more thoroughly removed from under the surface, but, more important, many people had built homes and other structures over the fields. "The restriction here in question is merely the prohibition of a noxious use," he said. Under these conditions he felt that neither grant nor contract could prevail against the police power of the state. And if Pennsylvania was only exercising her police power, the companies need not be paid for their coal.

Holmes conceded one thing. Government hardly could go on if to some extent property values could not be diminished without paying for every such change. Some property values must yield to the police power.

"But obviously"—and Holmes unquestionably threw this next point up to Brandeis before he wrote it down—"[this] must have its limits or the contract and the due process clauses [in the Constitution] are gone."

Brandeis tried to answer by making up a concrete example of what he meant. "If by mining anthracite coal the owner would necessarily unloose poisonous gases," he said, "I suppose no one would doubt the power of the State to prevent the mining, without buying his coal fields."

The implication intended by the younger justice was clear to Holmes, but Brandeis stated it anyway: "why may not the State, likewise, without paying compensation, prohibit one from digging so deep or excavating so near the surface, as to expose the community to like dangers?"

Holmes was not convinced, and Holmes, it turned out, represented the opinion of the majority of the justices. He spoke for them from the bench. The majority of justices did not agree with Brandeis or with the Supreme Court of Pennsylvania. They did not think the Kohler law was a legitimate use of police power. Holmes explained their point of view. As they saw it, the most important aspect of the case was the right of the State of Pennsylvania to protect her public streets and buildings.

> The rights of the public in a street purchased or laid out . . . are those that it has paid for [Holmes said]. If in any case its representatives have been so short sighted as to acquire only surface rights without the right of support we see no more authority for supplying the latter without compensation than there was for taking the [land to build the] right of way in the first place and refusing to pay for it because the public wanted it very much. . . . [The] Fifth Amendment presupposes that it is wanted for public use, but provides that it shall not be taken for such use without compensation. A similar assumption is made in the decisions upon the Fourteenth Amendment. . . . When this seemingly absolute protection is found to be qualified by the police power, the natural tendency of human nature is to extend the qualification more and more until at last private property disappears. But that cannot be accomplished . . . under the Constitution of the United States.

Holmes realized that the question was complicated. He tried to set up a guide to help lawyers like Davis and the men from Pennsylvania. "The general rule at least is," he said, "that while property may be regulated to a certain extent, if regulation goes too far it will be recognized as a taking." Holmes did not at that moment think it was necessary to emphasize the fact, but this would be equally true of every freedom we possess. Police power could be extended and extended until the right was gone. But Holmes did say, "We are in danger of forgetting that a strong public desire to improve the public condition is not enough to warrant achieving the desire by a shorter cut than the constitutional way of paying for the change." He could have added that the Court could not allow even the public or public-spirited official to be lawless in the name of progress, lest all our liberties disappear. Certainly this addition was in the mind of the many justices and attorneys who were to quote this opinion in the years to come.

The Mahons had lost their case, but their world did not come to an end, nor did their house. They lived there the rest of their lives. Harold went on to become a successful businessman. By the end of the 1920s he was the president of a bank. Later, in the thirties, Margaret—by then a lonely widow—was murdered in the house she had fought so hard to keep. Nobody knows who committed the crime or why. It is one of the unsolved mysteries of the State of Pennsylvania. At this writing, her house at 7 Prospect Place is still standing. It is owned by a plasterer who has turned it into a duplex and who keeps it up very carefully. As a result, it is considered a very desirable property.

John W. Davis, although he never became President of the United States, also went on to more adventures, and one of them is recounted two chapters later. Another Pennsylvania lawyer named Thomas Griggs has had a very special reason to be particularly grateful for the way the Court ruled in the case. As his strange story is another important tale in the evolution of property rights, it follows in the next chapter.

"By Federal Permission"

In 1944 Mr. and Mrs. Thomas Griggs were enchanted with a country home in the township of Moon, in Allegheny County, Pennsylvania. The grounds included a two-story stone house for them to live in, a large garage, and a little cottage for them to rent, and the place was conveniently near a fine macadam crossroad. They bought the property and enthusiastically set to work landscaping the grounds and making everything very pretty.

It especially delighted the couple that this was a quiet part of the country. A small airport, less than a mile away, served private planes, but the little craft did not bother them excessively. They and their cook settled down comfortably in beautiful peace—but not for ever after.

For a while they were not aware of it, but Allegheny County officials were engaged in negotiations that would bring about a shattering change. The county was working with the Federal Government and various airlines to turn the little airport into a huge commercial terminal.

In June, 1952, the Griggs couple became most painfully aware of it. A steady stream of heavy aircraft zoomed over the chimney. The floor vibrated, the windows rattled, plaster came down from the ceiling—and still more planes roared overhead.

On Sunday, June 15, Griggs was home from his Pittsburgh law office. He noticed to his horror that some of the big planes were barely skirting the tops of his trees. Something was going to have to be done about this! He decided that the first thing to do was to get the facts. By late afternoon he was making a record of the flights. An Allegheny ship went by, next one from Capital Airlines, then a T.W.A. plane; Mr. Griggs marked them down in his record. At dinnertime on Monday, there were more planes. Each one sounded like a steam hammer or an electric drill passing overhead. When Griggs was called to the phone he couldn't hear over the noises descending on him from the heavens. He was awakened by planes three times during the night and again in the early hours of the morning. Later Griggs put a calendar in the kitchen and asked his wife and cook to keep the record during the day when he was not at home.

Back at the office, his nerves somewhat shaken, he described his unpleasant predicament to his law partner, an able citizen named William A. Blair. Griggs showed Blair the record he had made, with T.W.A., Allegheny, and Capital marked down. Blair was amazed and certainly put the same questions to his friend that he later used at a hearing.

"How did you know those planes?" he asked.

"I could see the designations on the ships," Griggs told him.

"You mean you could read the letters on the planes?"

"Yes, sir."

Blair was sympathetic. If the planes were flying that low, his partner had a legitimate grievance. The two men started a vigorous chase all over town. They learned a lot from various officials but got no relief.

The Griggs' place, it turned out, was on a direct line with the northeast runway. Rules had been set by a federal agency (later the Federal Aviation Agency) directing the flight patterns of planes taking off or coming in. At the time when this, the Greater Pittsburgh Airport, was opened, the planes were ordered to go forty feet forward for every foot they rose. This was called the "glide angle." If any plane had started at the very tip of the northeast runway and stayed at the bottom of the glide angle it would have cleared Griggs' chimney by less than twelve feet. Actually the big ships were passing between thirty and three hundred feet over the house. Their heights varied a little according to their weight and the weather.

Blair and Griggs went on questioning everyone they could. One pilot was most responsive. Yes, he thought Griggs was in a bad spot. "If we had engine failure," he said, "we would have no course but to plow into your house."

That was interesting! It was also another blow to the nervous system of Thomas Griggs, but the trouble with it was that the airlines did not consider themselves responsible to the homeowner.

Years ago the Supreme Court had said:

> Today the landowner no more posses a vertical control of all the air above him than a shore owner possesses horizontal control of all the sea before him. The air is too precious as an open highway to permit it to be "owned" to the exclusion or embarrassment of air navigation. . . .
>
> Congress has recognized the national responsibility for regulating air commerce. Federal control is intensive and exclusive. Planes do not wander about in the sky like vagrant clouds. They move only by federal permission.

As the airlines saw it, Congress had made the skies a public highway. So long as they obeyed the federal agency they were safe from suit. In any case they had to obey, so they had to fly low over the Griggs house.

In view of all the facts it would have been useless for Blair and Griggs to go to the state legislature. Later, in 1956, suburbanites living in Cedarhurst, Long Island, did try passing a municipal ordinance, ordering all planes flying over their town to stay a thousand feet up in the air. These people had a noise problem, but they were told by the court that flight patterns were federal business. Their ordinance, if obeyed, would interfere with air safety. Planes could not come in to International Airport from that height. Besides, the town could not enforce any ordinance that was contrary to the exclusive power of Congress to regulate interstate commerce.

Blair knew about the federal rules, but he still thought the county had an obligation to his partner. The county owned the airport.

The county had received funds from the United States to build the field to its present size. The county should have condemned or taken his partner's house because it was in the glide path. Blair reasoned that the county had in fact "taken" the house. It had planned the airport in such a way as to make this home an unbearable place in which to live.

The county officials denied that they were responsible. Their design for the airport had been approved by the federal agency and they had no control over flight patterns. And, they said, they had not made a "taking." They knew that at one time a man owned all the air over his property, all the way to the heavens, but, as they saw it, that had changed. Congress was protecting air travel the way it once had protected the railroads. Railroads are a legalized nuisance; you can't get compensation from them if you are inconvenienced by their coming too near your property.

The county officials may or may not have remembered that there were exceptions to this rule. In 1883 worshipers in the Fifth Baptist Church in Washington, D.C., had won compensation for their property when the Baltimore and Potomac Railroad set up its repair station right next to their church. Rumbling locomotives clanged their bells and shrieked their whistles constantly during services. The worshipers couldn't hear the pastor and their clothes were sprayed with soot. The Supreme Court thought this an unusual and particularly unreasonable interference with the parishioners' use of their property. It was more of a hardship than the rest of the population had to endure, because of the trains. Therefore, the payment of compensation was in order.

After that, a Mr. Richards in the District of Columbia had won a similar battle. Trains authorized by Congress passed through a tunnel close to his house on their way to the Washington terminal. A fan in the tunnel blew the soot into his house, permeating everything with grime. The justices of the Supreme Court recognized that Richards was not entitled to any compensation of the usual loss of property values connected with having a train route move in next to him. They said he was nevertheless entitled to be compensated for the special and unusual damage due to the soot blown from the tunnel fan. How much of the destruction to the value of Richards' house was due to usual, and noncompensatable, effects of trains and how much of his loss was caused by the fan-blown tunnel soot was a worse-than-usual puzzle. The Supreme Court justices left it up to the lower court to figure out that one.

Griggs and Blair, both being lawyers, undoubtedly discussed this legal history together when they got back to the office after their trips around town. There was one case that Blair thought was important. It had its drawbacks as far as they were concerned, but still it might be helpful. It was called *United States v. Causby* and involved a South Carolina chicken farmer. Causby's troubles had arisen during World War II. His place was also in a glide area. The United States Army had rented an airfield 2,200 feet from his barn. The big planes passed over his chicken houses at frighteningly low altitudes. The farmer said the wind from the propellers blew the leaves off his trees. The noise and the glare from the bright lights so terrified the chickens that they flew into the walls. Six to ten of them were killed every day. The rest of them were too upset to lay many eggs.

Causby and his wife Tinie went into the Court of Claims. A majority of the five judges sympathized with their plight. The frequency of the low flights had interfered with the chicken farmer's use of his own land. The government had therefore made a taking and must give just compensation.

The Army objected that the flights were a temporary wartime necessity.

The presiding judge answered, "The Constitution is not set aside in time of war. Indeed, the restraints of that instrument are especially necessary . . ." and Causby should be paid.

One of the judges, Judge J. Warren Madden, dissented. Airplane flights, he said, should not be considered a taking. "When railroads were new, cattle in the fields . . . were alarmed. . . . Horses ran away. . . . The farmer's chickens have to get over being alarmed at the incredible racket of the tractor starting up suddenly in the shed. . . . These sights and noises are part of our world, and air planes are now . . . likewise a part of it." In other words, society could not pay for every individual's loss occasioned by mechanized progress.

Encouraged by Madden's dissent, the United States Army appealed to the Supreme Court. The justices heard the argument: So long as the planes flew only at the safe altitudes set by the federal agency, they were in the "navigable airspace." Congress had declared the safe navigable airspace to be a public highway in interstate commerce. Therefore, reasoned the government lawyers, nobody was liable to the chicken farmer.

The majority of the High Court justices disagreed. Congress, they thought, had said that the "navigable airspace" was the same as the federally-set safe flying height. The federal agency had declared the safe flying heights to be one thousand feet over congested areas and five hundred feet over more rural terrain. Planes taking off or coming in were below the free highway of the skies.

Causby had to be paid for his losses. The majority ruling in the Court of Claims was correct.

There were only two difficulties with the case as far as Blair and Griggs were concerned. For one thing, the Army had both rented the airfield and employed the pilots, so there was no question as to who was liable if payment was in order. Secondly, and more devastating, while Griggs and Blair were still arguing with the county over their rights, Congress amended the law to include in "navigable airspace" the space needed for take-offs and landings.

To offset these discouraging facts, Blair noted that Justice Douglas, who gave the Court's opinion in the Causby case, had intimated that if the federal agency had called eighty-three feet above the ground "navigable airspace," the validity of the ruling might be legally challenged. If a man no longer owned all the air above his ground, he still had to be allowed to keep enough footage to run up his fences, plant his trees, and erect his necessary buildings. Later Douglas wrote about the chicken farmer's case in his book, *Almanac of Liberty*. He compared the legal principles involved to the old English doctrine on property rights spelled out in the Magna Carta and forced on King John by his barons of Runnymede on the fifteenth day of June in 1215. One provision says, "No constable or . . . bailiff shall take corn or other chattels of any man without immediate payment for the same."

Studying all the facts and factors, Blair and Griggs could be optimistic, but they could not be sure what was going to happen to them at the hands of the law. As it turned out, much time was wasted when the Griggs couple joined a group of neighbors who were trying to fight the problem. When this was unsuccessful, Blair finally went and asked for help in the Pennsylvania Court of Common Pleas.

As is the custom in Pennsylvania, the court appointed three viewers to look into the matter. They were to visit the property in question. They were to hold hearings, study the law, and report back to the judge. Of course this would all take time. It was exasperating.

The family had already given up and moved out of the house. Living there was unbearable. Griggs waited impatiently for the viewers to do all their work. It took over a year.

Surprisingly, after all the talk, the viewers came back to court with a fresh approach as to how the problems in the case should be solved. Their position was based not on a federal but on a Pennsylvania case.

They remembered that in 1875, under an act of the Pennsylvania legislature, the authorities in Perry County were required to cooperate with the people in Dauphin County and build a bridge across the Juniata River. The workmen obediently built the arch. Then it was found that on the Penn Township side in Perry County they had built the abutment (which was like a foundation and came above the level of the road), but they had not filled in or raised the level of the road to meet it. The people stared. No traveler on horseback or driving a wagon could get up onto the bridge. The officials evidently expected the people of Penn Township to attend to this detail themselves. Instead, the township people went to court. Justice Isaac Gordon asked the Perry County officials if a house was finished before you built the steps up to the door. He thought not. He decided that if the county was obligated to build a bridge, it was obligated to provide an approach.

The viewers entrusted with making a recommendation in the Griggs case thought Justice Gordon's ruling applicable. The county, in building an airport with the help of federal funds, was obligated to provide it with an approach area. In so doing, they had "taken" an air easement or pathway over the Griggs' house. They should pay Griggs $12,650.

The recommendation satisfied neither side. Griggs, badly hurt, protested. He had been deprived of his home, which was worth a lot more than that, and he should be paid for it. Maurice Louik, the attorney for the county, was not willing to see the homeowner get even twelve thousand. Louik was still harping on the federal regulations. None of the flights Griggs objected to were any lower than was necessary to make a safe landing. They were therefore in airspace which Congress had placed within the public domain.

The judge was not impressed and said so. In the end he discarded the objections made by both Griggs and Louik and upheld his viewers.

Blair appealed to the Supreme Court of Pennsylvania, and so did Louik for the county. The majority of the justices were impressed by Louik's argument. Since the county had no control over flight patterns, they decided that Griggs had no case against the county because the county had not taken his land.

Two justices disagreed. One, Justice John Bell, soon to become Chief Justice of Pennsylvania, wrote his dissent in loud clear terms.

With piercing vision Bell tackled the entire problem of property rights in the air age. Some of his words were his own; some were quotes from other cases. "The law as to what constitutes a 'taking' had been undergoing a radical change during the last few years," he said. "Until the opening of the air age the owner of real property owned . . . to the sky. . . . It is now held that the owner of land owns from the surface . . . to whatever height may be needed for the use and the enjoyment of his property." Here Bell was referring to Douglas' ruling. He accepted it: ". . . we are faced with the task of reconciling traditional common law concepts with the realities of modern day life," he said. That, however, in no way justified what had happened to Griggs.

"In our desire for progress we must not overlook or extinguish the inherent and inalienable constitutionally guaranteed rights of private property which is one of the bedrocks of our Federal and State Governments, and indeed one of the two great hallmarks of western civilization," the justice warned.

Bell quoted what Holmes had said in *Pennsylvania Coal Co. v. Mahon:* "We are in danger of forgetting that a strong public desire . . . is not enough to warrant achieving the desire by a shorter cut than the constitutional way of paying for the change." Blair was delighted, for here, of course, was the main point of the case.

There was another basic concept relevant to private property rights, which as Bell saw it, could not change. "All that is beneficial in property arises from its use and the fruits of that use, and whatever deprives a person of them deprives him of all that is desirable or valuable in the title and possession. . . ."

In the light of this unalterable fact, Bell found it as clear as crystal "that flights over private land which are so low and so frequent as to be a direct and immediate interference with the enjoyment and the use of the land amount to a 'taking.'" In this instance, Bell said, "I am convinced . . . that there was a 'taking' of plaintiff's entire property."

Bell felt that the contention of the county was without merit. "Even if it be conceded," he said, ". . . that the air space in question, namely, 12 feet above plaintiff's home and buildings, is . . . [now] public . . . it could not . . . be taken for public use without proper compensation. . . . The government simply cannot arbitrarily declare that all of the airspace over a person's land is public domain and then, cavalierly, claim absolute immunity against property owners' claims for any and all possible damages. . . ."

As to who was responsible, Bell thought that too was clear. "Clearly an adequate approach way is as necessary a part of an airport as is the ground on which the airstrip, itself, is constructed," he said. Bell, like the viewers, saw the similarity between acquiring an approachway to an airport and building a road leading to a bridge.

He warned the court, "We must not allow, in the appealing name of progress or general welfare, a property owner to be deprived by the Federal, State or County Government, or by anyone, of his property or any rights occurring therein and thereform."

Blair, having lost his case, did the obvious. He placed a copy of Bell's dissenting opinion in a carefully written brief and asked the justices of the Supreme Court of the United States to grant certiorari (review the case).

This the justices agreed to do. In January, 1962, the case was argued. In March, Justice Douglas gave the Court's opinion. He reviewed the facts of the case. He then summarized the situation in a few words and upheld the position taken by Justice Bell. The county had been authorized to acquire property for the airport. It simply did not acquire enough. Instead, it had made a taking without just compensation. This it could not be allowed to do. It had to pay for what it had acquired. How much the estate was worth the lower courts would have to decide.

Blair gave a weary sigh of relief. The lower courts would still have to decide the amount due Griggs, but the principle had been established. There had been a taking for which compensation must be paid. Later, when he was discussing the case, Blair said, "People in their zealousness to serve the public forget that the individual has rights too. That is what we have the Constitution of the United States for. Let's hope that it doesn't disappear!"

"The Particular Emergency"

EVERYONE who still talks about *Youngstown v. Sawyer* still talks in superlatives. It was "the biggest lawsuit in years," "the worst constitutional crisis" since Franklin D. Roosevelt tried to "pack" the Supreme Court with justices who shared his own frame of mind. President Truman was "a usurper . . . seizing private property with-

out the slightest shadow of legal right." To those working with
the President, the case was a "peak of frustration."

Truman, himself, was an unpretentious man, given to direct
speech and direct action. His attitudes entered into the crisis he
tried to resolve.

Born on and raised on a Missouri farm, he was thrust into the
Presidency when Franklin D. Roosevelt died in office in 1945. At
first he seemed like a man bewildered. It was like having "a load of
hay fall on you," he told a reporter.

Then in a short time it was Truman who had to decide whether
to drop the atomic bomb. Later it was Truman who started America's vast aid program to foreign countries.

Gifted with native intelligence, he grew in wisdom but his personality did not change. Warmhearted, plain and homey, blunt, direct, and unpolished, he answered the Republicans' campaign
claims by telling the voters that "if you believe that you are bigger
suckers than I think you are."

Few politicians ever expected Truman to be elected President.
Truman surprised them. In 1948, he took a campaigning train trip
across the land and talked to the local people, calling the conservative Congress "the worst in my memory." In the fall elections the
people sent him back to the White House, but the conservative
Congress did little to cooperate with him. This unfortunate relationship between President and Congress played a significant role
in Harry Truman's desperate and historic "seizure of private property."

There was another and even more compelling factor. In June of
1950 the President had ordered American air, naval, and ground
units to help the South Koreans stop a Communist invasion. Technically, the war in Korea was a "police action" and our servicemen
were part of a United Nations fighting force. In fact, Korea was a
war and the United States contributed most of the troops other than
the South Koreans themselves.

As the President saw it, "Our national security and chances for
peace depend on our defense production." Arms and munitions depend on steel.

Toward the end of 1951, a possible steel strike by 600,000 workmen was on the C.I.O. calendar. If it happened, it would tie up
most of the industry and cut off 95 per cent of all steel production.

The President talked the problem over with his Cabinet. Defense
Secretary Robert A. Lovett echoed the President's own thoughts.
"The cessation of production . . . would be catastrophic. . . . It

would prevent us from adequately arming the military . . . ," he said.

"All the members of the Cabinet agreed with Lovett . . . ," Truman later recalled. He also said, "The demands of the workers did not seem out of line to me."

Even though the unions' demands created a terrible problem, the President still understood the men. With the country at war, its industries were busy with defense orders, and fewer consumer goods were being made. As goods became more scarce, prices went up. The purchasing power of a workman's pay went down. The steelworkers, as Truman knew, were making less than auto workers or coal miners. The situation forced on the President a serious conflict of responsibilities. As commander in chief he was responsible for the war effort, but he was also in command of the government's effort to stop the rising spiral of prices and wages threatening the economy.

To this end, the government had set up a series of war agencies under the Office of Defense Mobilization. They were to regulate and hold down both prices and wages so that the war effort would not be defeated by an economic crisis. If the price of steel went way up, the agencies could not do their job. The whole war effort would skyrocket in cost. Airplanes, ships, and guns all used steel. Consumer prices would fly upward in devastating degree. Everything made of steel or with steel tools or equipment would be affected, everything from egg beaters to public roads.

As the terrible year of 1951 came to an end, Philip Murray announced that his C.I.O. steelworkers would go on strike December 31. There was something the President could have done but the idea repelled him; he could have used the Taft-Hartley Act, which Congress had passed in 1947, and instructed the Justice Department to ask for a court order to enjoin (stop) the strike for eighty days while labor-management negotiations continued. Instead, Truman persuaded his friend Philip Murray to postpone the strike voluntarily while the Wage Stabilization Board (W.S.B.), headed by Nathan Feinsinger, looked into the matter. The W.S.B. was to study, hold hearings, and make recommendations as to how the matter might best be settled. All this took time. Again and again Murray and the unions postponed the date of the strike. Meanwhile, they were not getting their increase and they were not getting another thing they wanted—a union shop.

In March, the W.S.B. finally made its recommendation: The men should have a few not-too-costly fringe benefits, plus a 17½ -cents-an-hour increase, some of it to be paid at once and some later. It wasn't all the union people wanted but they accepted it. The companies did not accept it. They replied that they would have to have a price increase of twelve dollars a ton, six dollars to pay the wage boost and another six because other workers would immediately want more and thus increase the prices on the goods which the steel companies must buy.

The company executives were not alone in objecting to the W.S.B. recommendation. Director of Defense Mobilization Charles E. Wilson saw the recommendation as "a serious threat in our effort to stabilize the economy." He had come to the government from the General Electric Company and he agreed with industry's position; it would need a big price increase to pay for the raise. One of the agencies under Wilson was the Office of Price Stabilization, headed by Ellis Arnall. Mr. Arnall emphatically claimed the companies could pay the additional labor costs without any price increase.

A long and heated exchange between Wilson and Arnall took place in a meeting with the President near the end of March. The harassed President decided to take Arnall's advice and allow an increase in wages without giving the companies an extra price increase.

Wilson quit.

A week later, on Thursday, April 3, the industry officials met with representatives of the union. The companies offered to pay the workers an additional nine cents an hour, about half the increase that the W.S.B. had recommended. The union men turned this down. Murray sent the companies a strike notice. Friday, W.S.B. head Feinsinger rushed to New York to see if he could keep both sides talking and head off the strike. Newspaper reporters caught sight of his dapper, well-tailored figure coming through the Biltmore Hotel. Murray and his counsel, Arthur J. Goldberg—the future Supreme Court justice and United States U.N. representative —had set up the union negotiation headquarters in the hotel. Feinsinger had obviously been talking to them.

"Any progress?" a reporter asked.

"I haven't lost any ground," Feinsinger answered.

Meanwhile the union locals began setting up soup kitchens and getting picket signs ready. The companies began banking their furnaces for a shutdown.

Murray set Thursday night at midnight as the time for the strike to begin. A steel executive later said the companies raised their nine-cent offer to twelve and a half cents and that this too was not accepted.

The President had a last-minute conference with his advisers. The Secretary of Defense must have been quite upset. "We are holding the line with ammunition, and not with the lives of our troops," Lovett said. In other words, curtailment of steel would mean more American deaths in Korea.

Tuesday night the President called the radio stations and said he wanted to go on the air. At 10:30 the public heard him saying, "My fellow Americans: Tonight our country faces a grave danger." Then the President announced he was seizing the steel mills. He had instructed Secretary of Commerce Charles Sawyer to take possession. The "greedy" steel companies, he claimed, had never been so prosperous since World War I. He referred to their demand for an increase of twelve dollars a ton as "about the most outrageous thing I ever heard of." He explained that under an amendment to the price law, the companies could get three dollars more a ton. Truman's disposition was not being helped by the exasperating position he was in. If he had used the Taft-Hartley Act in the first place, he could have stopped the strike for only eighty days. Instead, he had used persuasion, and thereby he had talked the union into putting off the walkout for ninety-nine days. Truman's sense of integrity would not permit him to resort to the Taft-Hartley court-order method when Murray and his union members had already waited for a much longer period than the law could have required. But the hard legal facts remained. Aside from W.S.B., it was the Taft-Hartley law—and not seizure of private property—that was the machinery which Congress had provided for the President's use in a labor dispute.

The policies of the lawmakers were abundantly clear. They were printed in congressional records, and they were amply stated during the debate on the Taft-Hartley Act, which was written in 1947, at a time when the war seizure powers that Congress had granted to President Roosevelt had been allowed to lapse.

Senator Robert A. Taft of Ohio, a brilliant conservative, speaking for the committee which had worked on the bill, told the full Senate:

> We did not feel that we should put into the law . . . an ultimate resort to compulsory arbitration, or to seizure. . . . We feel that it would interfere with the whole process of collective bargaining. If such a remedy is available as a routine remedy, there will always be pressure to resort to it by whichever party thinks it will receive better treatment through such a process . . . [this party] will not make a bona-fide attempt to settle. . . .

I have had in mind drafting . . . a bill, giving power to seize the plants . . . to seize the unions, their money, and their treasury. . . . But while such a bill might be prepared, I should be unwilling to place such a law on the books until we actually faced such an emergency, and Congress applies the remedy for the particular emergency only. . . .

The lawmakers had decided what was to be done. If a serious labor dispute endangering the nation was not resolved during the eighty-day period in which the Taft-Hartley court order was in effect, the President was to lay the matter before Congress. He was to ask for what emergency legislation he needed to cope with the catastrophe.

President Truman had not gone to Congress. He had acted. He probably was afraid that Congress would tell him to use the Taft-Hartley Act. At least, the lawmakers would waste time debating whether that was the proper remedy. Meanwhile, the steel furnaces would remain cold. The nation's stockpile of steel would disappear and factories making shells and airplane engines would come to a standstill. Truman said later he thought of President Abraham Lincoln, who had acted on his own when the Confederates fired on Fort Sumter. But there were several differences, as Mr. Truman must have realized. In 1861 the actual theater of war was in the United States and enemy soldiers were drilling outside of Baltimore. Moreover, Congress had not provided President Lincoln with any usable alternatives to his action. Furthermore, Lincoln's actions were eventually upheld by Congress—although not without debate. Truman was not destined to be that fortunate.

No sooner were the President's words on the air waves than Secretary Sawyer telegraphed to the heads of the steel companies:

"The President of the United States . . . has directed me, as Secretary of Commerce . . . to take possession of all properties of your company which I deem necessary . . . . I hereby do take possession effective twelve o'clock midnight, Eastern Standard time, April 8, 1952. . . ." The company chiefs were then given their orders: Fly the American flag; post notices that the plant is now United States Government property; have all officers and employees perform their regular duties; and set up new account books on the Government's operation.

The next day President Truman sent a message to Congress explaining what he had already done. He stated, "Sound legislation might be very desirable. . . ." He promised to cooperate with whatever the lawmakers decided but added, "If Congress does not deem it necessary to act at this time, I shall continue to do all that is within my power to keep the steel industry operating. . . ."

Both houses began heated debate. Behind the argument were wishes to censure the "highhanded" President who had "usurped power" he did not have. This was a country of laws, not of men. If you could seize the steel mills you could seize the cattle on the farms.

Industry and government lawyers faced each other in court. The bevy of company attorneys asked Judge Alexander Holtzoff for a preliminary injunction to stop Secretary Sawyer. Holtzoff refused.

A preliminary injunction is a court order which can be issued before the case is fully heard. Holtzoff felt that enjoining Sawyer would really be enjoining the President. He said it was "very doubtful, to say the least," whether a federal court should issue such an injunction against the President of the United States. Besides, Sawyer had left the management in charge of the plants. The companies as yet were not suffering any irreparable damage, as Judge Holtzoff saw it. If they did suffer any damages they could later go into the U.S. Court of Claims.

The company lawyers insisted that if Sawyer was acting illegally —and they were sure he was—they could not go into the Court of Claims.

After the Holtzoff ruling, negotiation between labor and management continued fruitless. On Friday, April 18, Sawyer announced he would take up the wage question with the union himself. The company executives had visions of his giving the workers a "wage boost" and then returning the plants so they would have to pay the bill. Sawyer would probably make acceptance of the government-made contract a prerequisite to returning the mills.

The suggestion that the companies could rely on going to the Court of Claims to recover this damage seemed utterly worthless. In the first place, as the lawyers saw it, at least two Supreme Court decisions stood in their way. In 1910 the justices had said, "The constitutional prohibition against taking private property for public use without just compensation is directed against the government, and not against individual or public officers proceeding without the authority of legislative enactment." Legislative enactment meant act of Congress. As if that ruling was not already clear enough, in 1920 the justices had said much the same thing again.

For the steel companies to hope to sue Charles Sawyer personally, to recover the astronomical amounts that they would have to pay out in the years ahead because of his "wage boost," was absurd.

The lawyers went before Judge David A. Pine. Sawyer's announcement had changed the picture since Holtzoff ruled, they said. Surely they were entitled to an injunction which would prevent Sawyer from raising wages with their client's money.

Judge Pine said that if he found the defendant had acted without the authority of law he would grant a preliminary injunction against the seizure itself.

It was true that at the time there were two war measures that did permit seizure. Where the Government was desperately in need of certain equipment or certain real estate holdings, there was a sort of condemnation statute making it possible to force owners to sell to the United States. And when the President had given a plant an emergency order for goods needed by the armed services and the company had failed or refused to fill the order, a seizure could take place. But neither of these acts could be interpreted to apply to the steel seizure case.

Assistant Attorney General Holmes Baldridge, arguing for the Government, based his claims solely on the Constitution of the United States. He claimed that its provisions were sufficiently broad to grant the President all the executive power he needed to protect the United States in an emergency. He told the court that "when an emergency . . . arises . . . of such importance to the entire welfare of the country that something has to be done about it and has to be done now, and there is no statutory provision for handling the matter . . . it is the duty of the Executive to step in and protect the national security. . . ."

The President, Baldridge said, decided when there was such an emergency. It was not up to the court.

Judge Pine was shocked. "So you contend the Executive has unlimited power in time of an emergency?" he asked.

Baldridge pointed to two brakes on the President's power—what might happen at the next election as a result of his action and the possibility that he might be impeached by Congress.

The judge brought Baldridge back to the immediate issue. "Do you have any case of a seizure except a seizure authorized by statute . . . [which was held constitutional]?" he asked.

Baldridge referred to a number of instances in which previous Presidents had made seizures without being authorized by law.

Judge Pine: "I mean where the Courts approved it."

Baldridge: "I do not know of any."

Judge Pine: "I do not think a seizure without judicial interference is relevant. The fact that a man reaches in your pocket and steals your wallet is not a precedent for making that a valid act. . . ."

The judge's decision was no surprise. On Tuesday, April 29, he issued his injunction which ordered Secretary Sawyer to return the mills to the companies; "the contemplated strike . . . with all its awful results, would be less injurious to the public than . . . unlimited and unrestrained Executive power . . . ," he said. According to various polls, Congress and the public agreed.

The C.I.O. steelworkers had gone to work for the Government, but when they heard the court news, they went right back on strike.

The President and his Acting Attorney General, Philip Perlman (who was also Solicitor General), decided to rush an appeal. On the night of Judge Pine's decision, the lights burned late at the Department of Justice Building on Pennsylvania Avenue. Eight lawyers and six stenographers worked until four in the morning preparing the Government's appeal brief.

Only a few hours later Perlman was fighting the injunction before all nine judges of the U.S. Court of Appeals. Most often only three judges sit on a case. On this Wednesday morning they were all there.

Perlman told them, "This case may involve the very existence of this Nation . . . [and] every minute counts. . . . We can get the men back [to work] before the furnaces get cold."

The judges of the Court of Appeals then wanted to know how quickly Perlman could be ready to go to the Supreme Court for a final ruling on the legality of the seizure. Could he be ready by Friday?

Perlman turned and called out to a heavy-set young attorney, "Can we do it by then, Jamie?" Trying to sound casual and knowing that papers to that effect were already being prepared, the young man called back, "I guess so." At 6:30 the court recessed and took the amazingly short period of ten minutes to decide what to do.

At 6:50 Chief Judge Harold Stephens announced that the court was divided but that Judge Edgerton would give the majority's decision. Judge Edgerton then stayed—that is, postponed—the injunction for exactly a day and a half, until 4:30 that Friday. He was giving the parties time to petition the Supreme Court for a hearing.

More formally, the court's position was that Judge Pine's injunction was only justified if the companies could not collect for any damages they suffered, if they couldn't go to the Court of Claims because the seizure was illegal. In a case called *United States v. Russell* the Supreme Court had said, "Extraordinary and unforeseen occasions arise . . . in time of war or of immediate and impending public danger, in which private property may be impressed into the public service . . . but it is the emergency, as was said by a great magistrate, that gives the right, and it is clear that the emergency must be shown to exist before the taking can be justified. . . ."

If the Supreme Court found that the taking was justified by the emergency, the companies could theoretically collect in the Court of Claims. Only the year before, the Supreme Court had made the Government pay compensation to a coal company it had seized temporarily during World War II. In the case called *United States v. Pee Wee Coal Company,* the Government had raised wages and run the mine so that the owner lost money. The Appeals Court judges saw a similarity between *Pee Wee* and the present case.

The trouble with the *Pee Wee* case, as far as the steel companies were concerned, was that the question of the legality of the seizure had not been the issue. Pee Wee merely wanted to recover its losses, and it demanded only what the Government had lost for it while the Government was holding the mine. Conversely, what worried the steel companies was how much they were going to have to pay out after their properties were returned. Moreover, their biggest loss, which nobody could repay if they did not win this case, was their loss of bargaining power with the union.

The companies wasted no time. They were at the Supreme Court door on Friday with their papers. On Saturday the Supreme Court told Secretary Sawyer he was to leave the work contracts as they were, at least until the justices had had a chance to rule. Before them the final and decisive battle would be fought.

With this finality in mind the companies hired as their counsel John W. Davis, by then seventy-nine years old. In the thirty years that had intervened since he won the Pennsylvania Coal Company case against the Mahons, his hair and eyebrows had turned as snowy white as the handkerchief that protruded from the pocket of his elegantly tailored dark suit. A Broadway theatrical producer with all the tricks of make-up at his disposal could hardly have devised an appearance better suited to the role. Looking like a fashionable sage who carried with him the wisdom of the ages, Davis represented the companies both by oral argument and by submitting a written brief. He told the Court that here we have a striking example of the maxim that history repeats itself.

The present claim of the Executive to an inherent right to do whatever he considers necessary for what he views as the common good—without consulting the legislature and without any authority under law—is not a new claim. It . . . was made more than three centuries ago by James I of England when he claimed for himself the right to make law by proclamation and asserted that it was treason to maintain that the King was under the law. It is precisely the claim for which Charles I lost his life and James II his throne. Most important, it is precisely the claim for which George III lost his American colonies. . . . The story is as old as Magna Carta.

First, the prerogatives of the English Crown, as understood at the time our Constitution was drafted, embodied no such right of arbitrary control over private property as those now asserted under the Executive Order.

Second, the Founding Fathers . . . fully mindful of the long and bitter struggle that had been required to place that Crown under the law . . . made it clear that, in establishing the office of Presidency, they were creating a position of far more circumscribed powers than those then attributed to the Crown.

Davis went on to look at what powers the President did have under Article II of the Constitution. The President was, admittedly, the Executive. In addition Davis assumed that Mr. Sawyer was relying on two other provisions in Article II. "The President shall be Commander-in-Chief of the Army and Navy . . . ; he shall take care that the laws be faithfully executed. . . ."

As to the first sentence, Davis said, "The President's military functions do not encompass any power to legislate. . . . On the contrary. . . ." He referred to Article II, Section 3, of the Constitution which provides that from time to time the President shall "give to the Congress information of the state of the Union, and recommend to their Consideration such Measures as he shall judge necessary. . . ."

Thus, as Davis saw it, the power to devise legal remedies for labor disputes rested in the legislative branch, not in the commander in chief. Secondly, as to taking care that the laws be faithfully executed, that was exactly what President Truman had not done. He had ignored the law and, inventing a procedure of his own, had seized private property.

Davis went on to quote from earlier Court cases. In *Lichter v.*

United States the Court said, "In peace or in war it is essential that the Constitution be scrupulously obeyed, and particularly that the respective branches of the Government keep within the powers assigned to each by the Constitution."

He gave a dramatic example. In 1799 this country was in an undeclared naval war with France. Her attacks on our shipping were a by-product of her greater war with Britain. Congress provided that no American vessel should proceed to any French port, under penalty of forfeiture. President Adams in his orders to United States commanders directed them to seize ships bound both *to* and *from* France. Captain Little obeyed and seized a ship coming from a French port. When the case reached the Supreme Court in 1804, the justices ordered the vessel returned to its owner. The justices explained that it was not clear what the President as commander in chief could have done to protect the nation if there had been no law. It was clear that he could not thus expand the law once it was enacted by Congress.

Finally Davis came to the most difficult part of his argument. The Court of Appeals had referred to "immediate and impending public danger, in which private property may be impressed into the public service. . . ." The Appeals Court had also said the emergency must be "such as will not admit of a delay or a resort to any other source of supply."

"The Korean hostilities," said Davis, "have continued for close to two years. It is clear beyond argument that the present controversy does not present a situation of a sudden emergency . . . [and does not involve] sudden and imminent threat of military disaster which justifies the exercise of presidential power as Commander-in-Chief." This was no seizure in the course of battle.

In effect, Davis argued, the problem of labor disputes and their relation to vital defense supplies had been with us for two years and had received extensive consideration by Congress. Besides, the President had had ample warning that negotiations were about to collapse. He could have gone to Congress in the weeks before the strike started.

Above all, there could be no legal basis for using the power of commander in chief to raise wages. Davis ended by showing that there was no way under the Fifth Amendment by which his clients could be compensated for their financial losses if Secretary of Commerce Sawyer appropriated their funds by awarding increases to their help. Constitutional guarantees of private property rights would be meaningless if the President could do this by merely claiming the existence of an emergency. The old gentleman at last closed his notebook and concluded.

To all this formidable material, Acting Attorney General Perlman had to try to give an answer. He reviewed the history of the seizure. He stressed that it was temporary and subject to what Congress would decide to do, as promised in the President's message to the lawmakers. He stressed the defense emergency brought about by the work stoppage. The President, he said, did not have to use the Taft-Hartley Act merely because it was available if it was not wise to do so. "It was extremely unlikely that the 'voluntary' method would ever be acceptable again" if the President were to follow it up by asking for an injunction. The President in war or national emergency could seize property—subject, of course, to just compensation. Perlman did not think his opponents really belonged in Court. They had not as yet been hurt. Besides, any injury to them was offset by the greater injury to the public if the strike continued.

Perlman thought there was historical precedent for the President's behavior. It was in this part of his argument that he got into trouble. Perlman mentioned a number of situations that the justices did not think were comparable to the present one. He then mentioned President Roosevelt's seizure of the North American Aviation Company before World War II. Justice Robert H. Jackson had been Attorney General at the time. He would have none of the comparison. None of these steel companies were under direct contract to the Government, as North American Aviation Company had been. In the North American incident there was government-owned machinery in the plant. Communist-led pickets, protesting United States foreign policy, stopped employees from getting to work. The example "cannot be regarded as even a precedent, much less an authority, for the present seizure," the Justice said. He was obviously irritated. Before Perlman sat down, the justices also aired the fact that we were not technically at war.

The Acting Attorney General was followed by Arthur Goldberg, who appeared for the United Steelworkers. Goldberg's major point was how unfair it would have been for the President to use Taft-Hartley after the workmen had waited so long. Hence, the President had to try something else. This was especially true, he argued, since the main reason for the continuing emergency was a dispute between the Government and the industry over a price increase for steel. Therefore, concluded Attorney Goldberg, the seizure was not "to settle a labor dispute," as claimed. He did not convince the justices. Not wishing to give the impression that the union liked government seizures, Goldberg expressed the hope that the case would be quickly decided.

Evidently neither the companies nor the union liked seizure. The President's reaction to this was typical. "They are not supposed to like it. . . ."

The justices, having heard all sides, retired to decide how to rule. Justice Frankfurter found it distinctly unpleasant to have to rule that the President had exceeded his powers and especially as "his purposes were dictated by concern for the Nation's well being. . . ." He said he felt "wary and humble." And yet he was forced to remember that, even when Congress had given the Executive the drastic power to make seizures, it had always added careful restrictions: It had granted the power only for limited times—times of war or public danger. It had written in detail under what conditions the seizure would be legal. It had not even left to implication that just compensation must be made but had said how the Fifth Amendment was to be enforced. This time Congress had carefully not given the President that power. Maybe they should have, but this was not up to the Court. To uphold Truman was to "disrespect the whole legislative process and the constitutional division of authority between President and Congress." This Frankfurter could not do.

Justice Douglas was also critical of what the Chief Executive had done, but not without understanding; "the emergency which caused the President to seize these steel plants was one that bore heavily on the country," he said. He recognized that the "President can act more quickly than the Congress . . . [and that] Legislative power, by contrast, is slower to exercise. There must be delay while the ponderous machinery of committees, hearings, and debates is put into motion." Douglas went on: "But as Mr. Justice Brandeis stated in his dissent in *Myers v. United States,* 272 U.S. 52, 293: 'The doctrine of the separation of powers was adopted by the Convention of 1787, not to promote efficiency but to preclude the exercise of arbitrary power . . . to save the people from autocracy.' "

Douglas thought the debates and committee hearings were necessary in a serious situation like this, even if they caused a loss of precious time and of war production. He was willing to pay a price for our system of checks and balances. He explained, "Today a kindly President uses the seizure power to effect a wage increase and to keep the steel furnaces in production. Yet tomorrow another

President might use the same power to prevent a wage increase, to curb trade unionists, to regiment labor. . . ."

There was even a stronger reason why Truman's actions could not be upheld. "The command of the Fifth Amendment is that no 'private property be taken for public use, without just compensation.' [But the] President has no power to raise revenues. . . . The branch of government that has the power to pay compensation for a seizure is the only one able to authorize a seizure. . . ." Douglas thought that settled it.

Chief Justice Vinson disagreed with both Douglas and Frankfurter. Over and above our own peril we had a legal obligation to produce steel for our allies, he argued. In addition, the President had by now sent two messages to Congress and Congress had not acted. The President should be deemed to be executing the military procurement program and the anti-inflation program, at least until Congress acted. Both programs needed to be faithfully executed, and faithful execution of the law was the President's function. Justices Reed and Minton concurred with Vinson. They were all three deeply impressed by the nation's critical need for steel and the dangers of the hour.

Justice Jackson was very dubious about the "need" argument as an excuse for Executive action; "emergency powers would tend to kindle emergencies," he said. He pointed to Germany. After World War I she had a constitution to secure her liberties but the President was empowered, without the concurrence of the legislature, to suspend any or all individual rights if public safety or order were seriously disturbed. This proved a temptation to every government, whatever its shade of opinion. "In thirteen years suspension of rights was invoked on more than 250 occasions," Jackson reported. Finally, Adolf Hitler came along and all rights were suspended indefinitely.

Jackson also noted that at the moment there was no "imminent invasion or threatened attack." He distrusted the "emergency" argument.

Justice Clark had also been thinking about the emergency aspect of the problem; "where Congress has laid down specific procedures to deal with the type of crisis confronting the President, he must follow those procedures . . . ," the Justice said. Then he added that "in the absence of such action by Congress, the President's independent power to act depends upon the gravity of the situation. . . ." This was the conclusion of the justices in 1804. It still seemed wise. When Justices Burton and Black also felt they could not uphold the seizure, that made a six-to-three majority.

On June 2, Black read the Court's opinion from the bench. He summarized all that had happened and much that had been said. He noted the relevant laws and the constitutional provisions involved in the case. He ended on a note of unmistakable finality: "this seizure order cannot stand."

That afternoon the news was flashed to the nation. The President on June 10 asked a joint session of Congress for seizure powers. The lawmakers refused. They wanted the President to use first the machinery they had provided.

On June 27 Pittsburgh Steel Company settled with its workers, giving them a twelve and a half cents an hour increase and, with modifications, a union shop. Congress urged the rest of industry to work out their differences. On July 24 the steel strike in the rest of the industry came to an end. The workers had won sixteen cents and fringe benefits.

The companies gained from the Government more than five dollars a ton price rise. Truman had granted it to end the strike but with a reluctant heart. By then the defense effort had suffered as a result of the shutdown. The whole situation had been most unfortunate. Would a different President with different advisers have handled it differently? Would a different Congress have handled it differently? These are matters of speculation. As far as the justices were concerned, they could not take over the work of either the President or the legislature. They had to rule not for this emergency alone but for all time. They had to decide whether the procedures being followed jeopardized the property rights and hence all the guaranteed rights of Americans. The decision they made sacrificed the objectives of the moment to the security of the future.

BIBLIOGRAPHY FOR PART IV

Principal Sources on the Property Owners

BOOKS

Black, Henry Campbell. *Black's Law Dictionary*, third ed. St. Paul, Minn., 1933.

Cahn, Edmond N. (ed.). *The Great Rights* (a collection of lectures written by Justices Earl Warren, Hugo H. Black, William O. Douglas, and William J. Brennan, Jr.) New York, 1963.

Douglas, William O. *Almanac of Liberty.* New York, 1954.
Lorant, Stefan. *The Presidency.* New York, 1952.
Randall, Clarence B. *Over My Shoulder.* Boston, 1956.
Truman, Harry S. *Memoirs.* Vol. 2: *Years of Trial and Hope.* New York, 1956.

UNITED STATES FEDERAL RECORDS

Congressional Records
    Congressional Record, Vol. 93, 80th Congress, pages 3835–36 (1947).
    Congressional Record, Vol. 98, 82nd Congress, 2nd session (1952).
    House Document 534, *Steel Seizure Case,* Parts 1 and 2, 82nd Congress, 2nd session (1952).
    Senate Report No. 105, Federal Labor Relations Act of 1947, 80th Congress, 1st session (1947).

Supreme Court Records (Transcripts and Records of Briefs)
    Allegheny Airlines v. Cedarhurst, 238 Fed. 812 (1956).
    Baltimore & Potomac Railroad Company v. The Fifth Baptist Church, 108 U.S. 317 (1883).
    Chicago B & O R. R. v. Chicago, 166 U.S. 226, 241 (1897).
    Griggs v. Allegheny County, 369 U.S. 84 (1962).
    Home Building & Loan Association v. Blaisdell, 290 U.S. 398 (1934).
    Hooe v. United States, 218 U.S. 322 (1910).
    Lichter v. United States, 334 U.S. 742 (1948).
    Little v. Barreme, 2 Cranch 170 (1804).
    Northwest Airlines, Inc. v. Minnesota, 322 U.S. 292 (1944).
    Pennsylvania Coal Co. v. Mahon, 260 U.S. 393 (1922).
    Richards v. Washington Terminal Co., 233 U.S. 546 (1914).
    United States v. Causby, 328 U.S. 256 (1946).
    United States v. North American Transportation & Trading Co. 253 U.S. 330 (1920).
    United States v. Russell, 13 Wall 623 (1871).
    Youngstown Steel & Tube Co. v. Sawyer, 343 U.S. 579 (1952).

NEWSPAPERS AND MAGAZINES

Business Week, April 12, 1952.
Current History, June, 1952.
Life, May 26, 1952.
Newsweek, May 12, 1952.
New York Times, January 3, April 3–30, May 1–10, 1952.

PART FIVE

SOLDIERS

AND CIVILIANS

"A well-regulated Militia, being necessary to the security of a free State, the right of the people to keep and bear Arms, shall not be infringed."
—Second Amendment

"No person shall be held to answer for a capital, or otherwise infamous crime, unless on a presentment or indictment of a Grand Jury, except in cases arising in the land or naval forces, or in the Militia, when in actual service in time of War or public danger; nor shall any person be subject for the same offense to be twice put in jeopardy of life or limb; nor shall be compelled in any criminal case to be a witness against himself, nor be deprived of life, liberty, or property, without due process of law . . . ."
—Fifth Amendment

"In all criminal prosecutions, the accused shall enjoy the right to a speedy and public trial, . . . and to be informed of the nature and cause of the accusation; to be confronted with the witnesses against him; to have compulsory process for obtaining witnesses in his favor, and to have the Assistance of Counsel for his defense."
—Sixth Amendment

". . . nor [shall] cruel and unusual punishments [be] inflicted."
—Eighth Amendment

THE RIGHTS AND THE ISSUES

The man with a gun and his Bill of Rights provide the American scene with three important and closely related topics of continuing concern.

In the first place, the determined men of our Republic have always insisted that, in order to preserve freedom, the military must remain subordinate to the civilian authority. From the very beginning, the Founders gave Congress and not the military the right to declare war. They made the civilian President the commander in chief over the generals. Their reasons are not hard to find. They intended these United States to have a government that derives its powers from the consent of the governed.

In contrast, as they realized, the purpose of an army hierarchy is to secure its present and future military objectives by preparing men to go obediently to their death, if necessary. Thus, military leaders are trained to demand unquestioning adherence to their wishes. Therefore, reasoned the Founders, the military could not be allowed to dominate the Republic or the Republic would be lost.

The issue was very much alive when this country wrote its Constitution. Foreign countries and hostile Indians were ready and eager to destroy the infant nation. It would have been easy to scream emergency and call for a garrison state. The people, remembering British military domination during the Colonial period, wanted no such thing. Yet the problems of defense had to be met. James Madison spoke for the majority when he recalled, "The veteran legions of Rome were an overmatch for the undisciplined valor of all other nations, and rendered her the mistress of the world. Not the less true is it that the liberties of Rome provide the final victim of her military triumphs. . . . A standing force, therefore, is a dangerous, at the same time that it may be a necessary, provision."

Here, then, was a problem that would be with the new nation forever. Standing armies were a necessity, but down through the ages they had always proved a threat to freedom. As a partial answer, the United States maintained the smallest possible force of professional soldiers and counted on turning her civilians into soldiers in time of trouble. With the passing of the decades, even this tradition could not keep down the necessary growth of the nation's armed forces. Less than eight hundred men made up the United States Army in the months following President Washington's first inauguration. When Dwight D. Eisenhower left the presidency in 1961, the United States armed forces numbered over two and a half million. The munitions industry required to supply them had grown at an even faster rate. As the retiring ex-general and ex-President said, 'We must not fail to comprehend . . . [the] grave implications . . . [and] we must guard against the acquisition of unwarranted influence . . . by the military industrial complex. . . . We must never let the weight of this combination endanger our libertes or democratic processes."

In other words, military necessity and the cry of military need coming from a huge military establishment was as much a cause for anxiety and as big a threat to freedom as it had been when the Constitution was written. Congress and the public must be vigilant "so that security and liberty may prosper together," said President Eisenhower. How real a danger exists will be illustrated by the episode in the chapter which follows.

Secondly, this being the century in which most youths are potential members of our huge military forces, another serious question which arose was inevitable. How much license to disregard the Bill of Rights must the war command have, by reason of military necessity, in handling the discipline of citizen soldiers? Since time immemorial man has expected military discipline to be harsh, often arbitrary, and, at times, unjust. In the past, military leaders have insisted that it must be stringent or wars would not be won. A body of men equipped with firearms must not be allowed to become an unruly mob. The professional soldier of old accepted his hard lot. The United States citizen soldier often felt differently.

Unless military discipline was fair, when he was called to the colors to defend the nation and its Constitution, he wasn't getting much of what he was being asked to defend. After both World Wars, senators and congressmen faced the problem of reviewing military justice. What they finally attempted to do in 1950, and why and what they achieved by their actions, make the story in the second chapter of Part V.

The third question is closely related to the first two. If America does not want a huge professional standing army, she must rely on her citizens to become soldiers when she needs them. Out of this fact comes the question of what happens when these same citizens, though not part of a well-organized army or militia, carefully governed and highly disciplined, still demand their right under the Second Amendment to the Constitution to keep and bear arms. Some of them merely want to go hunting; others live in rural parts of the country where predatory animals are still a problem; others feel the need to protect themselves and their homes. Still more insist that if we are to rely on a citizen army the civilian must keep up his target practice. He must keep a weapon and be ready to defend the local community in time of emergency—an idea as old as civilization itself. Now the contention is often challenged as outdated, and the challengers also point to those who want their guns for antisocial motives. What rights under the Constitution do people have to keep and bear arms and how free from restriction should they be? Debate on this question is still going on. In one of the next chapters we will look at the arguments on both sides of this dilemma.

"Precisely What the Bill of Rights Outlaws"

"ON the morning of December 7, 1941, Japanese aircraft temporarily disabled every battleship and most of the aircraft in the Hawaiian area." So read the official United States Navy report. The words were calmer than the Hawaiian community had been on that ghastly Sunday morning when suddenly, without warning, the thundering crash of exploding Japanese bombs shattered the balmy Sabbath quiet and gray smoke blurred the sky.

The terrifying attack on Pearl Harbor forced an unready American public into World War II. The nation had to fight. The Hawaiian Islands were not only United States territory but also the nation's key military outpost to the westward. Pearl Harbor was a United States naval base. Hit and disabled battleships and cruisers lay in the waters off Oahu, the largest of the Hawaiian Islands. In short, the nation was at war with Japan, and Hawaii was in the theater of that war.

The governor, a presidential appointee named Joseph B. Poindexter, had undoubtedly seen the Bureau of Census statistics of the year before. About one-third of the islanders were Japanese or had Japanese ancestors. These figures could not help but add to his anxiety over the fate of Hawaii.

Poindexter sent a radiogram to President Franklin D. Roosevelt.

December 7, 1941

The President the White House
Washington, D.C.
I Have Today Declared Martial Law Throughout the Territory of Hawaii and Have Suspended the Privilege of the Writ of Habeas Corpus. . . . Your Attention Is Called to Section Sixty-Seven of the Hawaiian Organic Act for Your Decision on My Action.

Poindexter

The Organic Act to which the governor referred had been passed by Congress in 1900, when Hawaii was officially made a United States territory. In referring to the powers of the governor, it said that "he may, in case of rebellion or invasion, or imminent danger thereof, when the public safety requires it, suspend the privilege of the writ of habeas corpus, or place the Territory, or any part thereof, under martial law until communication can be had with the President and his decision thereon made known."

Pending the approval of the President, Hawaiians were without the writ of habeas corpus and under martial law. If anybody wondered: What was martial law? they could find it described in *Black's Law Dictionary* as a system "arbitrary in its character, and depending only on the will of the commander of an army. . . ." Blackstone describes it further as "built on no settled principles . . . [and] in truth and reality no law. . . ."

The nightmarish Sunday had still not spent itself when General Walter C. Short announced to the people that, in compliance with the request of the governor, "I have this day assumed the position of military governor of Hawaii, and taken charge of the government of the Territory."

The next day both civil and criminal courts were forbidden to try cases. General Short established provost courts and military commissions to try civilians. Rules of evidence and the procedures of other courts of law were not to control these tribunals. As announced by the military, the rules for imposing penalties were simple. Penalties were to be commensurate with the offense committed.

On Tuesday the President sent a message expressing his approval of the content of Poindexter's brief radiogram. From then on the military governed the day-to-day activities of civilians, including their meetings, wages, hours, traffic conditions, and the sale of foods and consumer goods. In addition, the Army established evening curfews to keep people off the streets and ordered blackouts that required islanders to turn off their lights or to cover their windows so that the electric glow would not serve as a beacon to enemy planes. One regulation forbade interference with any member of the military personnel in the performance of his duties.

On December 16 the territorial courts were permitted to reopen to try a limited class of cases not requiring the calling of juries or witnesses. The civilian courts were thus open but the military in their own courts were trying civilians. By Christmas, places of amusement such as movie houses were operating. By February, the bars were serving the public, but the courts were still restricted.

In August, Poindexter formally left his post. He had long since abdicated in essence. He was replaced by Ingram M. Stainback, a former federal judge. Within days of Stainback's appointment an incident occurred. Harry White, a civilian, was accused of embezzling from another civilian. The case had no military implications but, like many other civilians, White was taken before a military tribunal. He challenged the authority of the military to try him. His objection was overruled. He demanded a trial by jury as called for by the Sixth Amendment to the Constitution. His request was denied. His attorney asked for more time to prepare his defense. The request was refused. White was sentenced to five years in prison, later cut to four by the commanding authorities.

As soon as he could manage it, Governor Stainback headed for Washington, hoping to persuade the President to have martial law revoked. He did not meet with President Roosevelt, but he did have a series of conferences with officials from the Department of the Interior, the Justice Department, and the War Department. It was now a full year since Pearl Harbor had been attacked, and Hawaiians were still being treated like a conquered people.

The people at the War Department could not be convinced but the other government officials were sympathetic to the governor's demands for a change. Finally, with their help, Stainback obtained a compromise. The writ of habeas corpus remained suspended. A modified form of martial law was to continue, but the courts were to take back their old functions—with important exceptions. One of these exceptions included the right of the military to try civilians for violating military orders. The new conditions took effect on March 10, 1943. In addition, Stainback told attorneys he had left Washington with the impression that "very shortly the whole [martial law] set-up would be abandoned."

It had not been abandoned when Lloyd C. Duncan got into trouble a year later, in February of 1944. Lloyd was a ship fitter of Scotch-Irish extraction, born in Sheridan, Wyoming, where he had gone through public school. He had come to the Islands when the war was new, and in 1944 he was a twenty-five-year-old one-hundred-ninety pounder. He worked the graveyard shift from eleven at night to seven in the morning at the Pearl Harbor Navy Yard.

On the evening of February 24, Lloyd had an unexpected pleasure. A friend of his, a young merchant seaman from Sheridan, was in town. The two pals had dinner at a restaurant. They also had a few drinks. Lloyd took his friend Bob back to the yard. It was still early—about 9:30—but Lloyd wanted to show him where to catch a truck to get back to his ship. They entered the gates of the Navy Yard and Bob asked the marine guard about the truck. The marine told him he could not reach his ship that way. As to what happened next, the marine corporal's story and Lloyd's account are somewhat different.

Lloyd later insisted, "When I said the marine don't know what he was talking about, I was talking to my friend."

As the marine guard reported, "He called me a vile name and said I was trying to foul his buddy up. . . . I placed him under arrest . . . for using profane language when I told him to shove off and he said he did not have to shove off . . . and [for] interfering with my duties." The marine said he was trying to give Bob the proper directions and Lloyd was interfering. In order to make the arrest, the marine corporal had to see Lloyd's badge and he asked, "Let me see your badge." As the marine remembered, Lloyd just stood there with the badge hanging face down from a string around his neck. "I tried to slip it over and he took a swing at me," the marine corporal said.

Lloyd denied the charge. However, in one part of his testimony, he said that "I was trying to make him let go of me. . . ." At this point another marine was called in to help subdue Lloyd, and according to the marines Lloyd hit both of them. He was turned over to the civilian police. They took down his story and later released him. Thinking this was the end of the episode, Lloyd made no attempt to corral his witnesses.

Five days later he was handed a summons to appear before the provost court at 8:30 in the morning on March 1. He appeared, but the Government's witnesses were not present and he was told to come back the next day at 8:30. The court was in the Navy Yard near his work. He finished his shift at seven and did not go home but hung around, waiting to go to court. By his own testimony he was terribly tired because they had been busy on a rush job at the yard. He was still in his work clothes and he needed a shave.

Although he had never been indicted by a grand jury as called for in the Fifth Amendment, he was immediately put on trial. There was no jury, as called for by the Sixth Amendment. The judge was a lieutenant commander; he asked Lloyd if he wanted advice of counsel. At the time Lloyd could not believe the charges would be serious enough to warrant calling a lawyer. When the judge asked him if he was ready, it sounded like a formality. He thought he had no choice but to say yes. The Sixth Amendment says the accused may have compulsory process for obtaining witnesses, but Lloyd testified later he did not know he could have forced the provost court to subpoena his witnesses.

The trial as he remembered it later took about ten or fifteen minutes. Both Lloyd and the marines stood and gave their testimony. The naval judge then said, "This appears to me to be a pretty serious case." He ordered the prisoner jailed for six months.

Lloyd had a brother, James, who also lived on the Islands. After Lloyd was jailed, James made various inquiries to find out what he could do about it. Evidently it was James who found his way to the law office of J. Garner Anthony. Mr. Anthony must have made up his mind he was going to make this a test case. On March 14, at 11:30, he telephoned United States District Judge Frank McLaughlin. In spite of the suspension of the writ and the continuance of martial law, the attorney still wanted a writ of habeas corpus. In other words, he wanted the sheriff ordered to bring Lloyd and the record before the judge so that Anthony could challenge the legality of the provost trial. Judge McLaughlin gave him an appointment for two o'clock. As the court rules required, Anthony notified the United States Attorney for the District of Hawaii, G. D. Crozier, who also came to the two o'clock meeting in the judge's chambers. Following their discussions, the texts of three interesting messages appear in the records of the case.

The first is a court order "to show cause" directed at Duke P. Kahanamoku, sheriff of the city and county of Honolulu. It ordered the sheriff to "appear before this court on Monday, the 20th day of March 1944 at 10 o'clock A.M. to show cause if any he has why a writ of habeas corpus should not be issued. . . ." It was signed by Judge McLaughlin who, because of the arrangement of the court calendar, later turned the case over to another judge.

The second message printed in the records is another radiogram from Washington, signed by Attorney General Francis Biddle and addressed to Crozier. "Representatives of War and Justice Departments . . . being sent at once to Hawaii to participate in presentation of Government's position in pending Duncan habeas corpus proceeding. Please request ten-day adjournment for response to Order to Show Cause. . . ."

The third text is quite long and is the sheriff's answer to the court order. It reviews the events of December 7. It then goes on to claim that the public safety at all times since December 7 required the continued existence of martial law and the suspension of the writ as proclaimed by the governor. Provost courts, it says, are necessary for the successful prosecution of the war. The military action of punishing persons for assaulting sentries to hinder them in the performance of their duties was not unreasonable or arbitrary. The U.S. District Court was without jurisdiction to issue the writ.

The judge refused to be so easily convinced that he was without authority, and Anthony arranged bail for his client while the case went to trial.

The facts were reviewed but only over the Government's objection. Anthony was not convinced that Lloyd was guilty.

Judge Delbert E. Metzger listened to the story and the witnesses and then commented, "The questions in this case are not whether Lloyd C. Duncan created a disturbance . . . or whether he committed an assault on marine guards or was assaulted by marine guards. . . . The question here is: Has a Provost Court . . . lawful power to try and convict a civilian. . . ?"

This being the question, the government lawyers concentrated their fire on the continuing threat of Japanese attack, which they insisted necessitated martial law. They relied, as Poindexter had, on the Organic Act as it related to the dangers of invasion or rebellion.

Admiral Chester W. Nimitz was asked to testify. Under questioning, he admitted that invasion by sea-borne troops in sufficient numbers to establish a beachhead was no longer likely, but he thought invasion by stealth, commando raids, espionage parties, and submarines was still imminent.

Lieutenant General Robert C. Richardson, Jr., now in command of Hawaii, agreed when he also took the stand. He had to have provost courts to enforce his orders, he said. Going into civilian courts would mean intolerable delay. He found it inconceivable that he, as military commander, should be subjected to relying on another government agency for the enforcement of his commands. As far as Lloyd was concerned, he said that "we have to uphold the authority of our sentinels. . . ."

Anthony called Governor Stainback, who said he saw no reason why Lloyd should not have been tried by a civilian court. The courts were functioning. There was no public disorder, nor had there been any since Pearl Harbor. As far as imminent danger of invasion was concerned, Stainback said "imminent" meant "about to happen." Anthony then pointed out that our battle line against the Japanese was now over three thousand miles west of Hawaii. Judge Metzger listened and then gave his ruling:

> With due respect to the opinions of General Richardson and Admiral Nimitz that martial law is desirable and necessary . . . I

find myself bound not by their opinions, but by the laws of the land. . . .

The United States of America, of which Hawaii is an integral part, are governed by constitutionally established laws. . . . There can be no question that martial law depends for its creation and existence upon a condition of disorder so great as to disrupt the orderly performance of civil government. . . .

No part of the Island of Oahu in the Territory of Hawaii is in a battlefield today, nor has it been for over two years. . . .

If the military commanders still needed special regulations for the island's safety and defense, the judge thought they should ask the legislature to enact such regulations "instead of insisting upon holding by force of arms an entire population under a form of helpless and unappealable subjugation called martial law. . . ."

Only conditions of disorder and not mere military convenience could justify such a system, Judge Metzger decided, and on the basis of this decision he announced, "I conclude. . . . That martial law did not lawfully exist in the Territory . . . after March 10, 1943. . . . That the office of Military Governor . . . is without lawful creation. . . . That the . . . Provost Court . . . possessed no authority in law to try, find guilty, and sentence the civilian . . . to imprisonment in the county jail. . . ." It was a bold and far-reaching decision.

No sooner had Lloyd retrieved his bail money than the Government arranged to appeal. Judge Metzger then utilized Supreme Court rule 45 (now 49), allowing Lloyd Duncan to stay out of prison pending a final determination of the case. When the appeals judges reversed Judge Metzger, the case went to the United States Supreme Court.

The justices heard the case in December, 1945. They of course saw the case in its historical context; the Declaration of Independence states as one justification for the colonists' rebellion against King George III: "He has affected to render the Military independent of and superior to the Civil power." They listened at the same time to the arguments in the White case; Harry White was appealing his four-year sentence. Then they took their time and discussed the cases among themselves before at last giving their ruling on February 25, 1946. By then the war was over and the United States Government had long since restored the privilege of the writ of habeas corpus to the islanders. The remaining question was the legality of the trials.

Justice Black summed up his feelings very quickly. "Our system of government clearly is the antithesis of total military rule . . . [and] the founders of this country . . . were opposed to governments that placed in the hands of one man the power to make, interpret and enforce the laws." Such, however, had been Richardson's power, and he had used it to continue the provost court trials. As Black noted, Lloyd had been tried by the military two years and two months after the Japanese attack, and he had been given a military trial in territory which was not captured or recaptured from the enemy but which had all through the war been loyal to the United States.

Said Black, "We have always been especially concerned about the potential evils of summary criminal trials and have guarded against them by provisions embodied in the Constitution itself." He quoted from *Dow v. Johnson,* an 1879 case: "The established principle of every free people is, that the law shall alone govern; and to it the military must always yield." The law in the United States was that when the courts were open the military could not try civilians.*

It was no answer to this to say that Poindexter had been guided by the Organic Act. As one lawmaker said in 1900 when Congress passed the Organic Act, "This bill, in so many words, extends the Constitution to Hawaii." At that time the United States had already faced the question of the military's lack of authority to try civilians, and the constitutional principle was already well established. The problem had arisen during the Civil War. Under authority from President Lincoln, the military had tried and convicted a suspected rebel named Milligan. Finding the military to be without such authority under the Constitution, the Supreme Court subsequently ordered Milligan released on a writ of habeas corpus. Nevertheless, during Reconstruction, Congress had authorized military tribunals in the rebellious South and quickly acted to prevent the Supreme Court from passing on the constitutionality of the legislation. President Andrew Johnson, in his unsuccessful veto message, warned, "It is plain that the authority here given to the military officer amounts to absolute despotism." Surely that mistake should never be repeated. We are paying for it yet. Black may have thought as much, although his formal opinion was temperate.

In essence, he said, the Hawaiian Organic Act did not give the armed forces, during a period of martial law, power to supplant all

* See *The Supreme Court in American History,* pages 82–89.

civilian laws and to substitute military for judicial trials of civilians, at a time when it was not impossible for the civilian government and the courts to function.

Justices Frankfurter and Burton dissented. They called for a wider consideration of the military position at a time of great national peril. They added that an opinion such as the one Black was offering was all very easy to reach now that the war was over.

Their position was too much for Justice Frank Murphy, who said in a concurring opinion that "arbitrary power of conviction and punishment for pretended offenses is the hallmark of despotism." History had demonstrated that fact time and again. The American colonists "shed their blood to win independence from a ruler who they alleged was attempting to render the 'Military independent of and superior to the Civil power' and who was 'depriving us . . . of the benefits of Trial by Jury.' . . . [Thus] an impartial jury, was the only certain way to protect an individual against oppression. The Bill of Rights translated that belief into reality by guaranteeing . . . jury trials and other basic procedural rights foreign to military proceedings. . . ." Justice Murphy granted that civilian procedural rights, devised to protect the possibly innocent took time and this irked the military. But he maintained history had proved them necessary. "Our duty is to give effect to that heritage at all times, that it may be handed down untarnished to further generations. . . ." He went on to point to the facts in the particular case at hand.

There can be no question but that when petitioners White and Duncan were subjected to military trials on August 25, 1942, and March 2, 1944, respectively, the territorial courts of Hawaii were perfectly capable of exercising their normal criminal jurisdiction had the military allowed them to do so. The Chief Justice of the Supreme Court of Hawaii stated that after the month of April, 1942, he knew of "no sound reason for denial of trial by jury to civilians. . . ." In short, the Bill of Rights disappeared by military fiat rather than by military necessity. . . .

From time immemorial despots have used real or imagined threats to the public welfare as an excuse for needlessly abrogating human rights. This excuse is no less unworthy of our traditions when used in this lay of atomic warfare or at a future time when some other type of warfare may be devised. . . . Martial law in relation to closing the courts cannot arise from a *threatened* invasion. The necessity must be actual and present; the invasion real, such as effectually closes the courts and deposes the civil administration.

This had been decided in the Milligan case, and Murphy and Black considered that it was still true. The majority of the justices agreed with Murphy when he said, "The swift trial and punishment which the military desires is precisely what the Bill of Rights outlaws . . . [for] it is a rank appeal to abandon the fate of all our liberties to the reasonableness of the judgment of those who are trained primarily for war. It seeks to justify military usurpation of civilian authority to punish crime without regard to the potency of the Bill of Rights. It deserves repudiation."

The majority thus agreed that the trials were illegal. Both Duncan and White were ordered freed.

As one law review article noted, no new principles had been developed by Duncan's case, but the decision was valuable for its reaffirmation that the military could not try civilians when the courts were open and that the military must remain subordinate to the civil authority.

What everyone realized was that once martial law had been established it was so convenient for the authorities that it was almost impossible for them to bring themselves to give it up. They recognized, too, that every emergency looks as if it differs from every other that has ever been—at least to the people who have to cope with it. We will always be faced with the cry of "special situation" to lure us into yielding ground on our liberties. To prevent this the Bill of Rights was put into the Constitution and the courts established to uphold it and preserve all our legal freedoms.

To fulfill this obligation the Court has taken the stand that it must stop even the civilian government from extending military control. Long after the Duncan case, the justices declared unconstitutional a law passed by Congress which automatically denaturalized citizens found guilty of wartime desertion by a court-martial. By the time the Court heard the test case on this issue, the men involved were civilians but without any of the rights of citizens.

The facts were such that another court-martial might easily have found them guilty of the lesser charge of being A.W.O.L. (absent without leave). They were walking along the road headed back toward the United States Army base at Casablanca when an army truck overtook them and they climbed into it willingly and said they had decided to come back. They had been gone less than a day. Four justices felt that keeping them forever stateless and without status in organized society was cruel and unusual punishment forbidden by the Eighth Amendment. Citizenship was not a license but a birthright. Furthermore, the denaturalization law gave the military complete discretion to decide who among the convicted should continue to be an American citizen and who should not. This was intolerable.

Black and Douglas concurred in calling the law unconstitutional and Black, speaking for both of them, added, "Even if citizenship could be involuntarily divested, I do not believe that the power . . . may be placed in the hands of military authorities. . . ."

Chief Justice Warren later said that the law extended military authority into other areas—in other words, civilian affairs. This the Court would not permit.

In line with this same thinking, the Court refused to let the military recall a veteran with an honorable discharge for the sole purpose of subjecting him to a court-martial. The picture of millions of veterans, now civilians, being forever in possible danger of being disciplined by the military for some belatedly uncovered military charge had ominous implications. It certainly would be a terrifying weapon in the hands of some future ambitious leader. The situation was filled with possibilities for extending military control over the civilian population. For the same reason, the Court has stopped the military in peacetime from trying civilian dependents and civilian employees of the armed forces overseas. What the military could do with their own personnel when they had proper jurisdiction (authority) was another matter. This question had to be faced by Congress.

"You Cannot . . . Run an Army That Way"

FOLLOWING the attack on Pearl Harbor, Germany declared war in concert with her ally, Japan, and United States citizen soldiers crossed the oceans to help defend the free world. Theirs was a long war fought against tremendous odds. Back home the news of their final victory, when it came at last in August of 1945, brought tears of relief mixed with pride unlimited. The veterans heading for home found things to remember in which they took no pride. Many a young man's plans included not only exchanging his uniform for the comforts of a sport jacket but also having a chat with his congressman.

Their stories pieced together like parts of a jigsaw puzzle. A Massachusetts lieutenant with a fine record remembered the case of a fellow officer and friend who was all too successful at a court-martial proceeding in defending an immature recruit. "The kid," a youth of Mexican extraction, had left camp without permission. Consequently he faced a charge for being A.W.O.L. When he remained missing for well over two weeks, the command changed the charge to desertion—a word which defines a major criminal offense. Then one day the culprit came back of his own accord.

The officer who served as defense counsel at the trial knew the law and did a brilliant job. The youth was undisciplined but not necessarily a deserter. There was no proof of his having intended to stay away permanently—on the contrary, he had voluntarily returned. The soldier was still only probably guilty of an extended A.W.O.L. offense. The court was convinced and ruled accordingly. The sentence was "only" six months at hard labor in confinement (prison). The commanding officer was furious.

For incurring "the old man's" displeasure, the defense counsel was transferred to hazardous duty. There was a lot of hazardous duty that had to be done, but using it as punishment for a counsel who put up an effective defense at a trial did not seem decent.

That was not all. Albin W. Norblad, Jr., a young Oregon lawyer in combat intelligence who had won the air medal, brought home more of the picture. Norblad had acted as defense attorney for a cook's assistant stationed in England.

The accused had left base and gone to London without a pass. Twelve hours later he was picked up by the provost marshal and locked in jail for being technically A.W.O.L. There he remained for two weeks before the case came to trial. The court members decided he had already served much of the necessary penalty for a twelve-hour jaunt and added only five days to the sentence. Immediately on receiving the results of the trial the commanding colonel made an announcement over his loud-speaker system. His voice carried to every officer and every enlisted man in every corner of the base. He wanted the court brought into his office at nine o'clock the next morning. At nine o'clock the anxious court members were brought in. "We stood at attention for fifteen minutes while he reprimanded the entire court," Norblad remembered. He was astounded when the colonel said that "after a man has been charged with a crime he is very probably guilty and . . . [the court] should . . . have kept that in mind." The colonel had pointed a finger at Norblad. "I'll have no lawyers orating in my court," he had said.

This older officer, in absolute control of his tiny force tucked away on a fog-bound foreign island three thousand miles from home, undoubtedly felt he was securing the traditions of United States military justice for the future. He was, but not in the way he intended. Veteran Norblad was to be elected congressman from Oregon. He was to carry with him to his seat in Washington the memory that every man on that particular base avoided court duty after that incident.

Unknown to Norblad, another young military attorney, Daniel F. Carney—redheaded and communicative—was getting ready to take up the same fight. Carney considered that he had seen too much disparity between the sentences handed out by different courts-martial, and he felt he had also seen pointless severity. He was going to have his say about these conditions, and so were a number of other citizens in khaki.

Later, a spokesman for the American Veterans Committee reported they were particularly aggravated by "the complete lack of trained legal counsel which characterized all too many courts-martial. . . ." A legionnaire strongly urged Congress to serve notice "that these courts of ours in the Navy and in the Army are courts and they are not administrative arms of the generals." As a signal corps technician reported in a magazine article, "The enlisted man felt that the cards were stacked against him from the outset." He also complained of the lack of habeas corpus. Men waited endlessly in jail to be tried.

Even though both the Army and the Navy were already studying the problem, in 1946 the Secretary of War, Robert Patterson, appointed a committee of eminently distinguished civilian jurists to conduct an investigation. Heading the inquiry was Arthur T. Vanderbilt of Newark, a former president of the American Bar Association and law school dean (later chief justice of the Supreme Court of New Jersey). Judge Alexander Holtzoff of the United States District Court for the District of Columbia was another member of this outstanding group, which was called the War Department Advisory Committee on Military Justice. Holtzoff— Russian born, American educated, and sixty years of age—was well aware that stories such as those now being pushed forward had followed every war, and they were not always justified. It also occurred to him that, unlike the situation in civilian life where only a few people are likely to be hurt by a lawbreaker, misconduct by a soldier in the face of an enemy could endanger the whole command. He started his committee assignment with a blunt attitude: "The principal function of an Army is to wage war."

On the other hand, he was not against the investigation. The Constitution says, "The Congress shall have power . . . To make rules for the government and regulation of the land and naval forces." Perhaps it was time to look at those rules and see if they were up to date or whether Congress should be urged to modernize them. Holtzoff plunged into a self-imposed review of military law and tradition. While he was thus busily absorbed he had plenty of uninvited company in his studies.

Sensing the public interest, gray-haired or nearly bald middle-aged editors with expanding waistlines resurrected incidents of severe penalties meted out during World War I, showing how much harsher the Army had been in their day. Free-lance writers delved into naval and military history. Our Articles of War and Articles for the Government of the Navy, they found, had originally come from the British, and the British had gleaned much from the successful Romans. These early systems were not as concerned with justice as they were with discipline. They listed offenses and proclaimed stringent punishments. Our own first naval rules, passed by the Continental Congress, authorized a commander to inflict on a seaman's bare back up to a dozen lashes with a cat-o'-nine-tails. This punishment was not considered so severe that a court-martial needed to be called to determine the man's guilt or innocence, but the seaman's lacerated body could and often did remain scarred for life.

Carney, who had swallowed his curiosity during the war but who was still wondering "how the service got that way," joined the researchers. He uncovered a Supreme Court decision written in 1887 in which Chief Justice Morrison R. Waite had reminded courts-martial that their findings must not be "subjected to the uncontrolled will of any man, but . . . must be adjudged *according to law.*" The Court did not apply the Bill of Rights to the military, but Carney felt that this application was badly needed. Veteran Carney pointed to the classic book, *Military Law and Precedent,* copy-

righted by Colonel William Winthrop nine years after Waite's ruling. Winthrop considered the application of the Bill of Rights to
servicemen and concluded that it didn't apply. Parts of it were applicable as a matter of grace or established practice, but not as a
matter of right. Carney resented this. The colonel's writings reminded him of the attitude of his own first sergeant—a six-foot 250-
pound man—who said, "Your soul may belong to the Almighty,
but the rest of you belongs to me." The fact was that the Bill of
Rights almost never had been applied to the serviceman, except to
the extent that Congress so decreed. Like all the lobbying veterans,
Carney knew it never would be more fully applied unless Congress
again acted.

While Carney was being stunned by "the old precedents which
lurked in the background of military thinking," another scholarly
American veteran, Robert E. Quinn, was making a searching study
of how slowly Congress had moved in the past. He came across an
incident that had happened as late as 1917.

Seventeen men were convicted of mutiny in Texas and were executed without having an opportunity to have their case brought up
on appeal. It was 1918 before all court-martial proceedings went to
the Judge Advocate General's office in Washington for review, and
for some time thereafter the findings of the Washington office as to
the legality of the proceedings were considered merely advisory and
generals in the field could disregard them if they chose. Not until
1916 had army regulations granted the accused the right to defense
counsel; it was 1920 before the Army was required to give this protection by act of Congress. Navy regulations as enacted by Congress had not been drastically changed since 1862.

Holtzoff, plowing through his own wealth of material, saw that
the proceedings to assign punishment had different names in the
Army and the Navy.

In the Army there was something nicknamed "company punishment," which was generally mild and did not require a court hearing. Beyond that there were summary courts-martial and special
courts-martial, which were strictly limited as to how heavy a sentence they could impose. Serious offenses in both services were
heard by general courts-martial, and here was where Holtzoff felt
he had to center his attention.

His attention was soon caught by various points which as a lawyer and a judge he could not endorse. In the Navy the officer acting
as prosecutor was also supposed to advise the court objectively on
points of law. As Holtzoff realized, the two responsibilities auto-

matically put the man in conflict with himself. It bothered Holtzoff even more that, in these courts, professional legal duties were being assigned to men who were not legally qualified.

When the advisory committee started holding its hearings, Holtzoff was told by one colonel that the "law member" (legal adviser) of a general court-martial did not have to be a lawyer. He could read the manual. Holtzoff later reported that he asked the colonel "whether he would be willing to designate a layman as a regimental doctor, if the latter would study a brief pamphlet on medicine." The colonel had no answer, but Holtzoff had a further comment to make in his report to his professional colleagues: "legal work is frequently entrusted to laymen, at times with results that are either ludicrous or disastrous. . . ."

At the same time Holtzoff—in a law review article—reminded the critical legal world that some of the reported shortcomings of military justice were due to our aversion as a nation to maintaining a large standing army in peacetime. All the services had expanded rapidly at the last minute when the nation's survival was already threatened. They took in untrained men and quickly trained officers. Like most amateurs these people made mistakes. In conducting military trials, errors were made which were already against the rules.

In spite of this Judge Holtzoff said he knew of no flagrant case of an obviously innocent man being convicted of a heinous crime. He wanted no one to forget to be grateful and impressed that we had won the war.

The members of the Armed Services Committee in Congress felt the same. They read the letters and listened to a long succession of statements by honorably discharged veterans. They also listened to Colonel Frederick B. Wiener, who tried to explain the other side. "Now, our whole civil government is based on the system of checks and balances, but you cannot fight a war or run an army that way," he said. "You have to have a supreme commander. . . . Our whole notion of government is based on the idea that we will discuss proposals before we enact them. There are discussions [here] in the committee; there will be discussions on the floor [of the House and Senate]." He quoted Winston Churchill's words about "broad happy uplands where everything is settled for the greatest good by the greatest number by the common sense of most after consultation of all!" All very lovely, Weiner agreed, "but we cannot proceed in an army that way. . . ."

Civilian life was run to keep everybody happy as far as possible.

Armies were organized to expend human life, if necessary, to block the enemy advance. A military man had to be able to make decisions quickly. That his soldiers did not like his decisions could not be allowed to matter. Punishment, then, had to be swift and sure. The worst thing that could happen to military discipline, as the colonel saw it, was to have a guilty man think he might have a chance to get away with his malefactions. The Congress should consider the effect of a deserter serving a short prison sentence while his law-abiding buddies marched off to the front, some of them never to return. In the past three wars in which this country had engaged, Weiner said, "only one man has been shot for desertion in the face of the enemy—one man. Yet think of all the men who died because they did not desert, because they obeyed orders."

His attitude explained some of the long and severe sentences imposed by military courts. These, however, were less of an issue because they were usually reduced by the commanding officer when he reviewed the case. The practice was part of the tradition of letting the command control discipline. It also served—it was thought—to scare others who heard about the sentence. Finally, Colonel Weiner included in his testimony the warning of one attorney who turned into a great Civil War general, William T. Sherman: "it will be a grave error if by negligence we permit the military law to become emasculated by allowing lawyers to inject into it the principles derived from their practice in the civil courts, which belong to a totally different system. . . ."

As he stood there reciting his quote, the colonel was addressing himself to lawyers. They understood the Army's problems, but they had also dedicated their own lives to the principles of American constitutional law and justice as epitomized in the civil courts. After hearing Weiner, the congressmen asked each other with no little anxiety: Could the necessary discipline for defending the nation be enforced without thwarting justice?

Many of them were themselves veterans. They decided to find out if more of the spirit of the Bill of Rights could be applied to the man in uniform without disastrous results. This time Congress made revolutionary changes in the rules. It drafted the Uniform Code of Military Justice to apply to all the armed services, keeping only parts of the old articles.

From the moment suspicion begins to dawn in the military policeman's mind, the new code begins to operate. The M.P. must not search a suspect's sleeping bag or other luggage without first obtaining permission—comparable to the warrant needed in civilian life under the Fourth Amendment. The suspect must not be forced to testify against himself. If questioned he must be informed of his right to keep silent, as called for by the Fifth Amendment. To substitute for a civilian grand jury in the Sixth, the code provides for a complete impartial investigation before a suspect can be brought to trial. This investigation cannot even be ordered by the company commander who frequently brings the charge. It must be ordered by a high-ranking superior, and only after the accuser has made his own initial checks of the facts. The investigating officer must be mature and impartial, says the code. During the investigation he must allow the accused to face and question the witnesses against him, as the Sixth Amendment lets civilians do only later at their trial. As soon as a soldier knows he is in trouble he can ask for a lawyer. He may hire his own or demand that the service assign to him a qualified attorney in uniform; in the Army and Air Force these are part of a judge advocate corps. Whenever possible the accused selects the attorney he wants, and at times the service has transported his choice from a distant base. Contrary to all precedent down through the ages, Congress has decreed that if the accused is an enlisted man he can ask to have enlisted personnel serve on the court.

The court is still convened only by the highest officer in command (who first consults with his own attorney). But the code strictly forbids the commanding officer to censor, reprimand, or admonish those performing judicial functions in relation to their findings. The commanding officer can still review the findings as to law and fact. He can disapprove the findings and dismiss the case, or reduce the sentence, or order a retrial. He cannot increase the penalty or reverse a sentence of innocent to guilty. He cannot have a man found innocent retried, which would violate the Fifth Amendment's mandate against double jeopardy. If he approves a verdict of guilty the case goes to the Judge Advocate General's office in Washington.

If a serviceman is sentenced to a bad conduct or dishonorable discharge or to more than one year in prison, his case must be reviewed by a board of attorneys. In cases of lesser penalties the Judge Advocate General may direct review. Consideration of the lesser penalty cases ends here unless the Judge Advocate General certifies them for further review by a new court. Men facing the more severe penalties can themselves appeal to the new court for rehearing; Congress instituted an innovation in military justice by establishing the United States Court of Military Appeals, manned by three civilian judges who have five commissioners to help them with the work load.

All this Congress brought into law in May of 1950. It gave the services a year to study and reorganize their systems before putting the new code into operation. Not everybody approved. Many people had their doubts. Veterans who had not come forward before now said they remembered nothing amiss in the administration of justice at their post. Still others insisted that civilian justice was too complicated, too full of technicalities. What went on in the field had to be simple and easy to administer. All these new procedures were going to be a bad idea; they might jeopardize discipline, and they were not needed. The large majority of the interested public waited. The first decisions handed down by the new court might show how much it was needed. The future alone would tell what damage, if any, all this protection for the accused would do to discipline. Meanwhile the commander in chief issued a manual setting penalties for the guilty and outlining the details of how the code was to be administered and carried into practice.

The new code was to go into effect on May 31, 1951. On the night of May 25, Raymond D. Clay, hospitalman U.S. Naval Reserve, was in difficulty. He was—or so the accusation said—"wrongfully engaging in a struggle on a street in Pusan . . . with Korean Nationals." The trial took place. A naval officer performed the functions of a civilian judge, instructing the court members on matters of law. He did not remind them that the accused was to be considered innocent until proven guilty, nor did he instruct them that the burden of proving Clay's guilt beyond a reasonable doubt rested with the government prosecutor. They found Clay guilty. The records went to Washington. Lawyers in the Judge Advocate General's office wondered whether the omission was not negligible. The attorney for the government said the officers who had served at the trial were intelligent men—surely they knew that much law. This time the Judge Advocate General decided to ask the appeals judges for a ruling which could guide future military trials. Nobody wanted to saddle the military with minute technicalities. If a court had made an error, surely it should be absolutely necessary for the defense to show that the mistake actually did prejudice the outcome of the trial. At least some of the interested officials thought that was not the situation here, and they wanted the new court to say as much.

The judges recently appointed by President Truman took the case under advisement. They were three eminently qualified men.

The chief judge was Robert E. Quinn. He was born in Phenix, Rhode Island, in 1894 and had held many public posts, including the governorship of his state and a judgeship on its superior court. He had been a legal officer and captain in the Navy. At the request of Secretary of the Navy James V. Forrestal, Quinn had collaborated with Arthur Ballantyne in reviewing the Articles for the Government of the Navy with the idea of looking for possible necessary changes. He was well versed in those articles and well prepared for his new assignment.

With Quinn on the court at the time was a Republican, Judge George Latimer from Salt Lake City, Utah. Latimer had been a combat colonel in the Philippines, had been awarded combat stars and the Legion of Merit, and had served on his state's supreme court. The third judge—like Quinn, a Democrat—was Paul W. Brosman, a law professor who originally came from Illinois. He had one qualification the others did not: He had served as a private in World War I. Since then, in World War II, he had been chief of a Military Justice Division in the Office of the Air Judge Advocate and was a Legion of Merit winner. Like the other judges reviewing the questions in the Clay case, he well understood the problems faced.

For one thing, the offense had been committed before the code went into effect. The judges, nevertheless, decided to take the case because the proceedings had gone on after that date. They next considered the seriousness of the officer's omission.

Judge Latimer wrote their agreed-on decision and read the carefully chosen words from the bench. At this point the new court became a teacher. It was necessary, the court said through Latimer, to remember what Congress had intended. "Congress granted the accused the right to be informed of the charges against him, to be confronted by witnesses against him, to cross-examine witnesses for the government . . . to be represented by counsel . . ." and the right to have the court members told that he was to be presumed innocent until proven guilty. Congress in other words expected the military to abide by the spirit of the Bill of Rights. Even though not every procedure used in civilian life was necessary, even though minor errors should be overlooked when they did not prejudice the rights of the accused, the military still could not assume that the court members did not need to be charged with their obligation to uphold the values Congress had established. They had not been so instructed. The court reversed the action of the court-martial and sent the case back to the board of review, which there-upon set aside the penalty.

The court went on with its work and was soon faced with a case involving Private First Class Carmen DeCarlo, stationed in Korea. DeCarlo's unit was about to move in trucks to a new location. Pae, a young native boy—often with the soldiers—was sitting on top of one of the trailers. Private DeCarlo had his right foot on the trailer tongue. His carbine was resting on his knee, and spectators said later he was joking with the boy.

"If you don't give me some candy, I'll shoot you."

"I don't care if you shoot, I have no candy," Pae told him.

The carbine fired. The boy, fatally wounded, fell from the trailer. Nobody had seen DeCarlo pull the trigger. Pae was asked before he died what happened. He said it was an accident.

The court-martial did not think Pae's testimony was reliable. It was merely opinion, and Pae was not alive to swear to it or be cross-examined. The court had the statement stricken from the record. The private was found guilty of murder.

The United States Court of Military Appeals reversed, finding that the exclusion of Pae's dying statement was a serious error. In the face of impending death Pae would have no reason to tell an untruth. Seated where he was, he might have observed a step or motion which caused the accidental discharge of the carbine. The testimony of other witnesses established that his conclusion that "it was an accident" was not improbable. The accused was entitled to a rehearing.

The case was reheard by general court-martial convened by the commanding general at Yokohama, Japan, in April of 1952, and it was reheard under the proper procedures. This time the court found the soldier guilty of carelessness in the use of firearms but not guilty of murder. He was sentenced to six months at hard labor in confinement and to forfeit $50 a month for a like period. The convening general approved and directed that DeCarlo be credited with the penal time he had already served before the appeal. The papers went to Washington, where the Judge Advocate General did not feel any further review was necessary.

In another episode a New Jersey boy was tried under incorrect procedures, found guilty, and given a ten-year sentence. The Court of Military Appeals again reversed, and at the second hearing the young man was completely acquitted. In still another instance the court reversed a Navy trial because the convening officer did not outrank the accuser. The court was blocking any opportunity for a future return to "command control."

On and on the cases came. In 1953 the court received 2,160 cases. However, after careful examination, only about 10 per cent of these warranted a hearing and a written opinion by the court.

Of those cases heard and ruled upon in the beginning years, about half had to be reversed. After the first two years, however, the number of cases filed with the court began to level off. Among other reasons, the court had established the law on many points. It had developed a new concept in the minds of those administering courts-martial.

Judge advocates today talk about "military due process." They mean those procedures which the judges insist are essential to a fair trial and to carrying out the will of Congress that military justice should reach the same high standards afforded to civilians. As an example of this, the military authorities know that if it takes them too long to give an accused a speedy trial, and if they can show no satisfactory reason for the delay, the United States Court of Military Appeals will not merely reverse, it will dismiss the charge entirely.

As the years have gone by time has wrought changes. One bitter frosty December day in 1955 Judge Brosman, working in his chambers on the second floor of this court building, had a sudden and fatal heart attack. His contribution to the court was long and sincerely missed. Six years later, in 1961, Judge Latimer's term expired and he also left the bench.

Two new judges had to be appointed to carry on the work. They were Judge Homer Ferguson, a one-time United States senator from Michigan and our former ambassador to the Philippines, and Judge Paul J. Kilday, formerly on the House of Representatives Armed Services Committee and the winner of many distinguished awards for outstanding service to the nation. Chief Judge Quinn, although he was already seventy-two, was reappointed in 1966 for another fifteen years by the President with the advice and consent of the Senate. When Daniel F. Carney came back from being a judge advocate in the Korean war, he too joined the court as a commissioner intent on helping to carry out his dream of military justice.

During all these years, reaction to the court's work with the code has been mixed: It has been praised; it has been criticized for adversely affecting discipline; it has been ridiculed. In a book called

Now Hear This, Daniel V. Gallery, Rear Admiral U.S.N. (Retired), refers to the code as "a Philadelphia lawyer's dream" and describes a fictitious captain who isn't "used to the new code under which a sailor who fails to turn out at reveille is entitled to a lawyer." In spite of the fact that the admiral is intentionally (and hilariously) funny, his wit reflects the hard adjustment that many old-time commanders had to make. Some of them seem to have made it very well.

The Army and the Navy have added a refinement of their own to the code. The law officer who fills the judge's role at the court-martial now belongs to a field judiciary system and is in no way subject to the authority of the commanding officer who convenes the trial. At this writing the Subcommittee on Constitutional Rights of the United States Senate—working with a special Subcommittee on Armed Services—is drafting a bill to turn this voluntarily adopted safeguard into law and extend it to cover the Air Force.

That isn't all. There is more evidence of acceptance of the code.

In 1959, General Lyman L. Lemnitzer, chairman of the Joint Chiefs of Staff, stated, "I believe that the Army and the American people can take pride in the positive strides that have been made in the administration and application of military law under the Uniform Code of Military Justice. The Army today has achieved the highest state of discipline and good order in its history."

A year later General G. H. Decker made a similar remark. In 1966 this writer asked a major in the Judge Advocate's Office if there were still a good many people who were fearful or critical of the code. He did not want to say there were not, but he added, "People like that are often the first to scream when their own rights are jeopardized."

The senators on the subcommittees must agree. They are making plans to extend protections now granted the accused at general courts-martial to make them apply to the special courts-martial where lesser offenses are considered. They also plan to extend legal protection to men facing "undesirable" administrative discharges. If the subcommittees have their way, a serviceman will be able to demand a court-martial to challenge the justification for such a discharge. On goes the work of making the spirit and the lessons in the Bill of Rights apply to all.

Maybe all this is not the way armies and military forces have been traditionally run, but this is our army and its military justice is in keeping with our way of life.

"Our Fundamental Aim is to Prevent Crime"

On Friday, November 22, 1963, a President of the United States was murdered. The alleged killer obtained his rifle through the United States mail. This procedure did not make it necessary for Lee Harvey Oswald to prove his identification, and he used an assumed name. President John Fitzgerald Kennedy was only one of over five thousand homicide victims that year who were killed with a firearm.

Under the federal Firearms Act of 1938 the dealer who shipped Oswald his weapon was completely within his rights. He was restricted from selling to someone whom he knew to be a felon. He was also forbidden to ship to anyone living in one of those few states which require a gun purchaser to obtain a permit, unless the purchaser showed his permit or was a federally licensed dealer. Due to the ease with which people could travel across a state line in order to make a purchase, the requirement of a permit was almost worthless. In addition, a federal dealer's license was obtainable from the Internal Revenue Service by merely paying the nominal fee of $1.00.

After President Kennedy's death, people asked each other, "Isn't there some way of keeping firearms out of the hands of people like Oswald?" And they are asking still. The legal question is complicated, and gun legislation is always highly debatable.

The Second Amendment to the Constitution reads, "A well regulated Militia, being necessary to the security of a free State, the right of the people to keep and bear Arms, shall not be infringed." In 1789 when the amendment was written, the states, far from preventing able-bodied adult men from owning weapons, required them to do so. The militia comprised all physically capable males available for the common defense. When called to service, they were expected to appear bringing their own guns and ammunition. Lawyers, nevertheless, do not agree as to whether the right to bear arms was intended to be an absolute individual right to keep guns for one's own use. Justice Black, during a lecture at New York

University, told the audience, "Although the Supreme Court has held this Amendment to include only arms necessary to a well-regulated militia, as so construed, its prohibition is absolute." According to other jurists, the Second Amendment does not give anyone an individual right to have arms. Included in this group are officials of the departments of Justice and Internal Revenue. They say the amendment's guarantee is limited to the right to keep weapons in connection with the defense of the state or participation in the militia, and the amendment was designed merely to prevent the Federal Government from blocking the states in organizing militias.

Former Attorney General Nicholas de B. Katzenbach once argued that the wording "to bear arms" is military terminology and differs from what would have been said to describe an individual or nongovernment-sponsored group from carrying weapons for their own purposes.

He pointed to an incident which happened in 1879. Herman Presser headed a band of reactionary vigilantes. Their German name, Lehr und Wehr Verein, implied that they were committed to "enlightenment and defense." When four hundred of them marched through the streets of Chicago carrying rifles, led by Herman Presser, who rode a horse and brandished a sword, Presser was taken into court. Illinois law forbade private clubs from forming themselves into military organizations or drilling with arms in cities or towns unless authorized by law. Presser cited the Second Amendment and said he was a citizen and a voter. Illinois said that made no difference, since he was not part of the regular organized militia.

The case went from the highest court in Illinois to the Supreme Court of the United States. It was decided in 1886, when the Court held the Second Amendment had not been violated by the Illinois law. The justices then ruled that the right to bear arms was related to a citizen's duty toward maintaining the public security under government. They noted that Congress, when it proposed the amendment, had in mind its power to call out the state militias in time of emergency under Article I, Section 8, of the Constitution. The Illinois law was upheld and Presser's guilt was affirmed.

Later, in 1939, the question of the meaning of the amendment came up again and the Court upheld the conviction of two men who transported a sawed-off shotgun in interstate commerce. They had not registered the weapon as required by federal law. The defendants challenged the constitutionality of the National Firearms

Act of 1934. The act is sometimes nicknamed the "machine-gun act" and is administered as a tax law by the Internal Revenue Service. It relates largely to the type of weapon in common use by the gangster element of the 1930s. The Supreme Court said that at this time the sawed-off shotgun had no "reasonable relationship to the preservation or efficiency of a well regulated militia," nor could its use "contribute to the common defense." The Court then concluded that "we cannot say that the Second Amendment guarantees the right to keep and bear such an instrument." The justices upheld the Firearms Act.

Based on these and numerous other opinions, Katzenbach went so far as to say that the modern tendency among scholars supports the view that any act of Congress which does not in fact prevent an eligible citizen from functioning as a state militiaman is not forbidden by the Second Amendment. He conceded there was opinion to the contrary.

People who agree with Katzenbach contend that the main reason why the Founding Fathers wanted to protect the existence of an armed civilian militia was to avoid the necessity of establishing large standing armies. Congress could call out the state militias when it needed to and thereby not maintain as many professionals.

These people point to the debates in Congress when the amendment was under consideration. At that time, lean, astute Elbridge Gerry of Massachusetts—who originally opposed the whole Constitution because it had no bill of rights—took the floor and asked his fellow congressmen his now famous rhetorical question: "What, sir, is the use of a militia? It is to prevent the establishment of a standing army, the bane of liberty."

As Blackstone had taught these visionary young congressmen who were now founding a new republic, "Nothing . . . ought to be more guarded against in a free state than making the military power . . . a body too distinct from the people. . . ." Nor was Blackstone's the only warning.

It was the mercenaries in Rome, according to the French philosopher Jean Jacques Rousseau, whose "swords were always at the throats of their fellow-citizens . . . [and] this was one of the principal causes of the ruin of the Roman Empire."

The only alternative was to keep up militias of laborers, artisans, tradesmen, and other local civilians.

All these citations, say the lobbyists who object to gun legislation, support their contention, not the position of the regulators. How are tradesmen, laborers, manufacturers, and the like to be capable soldiers in time of emergency unless they are proficient in the handling of guns? They quote from a letter written to the National Rifle Association (N.R.A.) by then-General Dwight D. Eisenhower during the heat of World War II. "Any young man that has ahead of him prospective service in the Armed Forces will do well to learn all he can about the American military rifle. If he can become a really capable rifleman, so much the better. Once he has donned the uniform, he will find his hours and days so packed . . . that he will find the time all too short to learn the many things he should know, for his own self-preservation. . . ." *The American Rifleman,* a magazine published by the N.R.A., is filled with examples of situations where an armed citizen either did, or could have, stopped a criminal at a time when no policeman was available. The N.R.A. tells its readers to be informed on gun legislation; " 'Be it Enacted' May Mean Goodbye Guns!" it says. Feeling this way, the association—although it claims to support ownership controls directed at felons, drug addicts, drunkards, mental incompetents, and unsupervised juveniles—is constantly finding objectionable features to proposed gun legislation. One of its readers, Harold Goodwin, a husky athletic author of outdoor material and fiction with a science background, feels it goes too far. "I'm a respectable citizen and I am willing to have the police know how many guns I own," he says. "I am also willing to put up with a waiting period so that the police can investigate me. But they had better have cause before they deny me a license and I would insist on having recourse to the courts to challenge their findings. The day they try to take guns away is the day when I will get excited. Law enforcement has not reached a point where the private citizen does not need to protect himself."

Other gun owners are not as tolerant of government interference. The best deterrent to a robber is the fear that the homeowner may have a gun, they say. And what regulatory legislation does is to discourage the honest citizen from owning a weapon with which to defend himself. No matter what law you pass, criminals will still get their guns.

In answer, J. Edgar Hoover wrote in the June, 1963, *Law Enforcement Bulletin* that "those who claim that the availability of firearms is not a factor in murders in this country are not facing reality."

Other writers have pointed to the number of deaths caused by gun accidents, over two thousand a year, including one woman who accidentally shot her husband thinking he was a prowler. Most

often, the experts claim, a gun in the house is worthless against an
intruder. By the time you are confronted by the criminal it's too
late to go after the gun. It certainly shouldn't be stored in easy
reach or you increase the likelihood of tragedy.

James E. Edwards of the Florida Sportsman's Association is one
angry lobbyist who not only cited the Second Amendment but also
the Ninth and Tenth Amendments. They read:

"The enumeration in the Constitution, of certain rights, shall not
be construed to deny or disparage others retained by the people."

"The powers not delegated to the United States by the Constitution, nor prohibited by it to the States, are reserved to the States respectively, or to the people."

If you read these two amendments carefully you will see the
problem Edwards raises for the regulators. Nowhere does the Constitution say that you can't have a gun. This, it can be argued, is a
right retained. Congress then may regulate firearms only under its
power to control interstate commerce or its tax power. In any case,
it must be careful to stay within the Constitution or it will be
challenged by people like Edwards.

Edwards speaks of "the hostile groups trying to disarm America." He says, "The Federal Government has the power and the
duty to protect military training and civilian marksmanship . . .
but not to disarm the people, either by direct action or by petty,
nagging, burdensome rules. . . ."

Various state officials and advocates of gun-control laws deny
that this is what they are trying to do. In July of 1965 the House
Ways and Means Committee scheduled eleven of the many hearings
that Congress has held on this issue.

At ten o'clock on July 23, the chairman, Arkansas's Wilbur D.
Mills, called the first witness for the day. He was Leonard E. Reisman, deputy commissioner of the New York City Police Department.
New York has stringent restrictions on the ownership of concealable
hand guns, embodied in its much-debated Sullivan law. No one, with
certain exceptions, may own a pistol or revolver unless he has first obtained a license, and dealers in these weapons must also be licensed.
Getting a license is a major undertaking. The applicant is investi-
gated both as to his character and his need to possess the firearm.
He is interviewed and fingerprinted, and a check is made with both
the State Department of Correction and the Federal Bureau of
Investigation as to whether he has a criminal record. While the police are verifying the truth of all the statements that the applicant
has made during his compulsory interview, the State's Department

of Mental Hygiene is searching its files to discover whether the would-be gun owner ever had a mental illness.

Naturally, the congressional committee wanted to know how effective all these procedures were. Commissioner Reisman was very frank: "our fundamental aim is to prevent crime . . . ," he began, and "only about 17,500 persons out of 8 million possess pistol licenses [in New York City]."

Mr. Reisman believed that New York's stringent laws had saved many lives. "However, as long as criminals can obtain weapons more easily in other States through the mails or by personal purchase, the effort to eradicate the illegal traffic in small arms in the State of New York can never be completely successful," he said.

Reisman, a friendly person with a sense of humor who expressed himself with ease, encountered much hostility to his recommendations for more far-reaching gun legislation. In addition to talking to senators and congressmen, he became involved in heated discussions with gun enthusiasts from the Middle and Far West. "They would rather give up their wives than their guns," he once quipped. More seriously, he added that "they take the position that the right to own a gun is basic to American democracy, and this is the way the west was won. They are hunters and sportsmen and some of them live in rural areas where they need the protection. I understand. I'm a gun nut myself. But they seem to think that any attempt to register guns is a stepping stone to abolishing all gun ownership. Nobody wants to do that. If we didn't get legislation when President Kennedy was assassinated I doubt that we're going to get it now." As a result, New York continues to find her gun laws evaded.

New York is not the only part of the country with this problem. The District of Columbia, where the listening congressmen work, had a similar complaint. The District maintains a police registration requirement and enforces a waiting period for the would-be gun owner. The idea is to stop the jealous wife or the angry unbalanced individual from committing a terrible crime before he or she has had a chance to calm down. Any resident who does not want to wait merely hops in his car, and in a very few minutes he is out of the District. Of the gun purchasers who patronized a particular store located close to—but not in—the Washington area, 40 per cent had criminal records. Massachusetts also has this difficulty. People simply cross the state line to avoid her firearm regulations.

Another witness, Sheldon S. Cohen, Commissioner of Internal Revenue, explained his problems with the present federal Law—or lack of it. One question which must be dealt with on the federal level, he said, is the staggering flow of imported weapons. Among these are cheap, poor-quality small arms as dangerous to the user as they may be to the victims being assaulted with them. Also included are cast-off military firearms. They come into this country because the exporting nations have adopted more modern replacements, but these discards being dumped on the American market have not lost any of their quality. They are, besides, enticingly cheap and a lure to anyone wanting the thrill of owning such a lethal instrument. The rifle Oswald used cost the importer $1.12.

President Johnson recommended that Congress enact legislation to halt this senseless deadly flow. To protect American hunters, his administration recommended legislation which would not preclude the importation of good-quality sporting-type firearms. Many Americans still supplement their diet by what they can shoot.

The Johnson administration also urged the use of the taxing power of Congress to impose additional controls over such highly destructive weapons as bazookas, bombs, antitank guns, and the like which have found their way into the channels of trade. As to these weapons, and the less expensive foreign guns, the N.R.A. agreed with the administration. Cohen pointed this out to the committee. He sounded as if that proved the recommendations were beyond dispute.

Cohen then came to what is probably his most difficult problem; he said that "existing law provides that upon payment of the prescribed fee the Secretary shall issue a license to the applicant which shall entitle the licensee to transport, ship, or receive firearms or ammunition in interstate or foreign commerce. There are no stated conditions to the issuing of the license except . . . the prescribed fee, and no discretion is granted under the language of the law."

He then cited the facts in an actual case which resulted from the present wording of the law. A young man, aged twenty-nine, applied for a license as a dealer. He was not under indictment nor had he been convicted of a felony. If he had been, the Internal Revenue Service would have refused him a license because, license or no, he could not legally engage in the firearms business. In this instance the I.R.S. had no such excuse in spite of what they learned. A check of police records disclosed two arrests, one of which—though the charge had not been pressed—involved assault with intent to kill.

More investigation uncovered that the assault charge had followed a maniacal attack on his parents. The applicant had tied his mother to a chair, gagged her, and stabbed her repeatedly in the back with an icepick. When his father arrived on the scene the applicant struck him on the head with a two-bladed ax. Both parents recovered and the applicant spent two and a half years in a state hospital. (This was probably why the charge had not gone to trial.) Now he wanted a license to deal in firearms. A doctor on the hospital staff stated that, in his opinion, the applicant should not be granted a license. Cohen continued with the exasperating observation, "Yet we, by virtue of the present wording of the law, are apparently without any alternative but to issue him a license to deal in firearms."

In this instance the Internal Revenue Service decided to wait and withhold the license until they saw whether the applicant could get a court order requiring them to issue the document. At this writing, he had not tried to litigate his rights and hence was still without his license. An unjustified "bureaucratic" action? Perhaps so, yet many will view it with approval.

On and on the discussion goes, both in the hearing rooms and outside. The Internal Revenue Service wants more discretion to issue or withhold licenses and yet, in other areas such as voter qualifications or the right to assemble peaceably, the courts have again and again thrown out laws where too much discretion was left to the enforcement officer. As a matter of history, this discretion has always offered a big invitation to abuse. Laws must apply equally to everybody. To achieve this the law, not the officer, must fix the qualifications for a license in any field. Thus, whatever Congress puts together in this area will have to be very carefully worded.

Various other suggestions have been made. Six of them follow. One: Prohibit the sales of firearms in interstate commerce except between federally licensed dealers and manufacturers. Then allow dealers to sell only to people who are residents of the state in which the gun store is located. If you have to get your gun in your own state, local regulations can be made to work. Two: Increase the license fees for dealers so that these licenses are only within the means of actual businessmen, easier to regulate than just anybody with a dollar. Three: Curb the flow of foreign weapons not suitable for hunting or target practice. Four: Extend the present federal law to cover the registration of more types of destructive weapons, such as bazookas and antitank guns. Five: Set a minimum age level for gun owners and gun purchasers and make all licensed dealers responsible for helping to enforce it. In New York, 43 per cent of the people arrested in 1964 for the illegal possession of dangerous weapons were under twenty-one. Six: Increase the penalties for crimes which involve the misuse of firearms.

Other recommendations have been made for strengthening the laws on the local level, but of course here each state will do what it thinks best, depending on local needs and conditions. Some states want to attract hunters to their forest preserves. Hunters are part of their tourist trade and hence bring money in to bolster the local economy. All these things must be taken into account. In the hope of dealing with them, Senator Thomas J. Dodd and his Senate Sub-committee on Juvenile Delinquency conducted hearings covering every section of the country. Bills have been introduced, although not passed, to deal with what some people call, "the tragedy and imbecility of our failure as a society to civilize the use of firearms." The attempt still goes on, and we may be hearing more about this problem in the congressional sessions ahead.

BIBLIOGRAPHY FOR PART V

Principal Sources on Military and Civilian Justice

BOOKS

Black, Henry Campbell. *Black's Law Dictionary*. St. Paul, Minn., 1933.
Cahn, Edmond L. (ed.). *The Great Rights* (a collection of lectures written by Justices Earl Warren, Hugo H. Black, William O. Douglas, and William J. Brennan, Jr.). New York, 1963.
Fribourg, Marjorie G. *The Supreme Court in American History*. Philadelphia, 1965.
Hanlon, Frederick R. *Ten Year Chronology of The United States Court of Military Appeals*, U.S. Court of Military Appeals. Washington, 1961 (Available from the court).
Lovette, Leland P. *Naval Customs Traditions and Usage*. 4th rev. ed. U.S. Naval Institute, Md., 1959.

UNITED STATES FEDERAL RECORDS

Congressional Records

House of Representatives, Armed Services Subcommittee, *Hearing on H.R. 2575 to Amend the Articles of War*, 80th Congress, April, 1947.
House of Representatives, Armed Services Subcommittee, *Hearing on H.R. 2498, The Uniform Code of Military Justice*, 81st Congress, 1st Session, March, 1949.
House of Representatives, Committee on Ways and Means, *Hearing on Proposed Amendment to Fire Arms Acts*, 89th Congress, 1st Session, July, 1965, Parts I and II.

Senate, *Joint Hearing Subcommittee on Constitutional Rights of the Committee on the Judiciary and a Special Subcommittee of the Committee on Armed Services,* 89th Congress, 2nd Session, January–March, 1966.

Court of Military Appeals Records
U.S. v. Clay, 1 USCMA 74.
U.S. v. DeCarlo, Carmen, 1 USCMA 91.

Supreme Court Records (Transcripts and Records of Briefs)
Burns v. Wilson, 346 U.S. 137 (1953).
Duncan v. Kahanamoku, 327 U.S. 304 (1946).
Ex Parte Milligan, 71 U.S. (4 Wall) 2 (1866).
Presser v. Illinois, 116 U.S. 252 (1886).
Reid v. Covert, 351 U.S. 487 (1956).
Runkle v. U.S., 122 U.S. 542 (1887).
Toth v. Quarles, 350 U.S. 11 (1955).
Trop v. Dulles, 356 U.S. 86 (1958).
United States v. Miller, 307 U.S. 174 (1939).

MAGAZINES

Holtzoff, Alexander. "Administration of Justice in the United States Army." *New York University Law Quarterly,* Vol. XXII, January, 1947, page 1.
Quinn, Robert E. "That Justice Shall Prevail." *The Reserve Officer,* Vol. 29, No. 9, September, 1953.
Reed, Macon. "The Court of Military Appeals." *Army Times Family Magazine,* July 21, 1965.
Ross, Irwin. "You Can Lead a Man to Khaki." *Pageant,* October, 1949.
Spindler, John F. "The Uniform Code of Military Justice." *Michigan Law Review,* Vol. 50, 1951–52.
Sprecher, Robert A. "The Lost Amendment." *American Bar Association Journal,* Vol. 51, June, 1965.
"The Uniform Code of Military Justice—Its Promise and Performance. (The First Decade: 1951–1961), A Symposium." *St. John's Law Review,* May, 1961.

CORRESPONDENCE, INTERVIEWS, AND MISCELLANEOUS

Carney, Commissioner Daniel F., United States Court of Military Appeals.
Hanlon, Frederick R., Clerk, United States Court of Military Appeals.
Krouse, Gale E., Captain, U.S. Navy, Director Litigation and Claims Division, Office of Judge Advocate General.
Quinn, Robert E. Graduation Address, U.S. Naval Base, Newport, Rhode Island, February, 1952.
Rubinowitz, Stanley H., Secretary of the United States Army Judiciary.

PART SIX

ADULTS OR

YOUTH ACCUSED

OF CRIME

"No person shall be held to answer for a capital, or otherwise infamous crime, unless on a presentment or indictment of a Grand Jury, . . . nor shall any person be subject for the same offense to be twice put in jeopardy of life or limb; nor shall be compelled in any criminal case to be a witness against himself, nor be deprived of life, liberty, or property, without due process of law . . ."

—Fifth Amendment

"In all criminal prosecutions, the accused shall enjoy the right to a speedy and public trial, by an impartial jury of the State and district wherein the crime shall have been committed, which districts shall have been previously ascertained by law, and to be informed of the nature and cause of the accusation; to be confronted with the witnesses against him; to have compulsory process for obtaining witnesses in his favor, and to have the Assistance of Counsel for his defence."

—Sixth Amendment

"Excessive bail shall not be required, nor excessive fines imposed, nor cruel and unusual punishments inflicted."

—Eighth Amendment

THE RIGHTS AND THE ISSUES

In 1948, the Supreme Court was shocked to learn that a secret trial had taken place in Michigan. The case was called *In Re Oliver*. Here was one abuse of a citizen's rights which the justices thought had disappeared from the English-speaking world in 1641. The abuse came about because Michigan allows a judge sitting alone to act as a one-man grand jury, investigate a crime, and if necessary indict the accused. After the indictment the defendant has all the traditional safeguards of a jury trial. Many people feel Michigan is acting wisely. A secret pre-indictment hearing protects the accused from publicity until it is determined whether or not the man ought to be tried for the claimed offense.

What happened as a result was this: When Oliver, a witness, seemed to be lying and refused to answer questions to the satisfaction of the lone investigator, the one-man grand jury suddenly changed character. He again became the judge and sentenced Oliver to sixty days in jail for contempt of court. There was nothing to protect Oliver from being repeatedly convicted in this manner—in secret. Oliver appealed.

The Supreme Court justices reversed the contempt conviction. Oliver, they said, did not have a proper public trial for his alleged contempt. A proper trial would have included reasonable notice of the charge and the right to offer testimony, call and examine witnesses, and be represented by an attorney.

We have had all these rights for so long that it seems strange that they still have to be protected, but suddenly something as well-meaning as Michigan's procedures for the man not yet indicted could and did put traditional American rights in jeopardy.

Reading about Peter Zenger, we say the printer could have profited from a speedy trial. He stayed in jail for a year before his case came to court. We think we have grown beyond such oppressions. But overcrowded court calendars can bring them back. In Chapter 18 we see Congress facing the problem of what should be done about those awaiting trial.

Furthermore, American authors love to point to the Star Chamber of England in the sixteenth and seventeenth centuries as an object lesson in the horrors which led our forebears to protect us against being tortured into accusing ourselves of a crime. In one of the next chapters we will see that a reluctant Supreme Court finally decided that the American people in the various states still had to be protected from this same abuse.

Finally, we pride ourselves that we all believe in a fair and impartial jury—such as the labor agitators needed but did not get after the Haymarket affair. But even this fundamental concept in our system of justice can still be in jeopardy, as we will see in the last chapter. The courts are alert to all of these problems. They keep watching to make sure that the citizen does not lose his birthright when he has been accused—but not proven guilty—of a criminal offense. The judges and justices will succeed only so long as the public knows why—and for whom—these rights and protections were established.

"The Purpose of Bail Is Not Punishment"

AT ten o'clock on Tuesday, August 4, 1964, five United States senators gathered in a seemingly overlarge hearing room to consider a particularly vexing problem: bail. This is the money or "bond" that defendants wishing to be released must leave with the court as a guarantee that they will come back for their trial. Professional bail bondsmen will often provide an accused person with the necessary bond. They take a risk that the government will demand its value in cash if the defendant becomes a fugitive. Naturally they charge a fee for their risk-taking.

Before going into all that has gone wrong with the system, Senator Olin D. Johnston—a gentle southerner and a former South Carolina governor—called the serious little group together with an explanation. "The meeting today is a meeting of the Constitutional Rights Subcommittee and also the Subcommittee on Improvements in Judicial Machinery, jointly. Other Senators on the subcommittee will be here shortly. They are at the full Committee of the Judiciary at this time."

Shortly after they had settled themselves, Senator Hiram L. Fong of Hawaii told a story to illustrate the problem under consideration. Fong, a Harvard graduate, spoke in clipped and unornamented style about "a man [who] was charged with robbery and held in lieu of $10,000 bail. His wife could not raise the money [probably to pay the bondsmen] since he earned only $50 a week. So he was kept in jail 55 days. During those 55 days, he lost his job and his wife felt obliged to move from their apartment because of the comments of neighbors about her 'jailbird' husband.

"It turned out that the police had picked up the wrong man and the charges against him were dropped. But having the charges dropped did not get him his job back, and he was not able to return to his old apartment with his wife."

There it was. Unfortunately, the story was not too unusual. The Senator knew of another case where a defendant, unable to raise bail, stayed in jail two years before he was ultimately acquitted by the appeals court.

Attorney General Robert F. Kennedy had been making strong efforts to arouse the public. The 1963 report of his Committee on Poverty and the Administration of Justice called for reform. Under Kennedy's direction, the Department of Justice cosponsored the National Conference on Bail and Criminal Justice which met in the State Department auditorium in Washington, D.C., in May of 1964. The meeting drew delegates—judges, prosecutors, defense lawyers, and professors—from every direction, four hundred strong. Many of them were already working on the problem in their own locales. Bail surveys had been conducted by law school students and dedicated private citizens as well as by the Attorney General's own staff members.

This morning Mr. Kennedy came to the Senate Office Building and spoke to the little group of deliberating senators to share his findings with them. He stated the bald facts simply: "the rich man and the poor man do not receive equal justice in our courts . . . [especially] in the matter of bail.

"Bail has only one purpose—to insure that a person who is accused of a crime will appear in court for his trial," said the Government's chief legal officer. "We presume a person to be innocent until he is proven guilty, and thus the purpose of bail is not punishment. . . .

"In practice, however, . . . in this country, thousands of persons are kept in jail for weeks and even months following arrest. They are not yet proven guilty . . . [and] most of them stay in jail because, to be blunt, they cannot afford to pay for their freedom [to pay a bondsman].

"I am talking about a very large number of Americans. In fiscal 1963, the number of Federal prisoners alone held in jail pending trial exceeded 22,000. The average length of their detention was nearly 29 days.

"Like figures can be compiled from State and local jurisdictions." Since these figures were in averages, the Attorney General felt compelled to point out that there were instances of people waiting in jail three to six months for their trials; "many of these individuals who spend this time in jail, maybe month after month, are ultimately found to be innocent."

The poverty-stricken defendant who might be innocent was the Attorney General's main concern, but he also wanted to make another point. "The system distorts justice even for the defendant who can afford the bail bond. . . . He must pass muster with the bondsmen."

Here, Mr. Kennedy was referring to the workings of the system, already familiar to the senators. A person who is arrested after court hours is taken to the police station. In one neighborhood in the District of Columbia the outside of the building looks like a small public school, with red brick walls, large windows, and an American flag flying from its roof. Inside, the hall is painted green and leads to a huge counter behind which stands a police officer in his shirt sleeves. Other policemen are busily milling about. Hidden from view are twenty prison cells. If the arrest had occurred during court hours the arresting policeman would probably have taken the accused directly to court. Now, late in the afternoon or at night, the prisoner is taken to the precinct to be "locked up."

At the defendant's request the police officer calls a bail bondsman, who is not a government employee but a private businessman and who comes to the precinct to talk to the prisoner, look him over, and see if he is a good risk. The bondsman must consider whether to put himself in the position of guaranteeing to the Government that this alleged offender will not run out of town but will appear in court. To do this the businessman will have to sign a bond for the desk lieutenant of the Criminal Investigation Division—a plainclothesman stationed behind the counter at the Detective Bureau downtown.

If the accusation is so serious that the bond which the lieutenant will have to demand (in compliance with the chief judge's schedule) is over $1,000, the bondsman requires the prisoner to pay $8 for every hundred dollars of bond up to $1,000 and $5 for every hundred dollars above that. Credit is sometimes given, but most transactions take place only if the prisoner can pay the fee. Once he pays it the prisoner walks out of the station house at liberty until court meets. If he disappears, the bondsman will have to pay the face value of the bond into court.

You can't blame the bondsman who avoids doing business with certain types—for example, narcotics addicts. "They usually don't wake up in time to get to court," he says. But Justice Department staff members say, "Because of the speed with which the bondsman makes his decision, it is often based on pure intuition."

Judge J. Skelly Wright, an outspoken United States Court of Appeals judge for the District of Columbia, once complained, "The professional bondsmen hold the key to the jail in their pockets. They determine for whom they will act . . . [leaving to the court] the relatively unimportant chore of fixing the amount of bail." Businessmen thus were taking over the function of deciding who was or was not to be released from jail, a duty which should belong to the Government.

At the time when the Attorney General faced the senators with this fact, the system functioned in the Washington courtrooms in somewhat the same manner as it did in the precincts. Bondsmen hung around during preliminary hearings while the judge decided which arrestees should be held for trial. If not released, those who could afford a bondsman's fee were bailed out of the cells hidden behind the courtroom. With exceptions, the others remained in jail.

A private Washington civic group, staffed largely by six young law school students, was helping seemingly "good risks," many of whom were poverty-stricken. After checking the defendant's references, the young men decided whether to suggest to the judge that the prisoner be let out on his word (called "his own recognizance"). The judge took the students' recommendations about 85 per cent of the time.

It was a tremendous responsibility for the young men. How the students came to be there and how wise their recommendations proved to be would play an important role in the history of American justice.

Meanwhile, Senator Samuel J. Ervin, Jr., of North Carolina, was particularly anxious about the handling of a very different group of young men—those who steal automobiles. Both as a former defense attorney and a former state judge, he had had experience with these offenders. He said that these boys "didn't have access to automobiles, and they saw other boys of their age having access to automobiles. In so many cases they took them on the spur of the moment, just in the adventuresome nature of youth. They were not really bad boys at heart."

The Senator felt these young men would make good cases to keep out of jail. He was thinking of their rehabilitation after they were arrested. Supreme Court Justice William O. Douglas had once so aptly said that jailing a youth for want of bail "is equivalent to giving a young man an M.A. in crime." Although not yet tried or found guilty, the youth may be sharing a cell with repeated offenders. His treatment may be worse than that which is experienced by convicted prisoners. Good recreational, educational, and training facilities are made available in numerous reformatories, but rarely in jail.

The concern shown by the senators was shared by members of

the Judiciary Committee of New York's State Assembly. In material put before both the senators and the bail conference, they were quoted as saying, "We doubt whether any innocent person (as all before trial are presumed to be) can remain unscarred by . . . the indignities of repeated physical search, regimented living, crowded cells, utter isolation from the outside world . . . [and the] outrageous visitor's facilities [in jail]." The Assembly report concluded that "surely . . . one unwarranted day in jail in itself can be a major social injustice."

The lack of visitor facilities and the isolation from the outside world were contributing to another and even more serious side of the problem; "a man forced to stay in jail before a trial is more likely to be convicted," the Attorney General pointed out.

Senator Ervin thought the reasons for this were obvious. "He cannot locate witnesses; he cannot consult his lawyer in the privacy of his law office." This was bad enough, but psychologically the detained defendant was at a terrible disadvantage. The Senator noted that "he enters the courtroom—not in the company of an attorney —but from a cell block in the company of a marshal."

Meanwhile, being in detention, he has often lost his job. Yet having a job, as Senator Fong reminded everyone in the room, is a factor considered in the granting of probation. The poor man therefore also has less chance after conviction of being let out of prison and merely being required to report to the probation office.

There was no question in the minds of the senators that something had to be done, but the Attorney General thought he'd further stimulate their concern. He recited the case of a California citizen who spent 207 days in jail before being acquitted; a Pennsylvania defendant who could not obtain a $300 bail bond and spent 54 days in jail awaiting trial on a traffic offense for which the maximum penalty was five days in jail; a New Yorker arrested on suspicion of robbery whose credit was lost and whose car was repossessed before it was discovered that he was the victim of mistaken identity—and then it took him four months to find another job.

Senator Johnston had a question on what he considered to be one of the main reasons why reform was needed, the point that "if you hold a man in jail and he is associating with criminals there over a long period of time in the jail, it makes him harder to rehabilitate; isn't that true?"

Kennedy answered simply, "Yes."

The question, then, was: How should Congress change the law

and improve the system? Senator Kenneth B. Keating of New York, a genial white-haired man (now a judge), had some remarks and then some suggestions to make. He felt that until recently the bail system had served its purpose in 90 per cent of all cases. Whether you agree with him depends on your definition of "recently."

It is true that the idea of bailing out pretrial prisoners is an old and long-honored custom. The word "bailer" originally meant "to deliver." In medieval England the accused was delivered to a respected citizen, who promised to be responsible for the prisoner's later appearance in court. The idea was a merciful innovation— except, at times, for the responsible citizen. He was called a "surety," and if his ward became a fugitive the surety went to jail. As the years went by, this harshness was slowly relaxed and the surety forfeited money or property if the defendant disappeared.

In spite of the risk involved, in the tight little communities of old England there were men of property and good will who—knowing the defendants—were willing to be sureties.

Aware of this, the lawmakers in the first United States Congress decided that, in order to protect the innocent, anyone arrested for a federal crime was to be permitted out on bail, except where the punishment may be death. In these capital cases they left the matter of bail up to the discretion of the judge. The Eighth Amendment added a protection: "Excessive bail shall not be required. . . ." But it was generally understood that the amount demanded had to be enough in the opinion of the judge to insure the appearance of the accused at the trial.

In the New World two tremendous hazards worked against this great humanitarian advance. The country was vast and for a long time offered the suspect a wilderness frontier. No one could fail to imagine the accused being lured by the woods into attempting an easy escape. If this made sureties hard to find and led to the development of the professional bondsman favoring the financially able, it did no more damage to the bail system than the growth of the cities. When hordes of men and women, born elsewhere and having abandoned their farms or craft shops, came looking for jobs in industry, they crowded the urban slums. Crowded living conditions led to crowded jails and court calendars. The Constitution might call for a speedy trial, but often it simply was not possible. A stranger or slum dweller in the city had no friend in a position to risk money or assets to obtain a pretrial release. He was at the mercy of the professional bondsman.

Most experts agreed that bail reform in the 1960s was long overdue. Actually, the issue came to a head only because of the dedicated efforts of a few sympathetic citizens.

One of these was a chemical engineer and successful industrialist named Louis Schweitzer. Mr. Schweitzer learned of persons accused of crime and held in pretrial detention in New York City for over a year. Bail seemed to him to be a device for the defendant with money or connections. In this city of many millions, the judges who set bail knew nothing about the accused individual but his name, his address, and the nature of the charge against him. The judges did the inevitable: the more serious the accusation, the higher the bail. Hardened criminals, grown rich in crime, could almost always raise it, but not the shabby little women accused of shoplifting.

As Schweitzer looked into the problem more deeply, he must have come across the findings of another humanitarian, Professor Caleb Foote of the University of Pennsylvania. Foote first studied conditions in his own state. He analyzed the cases of 528 people who were eventually released after their trials and found they had already spent an average of thirty-three days in jail.

Some magistrates candidly admitted they set high bail to break crime waves. Foote recommended lowering the standard amounts of bail and releasing more people on their personal bonds (their own promise to reappear or pay a forfeit). People who could not afford bail could thus be sent home to prepare for trial. "They won't run away," Foote said.

Schweitzer decided he wanted to see Foote's recommendations tried. He called on local judges and public officials, urging them to agree to give the idea a chance. Then he launched the Vera Foundation (named after his mother). In 1961 the foundation hired seven New York University law students and started the Manhattan Bail Project. The Department of Correction set aside a small cell and let the young men use it as a place in which to interview the prisoners. The law school students asked the arrestees a string of questions, which covered such matters as: How long have you lived in this area? How long at your current address? How long have you held your present job? What relatives and dependents do you have in New York? Have you ever been arrested before? Have you ever been convicted? Is there anyone we could call as a reference (employer, relative, religious leader, teacher, landlord, union official, credit reference)? If the answers sounded promising the student checked on their accuracy, usually over the telephone. At times, when necessary, the student went out looking for the reference whose word might give a clue to the defendant's character. At last the questionnaire was scored and the Vera Foundation decided whether or not to recommend another nonbail release to the judge.

By July of 1964, two years later, 3,200 persons charged with such major crimes as larceny, burglary, forgery, and assault had been released on their own recognizance, on the Manhattan Bail Project's recommendations. On Sunday, July 26, a *New York Times* staff writer, Gertrude Samuels, reported that "a whopping 99 per cent have appeared for trial."

Senator Keating was impressed. He knew that during the same period only 97 per cent of those released on bail appeared on schedule, and he said that "a new and better system has now been devised."

The Junior Bar Section of the District of Columbia Bar Association had long since reached the same conclusion. Working with another legal group, the Judicial Conference for the District of Columbia Circuit, they had decided to more or less duplicate the Vera experiment in Washington. With money from the Ford Foundation, they had launched the law school students on their work in the District courts. The eager dedication of these young men was helping to make the reform a success.

Other communities were also impressed with Vera. Bail reform projects were begun in Des Moines, Chicago, Los Angeles, St. Louis, and Nassau County in New York, and still more communities began to make similar plans. Here, say staff people from the Criminal Division of the Department of Justice, is the real key to the bail reform movement. When people realized that something could be done about the inequalities of the bail system they were interested; and Schweitzer's bail project had shown that something could be done.

The Attorney General was the most impressed of all. He ordered U.S. attorneys to recommend to federal judges that the greatest possible number of defendants should be at liberty during their pretrial periods. The default rate was very low.

The senators in the two committees met to discuss changing the law and in a new law to spell out the authority of a federal court or a federal commissioner to release a pretrial defendant on his own recognizance, thereby making the practice a matter of public policy.

To do this, the senators drafted a bill on bail procedures and then held hearings letting interested citizens comment on their work. They listened to Mr. Herbert Sturz, the paid director of the Manhattan Bail Project. They listened to James V. Bennett, director of the U.S. Bureau of Prisons, who further encouraged them. Bennett believes deeply that "large percentages of these people who get into trouble can be rehabilitated and restored to life." He spoke of the dirty, overcrowded conditions in many jails where good people are mixed with bad. He spoke of bail reform as a splendid movement in the right direction. He said it meant a larger number of people would be rehabilitated, because it meant that fewer people would be demoralized and contaminated, by remaining in jail, and embittered to the point where it was extremely difficult to work with them.

After hearing all the witnesses, the committee members made some further changes in the draft of their bill and in December of 1964 sent it along with a report to the full Senate. In the report the senators concluded, "Federal bail procedures [now] are in direct conflict with two of our cherished principles of justice—equality before the law and the presumption of innocence."

A year and a half later Congress passed the Bail Reform Bill of 1966. It specified that the accused be released on his own recognizance whenever this is justified by his past record or by community and family ties. It suggests other alternatives to bond, such as release in the custody of a person or organization or release with restrictions—on travel, place of residence, or association. The judge can release an accused person on condition that he stay away from the complainant.

When President Lyndon Johnson signed the bill into law on June 22, 1966, he paid tribute to Mr. Louis Schweitzer and his bail project and then said that "now . . . we can begin to insure that defendants are considered as individuals, not as dollar signs."

Two days before, the Vera Foundation had reorganized into the Vera Institute of Justice. They already had another experiment well under way, the Manhattan Summons Project. The idea was to give an arrested person a summons to come to court, instead of locking him up for the night. When the defendant was brought to the precinct station house, he was interviewed by a Vera staff member as he would be if he were taken to court. If the accused seemed to be a good risk to the staff member, a recommendation for his release would be made to the desk officer.

While Vera was thus going ahead, the new bail law was implemented in the District of Columbia. The private bail project was turned into a government agency.

The young men still had important work to do. Since Washington is a federal city, the new law applied here to cases which in other localities would come before the state courts. The situation provides an opportunity for Congress to demonstrate to local communities across the land what can be done, and many of them are watching.

On a week-day morning at 9:30 in the Court of General Sessions for the District of Columbia, the wooden seats are filled with desolate, shabby men and women who face the judge's bench and the witness chair, both of which are mounted on a platform inside a curved wooden rail. Inside the enclosure is a table for the court clerk and the marshal.

A law school student comes through the swinging door at the back of the chamber and heads for a desk at the far left-hand corner of the courtroom. He is emerging from the cell area and he carries a manila folder which he hands to a student seated at the desk. While taking the folder, the desk worker asks, "How about Raymond? Is he a good risk?" The reply is, "None better." The questioner nods. He thought as much. Raymond was arrested last night for purse snatching, but his references are good and the student will recommend his pretrial release.

One after another the cases are called before the judge. This judge has the power to try minor crimes called "misdemeanors," but in serious felony cases he can only approve the arrest. Such cases are tried in the District court. A nice-looking woman with soft curls, in a gray coat, is called forward from the pews. "First time up," says the marshal and adds, "Second-degree murder." Second-degree murder is a felony. The judge warns her of her right to keep silent and that anything she says may be used against her. He asks if she has a lawyer. She has, as it turns out—provided by her employer. The judge sets bail at $1,000. As her employer is also paying for her bond, there is no work on this case for the students.

A fantastic-looking girl with auburn hair, a purple wool dress, and huge round orange earrings is next to face the judge. She is charged with forgery. The students know her and are not going to recommend her release. They have helped her before, but since then she has been a fugitive from a charge in another court and this fact is in the report that one of them hands the judge.

The judge, nevertheless, addresses her courteously as Miss ————" and makes sure she has a lawyer. If she cannot raise her bail, she will stay in jail. An article in the *American Bar Association Journal* has suggested that, under the new law, it is now the duty of the lawyer to find reasons why this type of defendant should be released or paroled in a responsible person's custody.

Finally a young Negro in a yellow and black plaid shirt is brought from the lockup. He is charged with criminal assault. "First time up," says the marshal. The judge asks the prisoner if he has a lawyer. He says "No" in an almost inaudible voice, and the judge calls a lawyer from a group of men sitting in what looks like a jury box near the rear door. The students are already busy checking the Negro's story. He seems too young to be married, but evidently he has a wife with whom he has quarreled. She is bringing the charge. This is what the students call a "boy-girl case." Formerly the defendant would sit in jail, lose his job, and his dependents would most likely go on relief. Yet experienced court workers know that in most instances by the time a "boy-girl case" comes to trial the couple has patched up the row and the complainant wants the charge dropped. So say the records, even in histories of middle-aged couples and even when one of the married pair comes to court with an arm in a sling or a bandage over his or her temple. In this case, the young Negro's record is excellent and he walks out of court, a beneficiary of the new law.

"I Didn't Shoot Manuel, You Did It"

THE story does not begin when Danny Escobedo was arrested for murder in Chicago. It began when our distant ancestors decided that torturing a suspect was a good way to obtain evidence. It continued with the horrors devised in the Middle Ages by zealous Inquisitors determined to obtain the confessions of heretics. The tale includes the image of Galileo, summoned to Rome in 1632 and, on his knees, repudiating his teaching—dangerous to the faith—that the earth moved around the sun. For this is a story of forced confessions and a nation's search for the standards of a fair trial, a story kept alive by a great conflict in our own society.

To protect the public, the policeman must catch the criminal. For the officer and the prosecutor, the criminal's confession can be most helpful in solving the crime and establishing guilt. With all their evidence painstakingly organized, these officials of and for the state go before the judge who must uphold the law. There they find that the law embodies more than punishing the guilty. It embodies protection for the possibly innocent and it also provides a dam against official lawlessness—a force which, once released, could engulf and wipe out our system of orderly liberty.

Not everybody agrees that the accused needs all the protection we give him. There are many among us who hold the same opinion expressed by an impatient jurist half a century ago: "Our procedure has been always haunted by the ghost of the innocent man convicted. . . . What we need to fear is . . . the watery sentiment that obstructs, delays and defeats the prosecution of crime." Rephrased, this means: A little more leeway for the prosecutor would facilitate more convictions, protect the honest citizen, the women and children in our streets, and break crime waves.

The famous Star Chamber judges of England once had equally laudable motives. After the War of the Roses at the end of the Middle Ages, the great English barons were an overmatch for any local court, and in order "to bridle such stout noblemen or gentlemen who would offer wrong by force to any manner of men . . ." Parliament was induced to give the King's Star Chamber wide powers. This special court dispensed with the annoyances of a jury, conducted prosecutions on the basis of mere rumor, and forced many a suspect to testify against himself. Before it was abolished, the Star Chamber had changed from an instrument which upheld order against anarchy to one which upheld despotism and suppressed individual liberty.

It caused its own downfall when John Lilburne, a quarrelsome young man and a religious nonconformist with advanced ultra-democratic ideas, was brought before the awesome judges in 1638 Lilburne stood accused of importing books offensive to the official beliefs of the realm. He refused to take the oath to tell the truth concerning himself and his actions.

For this offense he was publicly flogged, stood in the pillory, thrown into prison, and fined. The episode ended when, in 1641, the Long Parliament abolished the Star Chamber, vacated the sentence, and paid Lilburne reparations, thus making illegal the attempt to obtain involuntary confessions for use as evidence.

The Founding Fathers, remembering such tortures of old as the rack and the thumbscrew, and the obvious fact that the innocent confessed as often as the guilty, said in the Fifth Amendment to the Constitution, "No person shall be . . . compelled in any criminal case to be a witness against himself. . . ."

This did not make the problem disappear. So-called voluntary confessions were still the mainstay of criminal law enforcement. Temptation remained for an enforcement officer, when he confronted what he believed to be an obvious robber or murderer, to use some kind of pressure to force a confession and then to believe the coerced admission—even if it was later retracted. The Fifth Amendment was written long before the invention of the "squeal room" in the big city police station, but for a long time the Fifth Amendment did not bind the states. Passage of the Fourteenth Amendment after the Civil War required the states to use due process. As time passed, the Supreme Court justices gingerly faced the problem of how much of the Bill of Rights they should declare to be required by due process. They should, they felt, enforce the fundamentals of orderly liberty and a fair trial. They should not, they decided, interfere with legitimate differences between federal and state procedures.

As to confessions, for a long time the Court relied on the fact that all but two of the states had some kind of prohibition against compelling a witness to be his own accuser. The two remaining states had judge-made rules against the practice. In 1908, Supreme Court Justice William H. Moody, a Republican from Massachussetts, explained the Supreme Court's position at that time. "The exemption . . . from disclosure as a witness of evidence against oneself, forced by any form of legal process, is universal in American law, though there may be differences as to its exact scope and limits." Moody thought these differences should be left undisturbed. At the same time, he described the privilege as "of great value, a protection to the innocent though a shelter to the guilty, and a safeguard against heedless, unfounded or tyrannical prosecutions."

Then in 1930 a shocking report to Congress exposed "the third degree," police violence used to obtain confessions. Shortly thereafter in 1936 the case of *Brown v. Mississippi* came before the Supreme Court. The three defendants had been whipped. Their backs had been cut to pieces with a buckle-studded leather strap, and the whipping had continued until they agreed to admit to a murder. It was the only evidence against the men, but they were convicted.

By the time the case reached the Supreme Court, the justices were in a most difficult position. They had already adopted Moody's position, having refused to reverse a case called *Twining v. New Jersey*. In *Twining* two bank directors elected not to testify to refute a charge that they had attempted to deceive a state examiner who was checking into the company's affairs. The state judge told the jury members they might draw their own conclusions from the failure of a defendant directly accused to take the witness stand. Thus the judge drastically cut down the legal value of the right to remain silent. If accused, a man could still remain silent but the jury could weigh that silence in determining his guilt. The Supreme Court justices, wanting to leave the people in the states free to govern themselves, held then that the Fifth Amendment rule did not apply in the courts of the states. (It was 1964 before the justices changed their minds.)

Thus, at the time of *Brown*, unless they wanted to reverse their own position, the justices had to say that their decision could not involve enforcing the Fifth Amendment's privilege against self-incrimination in a state case. Instead, the justices said, "Compulsion by torture to extort a confession is a different matter." Obviously the defendants in *Brown* had not had fair treatment under any standards of orderly liberty or fair trial. Therefore they had not had due process. After that, other forced confessions were thrown out by the Court as not meeting the standards of due process.

Meanwhile, the justices were facing a similar problem in the area of the defendant's right to an attorney, as called for by the Sixth Amendment. This amendment, quoted in full at the beginning of this section, is basic to the whole controversy over what is necessary to protect society from despotic methods which could be used to dispose of unpopular or seemingly suspicious characters (who might be innocent). It states, in part, "In all criminal prosecutions, the accused shall enjoy the right . . . to have the Assistance of Counsel for his defence."

In 1942 something happened which made the justices look over the records to see what the states were doing about a defendant's right to counsel. Justice Black noted, "In thirty-five states, there is some clear legal requirement . . . that indigent defendants in serious non-capital as well as capital criminal cases . . . be provided with counsel on request." In eleven states the law was indefinite, and only in Maryland and Texas was the requirement affirmatively rejected.

The question of what to do had to be discussed because that year a penniless unemployed farmer named Smith Betts was accused of robbery in Maryland. At the trial Betts asked for, but was denied, the help of a state-appointed counsel. When he was convicted, the Supreme Court agreed to review his case. Betts and those who spoke for him must have relied on the fact that, ten years earlier, the right to counsel had been imposed by the Supreme Court on the

State of Alabama. The case was *Powell v. Alabama.* Seven young, ignorant, and illiterate Negro boys had been condemned to death in a rape case, and the Supreme Court had reversed their conviction because they had not had the help of a lawyer in preparing their defense. Several justices later said that the Court acted not because of the counsel requirement on the federal level but because the help of a lawyer was essential to a fair trial in that particular situation. The boys were taken off a freight train and tried in a hostile community and, furthermore, their trial involved a matter of life or death.

The Court found no such compelling factors in the Betts trial and again decided not to impose the federal standard on the states. In other words, the justices were still limiting themselves to imposing what they considered to be the minimum requirements of fair procedures, in the name of due process. Betts lost.

In 1947 Justices Black and Frankfurter argued over whether to apply the Bill of Rights literally in these criminal cases. By now the Roosevelt era had come and gone. Labor laws once held unconstitutional were now being upheld by the Court. The First Amendment had been applied to the states via the Fourteenth. Much of the country had changed its attitude on states' rights. Black put up a memorable fight, reviewing the debates in Congress when the due process clause was put into the Fourteenth Amendment, but Frankfurter won. The Court moved slowly forward, judging each state case on its merits but being strict with federal enforcement officers.

In 1957 the Court imposed the "Mallory" rule on federal agents. There could be no unnecessary delay in taking a suspect before a United States commissioner or magistrate who would tell the defendant his rights and provide a lawyer if the defendant was poor. Admissions which were obtained by long-drawn-out questioning beforehand were not usable in court.

Then in 1959 the Supreme Court gave the states a fateful warning. "The abhorrence of society to the use of involuntary confessions does not turn alone on their inherent untrustworthiness. It also turns on the deep-rooted feeling that the police must obey the law while enforcing the law; that in the end life and liberty can be as much endangered from illegal methods used to convict those thought to be criminals as from the actual criminals themselves."

Confessions obtained by promise or trickery were not voluntary under due process. They were not reliable and did not protect society from future tyrannical lawlessness.

All this was history, and yet it was part of the environment in Chicago's west side slums when, late on the night of January 19, 1960, Danny Escobedo's brother-in-law, Manuel Valtierra, was shot in the back on his way home.

To the police a crime had been committed and had to be solved. They looked for a suspect and they looked at Danny, a short, almost skinny, sensitive youth of Mexican extraction. He loved his sister Grace, and Grace and her husband had been having brutal quarrels.

Two and a half hours after midnight the police, without a warrant, arrested Danny, Grace, and two of Danny's pals—Bobby Chan, seventeen, and Benny DiGerlando, eighteen. While detectives questioned the crew, Bobby's mother called a lawyer, Warren Wolfson. Mr. Wolfson had to go to a state court for a writ of habeas corpus that would order the four of them released, and it was dusk of the twentieth before they were all out of the police headquarters building.

Ten days later, on a Saturday night, Danny was again arrested. In the police car the arresting officer told him that Benny had named him as the killer and he might as well admit to it. Danny, who evidently had been coached, replied, "I am sorry but I would like to have advice from my lawyer."

Someone phoned Wolfson, who arrived at the big, gray, State Street detective headquarters about 9:30 P.M. There he engaged in an exasperating and tedious chase up and down stairs, from the Detective Bureau to the Homicide Bureau, introducing himself as Danny's lawyer first to a desk sergeant, then to various detectives, and then to Chief Flynn. Still he did not gain access to his client. He gave up and left State Street at 1:00 A.M. Sunday morning, phrasing his official complaint to the police commissioner. Danny, in the meantime, while being questioned—handcuffed and in a standing position—kept asking for him.

According to the Supreme Court record "during the course of the interrogation Officer Montejano, who 'grew up' in petitioner's neighborhood, who knew his family, and who uses 'Spanish language in [his] policework,' conferred alone with petitioner 'for about a quarter of an hour. . . .'" Danny later claimed that the officer had promised him in Spanish "that my sister and I could go home if I pinned it on Benedict DiGerlando . . . [that] he would see to it that we would go home and be held only as witnesses . . . if we had made a statement against DiGerlando . . . , that we would be able to go home that night." Danny then testified that he made a particular statement because of this assurance. Officer Montejano denied offering any such assurance.

Another police officer testified that during the interrogation the following occurred: "I informed him of what DiGerlando told me [that Danny did the shooting] and when I did, he told me that DiGerlando was [lying] and I said, 'Would you care to tell DiGerlando that?' and he said, 'Yes, I will.' So, I brought . . . Escobedo in and he confronted DiGerlando and he told him that he was lying and said, 'I didn't shoot Manuel, you did it.' "

With these words Danny admitted knowledge of the crime. As a layman who at that time had no record of previous experience with the police, Danny was undoubtedly unaware of how serious a statement he had made. Under Illinois law, mere complicity in the murder plot was legally as damaging as an admission of firing the fatal shot. It was too late to see Wolfson. The lawyer could do nothing more now but object to the admission of the confession in evidence. In this he was not successful. The only question before the jurors was whether it was a voluntary confession. Since they believed Officer Montejano when he claimed to have made no promises, they also believed that Danny had freely given his confession. They kept in mind that after the initial words "you did it," Danny had added more statements damaging to his case. Danny was sent to prison to start a twenty-year sentence.

Years ago the story would have ended there, but coming events were to make legal changes in Danny's favor. In 1961, a timely book written by Edwin M. Borchard, a Yale professor, and first printed almost thirty years before, was reissued. It carried the harrowing title *Convicting the Innocent*. The professor was angered by a district attorney who said, "Innocent men never get convicted. Don't worry about it—it never happens." The professor selected sixty-five cases from what he said were "a much larger number" in which innocent people had indeed been convicted. Among Borchard's reported defendants were men and women who had made confessions, including confessions of murder. In these documented incidents, supposed murder victims reappeared after the "murderer" had been convicted. Footnotes to later Supreme Court opinions showed that the justices had been reading Borchard's volume. Two other quite different publications also caught their attention. They were two "how-to-do-it" books for policemen and prosecutors on obtaining confessions. These manuals advised the policeman to rely on an oppressive atmosphere; to interrogate steadily and in an atmosphere of complete privacy. The justices were most concerned. Obviously under such conditions it was impossible for anyone to measure how much pressure had been applied.

Without knowing any of this, Danny, after spending two years trudging through the massive prison halls between the mammoth guards, appealed to the Illinois Supreme Court. Since he had no money, the Illinois court appointed a lawyer to handle his appeal. The lawyer was Eugene Farrug, who put the job of writing the appeal brief into the hands of his able young associate, Barry L. Kroll. While Kroll was working, time and history were working with him.

History took its first step for Danny in January of 1963. An already famous attorney, Abe Fortas (now a justice himself), told the United States Supreme Court, "I believe that this case [*Gideon v. Wainwright*] dramatically illustrates the point that you cannot have a fair trial without counsel." As he pleaded for the rights of Clarence Gideon, an indigent inmate in a Florida prison, Fortas indirectly was fighting for Danny. Gideon had been convicted of breaking into a poolroom and Fortas was asking the Court to rule that Gideon's trial fell short of the demands of due process because the judge had turned down the defendant's request for a lawyer. When Fortas convinced the justices, they overruled their earlier decision in *Betts*. (Gideon was acquitted at a retrial, where he had the help of an attorney.)

The Sixth Amendment's mandate on the right to advice of counsel at last bound the states. Consequently, Danny Escobedo, who had been denied advice of counsel at the police station (although he had had a lawyer at the trial), was one step nearer freedom.

Meanwhile exciting things were happening in the progress of Danny's appeal. In February the Illinois Supreme Court said, "It seems manifest to us . . . that the defendant understood he would be permitted to go home. . . ." A self-incriminating statement obtained in this manner should not be admissible in evidence. For a time Danny must have been elated. Then, in May, after a full rehearing of the arguments, the state's highest tribunal finally decided it ought not to disturb the trial court's finding that the confession was given voluntarily. Danny had lost again. But again time was working changes in his favor.

On the same day that discouraging words were being uttered in Illinois, the justices in Washington announced that they could review the findings of a jury as to whether a confession was voluntary. In a case called *Haynes v. Washington* they voided a confession obtained after the defendant had been questioned for long hours and denied the right to call his wife until he gave the police an admission of guilt.

Kroll, of course, prepared to take Danny's case to the Supreme Court. Significantly, seven days before the justices ruled on Danny's appeal, they handed down a landmark ruling in another case, *Malloy v. Hogan*. In it they said the Fourteenth Amendment prohibits state infringement of the privilege against self-incrimination, just as the Fifth Amendment prevents federal infringement of the privilege. Now, for all purposes, the Fifth Amendment's mandate against forcing a man to accuse himself bound the states as well as the United States Government. (Later the justices would forbid even the prosecutor in a state trial from adversely commenting on a defendant's unwillingness to testify.)

The justices were ready to rule on the Escobedo case. As they looked over Danny's history it became clear that the right to counsel and the right to remain silent had merged.

> We hold, therefore [the justices announced], that where, as here, the investigation is no longer a general inquiry into an unsolved crime but has begun to focus on a particular suspect, the suspect has been taken into police custody, the police carry out a process of interrogations that lends itself to eliciting incriminating statements, the suspect has requested and been denied an opportunity to consult with his lawyer, and the police have not effectively warned him of his absolute constitutional right to remain silent, the accused has been denied "the Assistance of Counsel" in violation of the Sixth Amendment to the Constitution as "made obligatory upon the States by the Fourteenth Amendment" . . . no statement elicited by the police during the interrogation may be used against him at a criminal trial.

Danny left prison and went home to Chicago. Spirited debate filled public newspapers and magazines. A New York police commissioner stated, "What the Court is doing is akin to requiring one boxer to fight by . . . rules while permitting the other to butt, gouge and bite." Angry editorials harped on the need of the innocent public for protection against the criminal element. A Los Angeles police chief stated that "a whole Pandora's box is opened as to under what circumstances . . . can a defendant intelligently waive these rights. . . ." For the benefit of these people and others who found the ruling confusing, the Supreme Court justices clarified their position in a case called *Miranda v. Arizona*.

In that opinion the Court said, "Accordingly we hold that an individual held for interrogation must be clearly informed that he has the right to consult with a lawyer and to have the lawyer with him during interrogation. . . . As with the warnings of the right to remain silent and [the warning] that anything stated can be used in evidence against him . . . [a lawyer's help] is an absolute prerequisite to interrogation." *

The question: "What are the fundamentals of a fair trial?" had not been born with Danny's story. It did not end with Danny's case or with the clarification of it which the justices gave in *Miranda*. On April 5, 1965, the justices ruled, "We hold today that the Sixth Amendment's right of an accused to confront the witnesses against him is likewise a fundamental right and is made obligatory on the States by the Fourteenth Amendment."

While the justices were so ruling, another case involving America's young people was working its way up through the Arizona courts. It was to come before the Supreme Court justices in December of 1966. What triggered it was this. On June 8, 1964, Gerald G.'s mother came home from work and learned from the neighbors that Gerald, aged fifteen, had been arrested and taken by the sheriff to the detention home for juveniles. Since the hearing was held the next day, Mrs. G. claimed she had never received proper notice—as the Supreme Court had insisted was the right of every adult criminal.

In answer, Darrell F. Smith, the attorney general of the State of Arizona, explained to the justices—when they questioned him— that the probation officer, Charles D. Flagg, was occupied with another matter away from the detention home for most of that day, but that when he saw Mrs. G. in the detention home, trying to find out about Gerald, "he explained the whole thing to her. . . ." She appeared without objection at the hearing next day in Judge Robert E. McGee's chambers. No transcript of the hearing was made, and exactly what Gerald admitted in testimony is still a matter of dispute. He and a friend were accused of making lewd phone calls to a Mrs. Cook. Mrs. G. wanted the complaining lady called in to testify as to which boy had used the dirty words. Judge Robert E. McGee said, "She [Mrs. Cook] did not have to be present at the hearing."

Mrs. G. could have called a lawyer to come to the hearings, but juvenile court procedures in Arizona did not automatically require

* At Miranda's retrial, his confession could not be used since the Supreme Court had thrown it out. He was nevertheless convicted a second time.

the state to furnish a lawyer for Gerald. Nor did the state code require a juvenile judge to advise an infant of the privilege against self-incrimination.

While trying to decide how to dispose of the case, Judge McGhee appears to have taken into account two previous complaints against Gerald. One complaint, on which no hearing was held, involved a missing baseball glove; in the other complaint Gerald was accused of being in the company of a youth who snatched a wallet in a theater. Finally, after the hearings on the lewd phone calls, Judge McGhee sent Gerald to the State Industrial School to remain there—unless released under state supervision—for six years until he reached twenty-one.

The justices wanted to know from Smith how long a sentence an adult offender would have served for the same offense—lewd phone calls.

Attorney General Smith answered, "Two months."

Smith, a nice-looking, intelligent, blond young man, explained the position many juvenile court systems take. The juvenile is not considered a criminal. He goes to the industrial school not as a punishment but to help him.

Justice Fortas said he did not care what you called the place; the boy had to stay there. He was deprived of his liberty. Juvenile court people argue that no minor is completely free. He is under somebody's custody, and when necessary for his own good it must be state custody. This attitude explains juvenile court procedures in many areas. As Smith explained, the judge asks the youth in a fatherly way exactly what he did do and generally the youth answers.

At this point, Justice Harlan wanted to know, "What does the judge say then in a fatherly way?" One may well wonder what is left to be said after the youth has admitted his guilt during questioning in which he is without advice or knowledge of his rights. Juvenile court authorities claim it is part of the "therapy" to have a juvenile admit his guilt.*

Other legal authorities have been arguing that the system pressures a young person either into lying or accusing others. Some minors are so inarticulate that they hurt their own case when they try to testify, and a good lawyer would advise them against it.

The Supreme Court justices faced the same problem here that they had faced in other areas. Many states had already begun to

* The Court decided that, on the contrary, the juvenile may feel tricked. He may therefore resist help. The fairness of due process may be more impressive and more therapeutic. Rhetoric cannot change the fact that on being found to be a delinquent, the youth goes to an institution as a criminal goes to jail. Since his freedom and his reputation are in jeopardy, he is entitled to the protection of the Fourteenth Amendment and the Bill of Rights: "neither . . . is for adults alone."

reform their own juvenile court systems. How rigid should the court be with the others? On May 15, 1967, the Court ruled that juveniles are entitled to have adequate notice of the charges against them, to remain silent, to have a lawyer, to have their lawyer cross-examine the witnesses, and to take their case to appeal.

Admittedly, this is a relatively new area of law, and time was needed to work out its special problems. Juvenile court systems— unlike adult criminal codes—were born around the turn of the century. They represented a need to save the "infant offender" from being lumped with adult criminals. They have developed since under such well-meaning phrases as "flexibility," "freedom from stigma," and "rehabilitate the child." Only since World War II has there been a growing chorus of voices crying out that fair procedures to establish guilt or innocence are not incompatible with helpful therapy later, after delinquency has been properly established under constitutional standards. Time has taught its age-old lesson. Well-meaning people burnt witches. Well-meaning prosecutors have convicted the innocent. Well-meaning objectives espoused by those not grounded in history can lure us from protecting our heritage of equal justice under law. They can entice us, faster than we like to believe, into endangering our liberties.

"A Fair Trial and a Free Press"

BY 1966, two of America's most treasured traditions, a fair trial and a free press, had run into a head-on collision. The *Wall Street Journal* commented on November 2 that "each side presents an overwhelming case . . . ," and the reader could almost see the editor shaking his head.

For a long time the justices of the Supreme Court had been most concerned. They were loath, as they had always been, to shackle the press. The press, like the defendant's counsel, could serve as a safeguard against abuse, subjecting the prosecutors and the courts to public scrutiny. It is an old adage that there is no more powerful brake on official misconduct than the knowledge that the public is watching. Equally important, a newspaper account of a trial might alert and bring forth unexpected witnesses, who could then be most helpful in the court's search for truth.

Long before 1966 it had become evident that there was also another side. In its search for a good story, the press could itself become the reckless abuser of the citizen's rights.

In 1959 agents of the United States Government on the West Coast brought an action against one Howard Marshall, who was handing out dextro amphetamine sulfate tablets (pep pills). Marshall wasn't openly selling the tablets, but he was soliciting "donations" of money from his contacts. Since no physician had prescribed the pills, Marshall was violating the Pure Food and Drug Act.

The government attorneys asked the District Court judge to allow them to introduce evidence that the accused had previously practiced medicine without a license. The judge refused, saying, "It would be just like offering evidence that he picked pockets . . . which would have no bearing on the issue . . . and I think would be prejudicial to the defendant."

This having been decided, the case was argued without the attorneys mentioning the prejudicial evidence, but two newspapers carried it in their accounts of Marshall's past, and a substantial number of the twelve jurors saw the papers.

As a result, when Marshall was convicted he appealed to the Supreme Court of the United States and the justices felt compelled to set aside the conviction, letting Marshall have a retrial. By the time the case started over again, the publicity had been forgotten. Even so, at the second trial the pill dispenser was again convicted and sentenced to a year in prison. Evidently this man was guilty. Nevertheless, the community could take pride. He had had his full fair day in court. The press unfortunately did not see the incident as a warning.

In December of 1961 the Supreme Court justices were even more annoyed with the newsmen. Six murders had been committed in the locality of Evansville, Indiana. Finally the police arrested a suspect and issued a press release to that effect. From then on, the Supreme Court justices found, a barrage of newspaper headlines, articles, cartoons, and pictures was unleashed against the accused. The barrage continued for the six or seven months preceding the trial. Crimes the accused had committed when a juvenile, a court-martial he had faced on A.W.O.L. charges during the war, all made good copy. News stories reported he had offered to plead guilty if promised a prison sentence instead of the death penalty. In many of these stories, the defendant was described as the "confessed slayer of six." The papers carrying these accounts were delivered to approximately 95 per cent of the residents in the county where the trial was to be held. Justice Clark, while describing the case, noted,

"Finally, and with remarkable understatement, the headlines reported that 'impartial jurors are hard to find.' "

The accused was convicted and sentenced to death. The execution was then delayed while the attorneys for the defense appealed. They wanted a change of venue—that is, they wanted the trial moved to another locality. This is one way of handling this kind of problem. Another is to delay the trial until the effect of the publicity dies down. The justices of the Supreme Court fully agreed with the defense attorneys that, as matters stood when the case came before them, the accused certainly had not had a fair trial.

The Court therefore sent the case back to the state, where the retrial was moved to a new locality and a more objective jury brought in a verdict resulting in the lesser penalty of a prison term for the defendant.

That seemed to take care of that trial. It still did not take care of the big difficulty. Over the past years the growth of national television and other communications media has materially intensified the whole problem of publicity and a fair trial. Not only can pretrial news be spread over the country, so that there is no place left to which a trial can be moved, but the radio, papers, or TV can pick and choose sensational bits of a story, leaving the public with so sharp and distinct an impression that the calm and often complicated deliberation of a courtroom can hardly be expected to erase the prejudice jury members have already formed.

In 1966, the justices were forced to admit, "From the cases coming here we note that unfair and prejudicial news comment on pending trials has become increasingly prevalent."

The case before them was *Sheppard v. Maxwell.* The story had been given wide publicity. On July 4, 1954, Sheppard's pregnant wife, Marilyn, had been bludgeoned to death in the upstairs bedroom of their lake shore home in Bay Village, Ohio, a suburb of the city of Cleveland.

Dr. Sheppard, an osteopath, had called a neighbor, the Bay Village mayor, who came at once and asked, "What happened?"

Sheppard answered, "I don't know, but somebody ought to try to do something for Marilyn."

Mrs. Houk, the mayor's wife, went up to the bedroom, and Mayor Houk commanded, "Get hold of yourself, can you tell me what happened?"

Sheppard said he had been dozing on a couch when he heard Marilyn cry out. He had hurried upstairs and in the dim light from the hall saw "a form" by Marilyn's bed. He was struck on the back of the neck by whoever it was and rendered unconscious. On regaining consciousness, he heard a noise downstairs and pursued the "form" to the lake shore, again grappled with it, and again lost consciousness. Later this story had to be repeated to the police from Sheppard's hospital bed, where the doctor was under sedation for his injuries.

A questioning police officer commented, "I think you killed your wife."

On July 7, the day of Marilyn's funeral, a newspaper story appeared in which the assistant county attorney, later the chief prosecutor of Sheppard, sharply criticized the Sheppard family for refusing to permit immediate questioning of the suspect. From there on headline stories stressed Sheppard's lack of cooperation, whereas the Supreme Court found Sheppard had indeed been available for frequent questioning.

Later, front-page headlines read: DR. BALKS AT LIE TEST, RETELLS STORY. Sheppard, said the papers, had refused to take a lie-detector test. On July 20 the editorial artillery opened fire, charging that somebody is "getting away with murder."

The inquest was staged in a school gymnasium with a long table provided for reporters and television and radio personnel and their broadcasting equipment. The newspapers then stressed Sheppard's friendship with a lady not his wife and the fact that at the beginning of the investigation he had once lied about their relationship. The papers further alleged other evidence to throw doubt on the doctor's testimony, some of which was never produced at the trial. On July 30, a front-page editorial asked: WHY ISN'T SAM SHEPPARD IN JAIL?

As soon as Sheppard was arrested, the publicity was intensified. When the jury picking began, the small courtroom contained a long temporary table especially set up for reporters inside the barred or railed-off area around the judge and witness box that is usually reserved for attorneys, litigants, and court officials. This time the trial participants had the company of the approximately twenty reporters seated at the table. Right behind them in the courtroom, television and radio people had front-row seats. Newsmen also used other rooms on the courtroom floor, in which they had private telephones and telegraph lines installed. Broadcasting facilities were set up next to the jury room and newscasts were made. In the corridors and on the court steps, cameramen took pictures of judge, jury, witnesses, and counsel.

Crowded to capacity, with people from the news media moving in and out, the courtroom afforded no opportunity for confidential talks between counsel and defendant—unless they left the room. It was, moreover, hard to hear the witnesses in the confusion. In this atmosphere of a Roman holiday for the news media, Sam Sheppard stood trial for his life.

While Sheppard was on the witness stand, a police captain who was not at the trial denied criticisms which the doctor had leveled at the city's detective forces. A headline appeared: BARE-FACED LIAR, KERR SAYS OF SAM.

Via such news stories, the jurors were able to read material that was not being presented in court where it could be properly evaluated (although the judge had cautioned the jurors against reading about the case in the papers). Moreover, the jurors were thrust into the role of public celebrities. Their pictures, names, and addresses appeared in the papers, thus exposing them to letters from friends and cranks alike, invading their privacy, and subjecting them to all the pressures of the news-fanned public prejudices. Finally, during the trial, a particularly damaging radio broadcast took place, vilifying Sheppard's character. At least two of the jurors heard it. The attorney for the accused asked for a mistrial, but the judge refused; "how are you ever going to prevent those things . . . ? I don't justify them at all. I think it is outrageous, but. . . ."

After Dr. Sheppard was convicted of second-degree murder and sent to prison, John H. Harrison, associate editor of the *Toledo Blade,* wrote an editorial on the conduct of the case. It appeared in the October, 1955, *Saturday Review,* saying that "almost everyone who watched the performance of the Cleveland press agrees that a fair hearing for the defendant, in that area, would be a modern miracle."

A number of years elapsed. Then an attorney by the name of F. Lee Bailey succeeded in getting the case reopened to challenge "the performance" of the press.

The justices of the Supreme Court did not think the modern miracle had occurred. They said, "Having assigned almost all of the available seats in the courtroom to the news media, the judge lost his ability to supervise that environment." The justices felt that the number of reporters in the courtroom should have been limited at the first sign that their presence would disrupt the proceedings. They certainly should not have been placed inside the bar. Furthermore, the judge should have more closely regulated the conduct of the newsmen in the courtroom, insulating witnesses from being interviewed. He should have controlled the release of information and gossip to the press coming from police, witnesses, and counsel for both sides and should also have imposed control over statements made to the papers by the prosecution and all other officials participating in the trial. He should have warned the press against printing prejudicial statements during the proceedings.

The Supreme Court justices therefore reversed the judgment, and ten years after the incident the state started over again with a new trial. Members of the press reading the justices' words were much disturbed. The opinion coming from the Supreme Court bench made it evident that it was not Sheppard who had been on trial before the country's highest court. It was the nation's press and its freedoms that the justices had considered.

Sheppard's new trial ended in an acquittal. Although this was obviously a very important matter to Sheppard and his family, it was even more important for the rest of us that the Supreme Court had again insisted that every man must have a fair trial.

The highest court of the land had served notice that trials are not to be decided through the use of radio and newspapers. Instead, the Court held that no one may be punished for a crime unless he is tried in an atmosphere free of prejudice, passion, gossip, and excitement.

Freedom of discussion must be given the widest range, but at the same time it must not be allowed to divert a trial from its purpose: to judge controversy in the calm solemnity of the courtroom, relying solely on the evidence examined by both sides and without considering rumors and accusations from without.

A fair trial being so vital to our way of life, the High Court has gone to great lengths to make sure that each deliberating jury be picked from a list that represents a cross-section of the population. Citizens may not be kept from doing jury duty by reason of their race or economic status. The courtroom door must be kept closed to class distinction. Years back, the Supreme Court had reversed the convictions of Negroes where members of their race were systematically excluded from the jury. In 1964 a white civil rights worker, engaged in Negro voter registration, was indicted for assault and the Georgia Court of Appeals invalidated the indictment because Negroes were excluded from the jury lists. There would be little use in all the requirements of a representative jury if television were allowed to lure a witness into becoming an actor— possibly distorting his testimony because he is conscious of the audience—or if jurors had to worry about what their excited neighbors (not at the trial) would say if they acquitted an unpopular defendant or convicted a popular one.

"Our system of law," says the Supreme Court, "has always endeavored to prevent even the probability of unfairness."

The news media must take note. Their rights are not so absolute that they may prejudice the rights of others. They too must have respect for the dignity of the accused individual and his presumption of innocence until he is proven guilty beyond a reasonable doubt.

With this clash between press and courts, we have come full circle. We started this book with officials bringing an unsuccessful libel suit to punish the press. We end with the press being warned not to disrupt the rights of citizens in court. The press, like everyone else, must have both rights and responsibilities and respect for the rights of others, or no one will be safe from tyranny.

Thus we have seen what endless challenge there is in this difficult, delicate, supremely sophisticated set of principles embodied in our Bill of Rights and our system of orderly liberty. We can also see why and for whom the great bill was written.

If you are never going to speak or write on a controversial topic; if you are never going to join the armed services, or be a member of a labor union, or own property the Government may want to take or regulate; if you subscribe to a religion that has never been the subject of persecution or slander; if you know you will never associate with any small or unpopular group or cause; if you will never wish to attend a public meeting; and if you can be sure that you will never be accused of a crime, even then you need the Bill of Rights. As a voting citizen you still need to hear all sides of a dispute, and the bill makes sure that the voices of dissent will not be silenced, so that you will not be prevented from hearing them and you will not be deprived of the right to judge for yourself the truth or falsity of any idea.

More likely you will not always be content to be a mere listener but will want to participate in community life. Thus at some point, now or in the future, you will doubtless find yourself a member of one of this country's myriads of small minority groups, of which there are so many that they make up the majority. In the United States this is their strength and it is the country's strength; for it means that no one can feel safe in the possession of his rights unless the rights of all others are also protected.

Mere opposition to another system is not democracy. The Constitution is an affirmative concept, not a negative one. It affirms and protects the integrity of the individual. It asserts his rights against other individuals, against groups, against even the majority and the Government itself; and it provides the imaginative and the dissatisfied with the machinery for peaceful change.

This concept of orderly liberty, even more than our constantly changing economic system, gives this country its vitality and provides room for its constantly greater ideas and achievements, triggered often by those with the courage to stand out from the crowd.

This is the concept for Americans to cherish and to bequeath. All of us need these rights.

BIBLIOGRAPHY FOR PART VI

Principal Sources on Adults or Youth Accused of Crime

BOOKS

Borchard, Edwin M. *Convicting the Innocent.* Connecticut, 1961.
Brant, Irving. *The Bill of Rights.* New York, 1965.
Lewis, Anthony. *Gideon's Trumpet.* New York, 1964.
Mitchell, Broadus and Louise. *A Biography of the Constitution of the United States.* New York, 1964.

UNITED STATES FEDERAL RECORDS

Congressional Records
    U.S. Congress, Hearing Before the Subcommittee on Constitutional Rights and the Subcommittee on Improvements in Judicial Machinery on "Federal Bail Procedure," 88th Congress, 2d Session, August, 1964.

Supreme Court Records (Transcripts and Records of Briefs)
    Betts v. Brady, 316 U.S. 455 (1942).
    Brown v. Mississippi, 297 U.S. 278 (1936).
    Estes v. State of Texas, 381 U.S. 532 (1965).
    Escobedo v. Illinois, 378 U.S. 478 (1964).
    Gideon, v. Wainwright, 372 U.S. 335 (1963).
    Haynes v. Washington, 373 U.S. 503 (1963).
    In Re Oliver, 333 U.S. 257 (1948).
    Irvin v. Dowd, 366 U.S 717 (1961).
    Marshall v. United States, 360 U.S. 310 (1959).
    Malloy v. Hogan, 378 U.S. 1 (1964).
    Miranda v. Arizona, 384 U.S. 436 (1966).
    Powell v. Alabama, 287 U.S. 45 (1932).
    Sheppard v. Maxwell, 384 U.S. 333 (1966).
    Spano v. New York, 360 U.S. 315 (1959).
    Twining v. New Jersey, 211 U.S. 78 (1908).

MAGAZINES AND PAMPHLETS

"Criminal Justice," *Time,* April 29, 1965.

Freed, Daniel J., and Patricia M. Wald. *Bail in the United States* (a government publication). Washington, D.C., 1964.

Harrison, John W. "The Press v. the Courts." *Saturday Review,* October 15, 1955.

McCarthy, David J., Jr., and Jeanne J. Whal. "The District of Columbia Bail Project." *Georgetown Law Journal,* Vol. 53, 1965, p. 675.

Paulsen, Monrad G. "Fairness to the Juvenile Offender," *Minnesota Law Review,* Vol. 41, No. 5, 1957.

Sturz, Herbert. "An Alternative to the Bail System." *Federal Probation,* December, 1962.

NEWSPAPERS

"The Suspect Confesses—But Who Believes Him?" *New York Times Magazine,* May 16, 1965.

New York Times, November 28, 1965, June 19, 1966.

INDEX

Index

Abington Township v. Schempp, 114

Abolition, 48, 49, 51, 55, 90, 92

Academic freedom, 32–35

Adams, John, 17, 18, 38, 136

Adams, John Quincy, 48

Adamson v. California, 99

Alabama, 15, 16, 55, 80–84, 226

Alien and Sedition Act, 17–20

Allegheny Airlines v. Cedarhurst, 147

Altgeld, John Peter, 65

American Federation of Labor, 61, 63, 66, 68

American Legion, 33, 187

American Veterans Committee, 187

Anarchists, 24, 61, 63–65

Anthony, J. Garner, 179

Anthony, Susan B., 51–57

Arbitrary power, 38, 72, 163, 166, 183, 184

Arbitration, 62

Areopagitica, 16

Arizona, 125, 231

Arkansas, 33

Armenians, 130

Arnall, Ellis, 156

Articles for the government of the Navy, 188, 194

Articles of War, 188

Assembly, freedom of, 48–106; limitations on, 72, 83, 103

Association, freedom of, 29, 31, 33

Atheists, 115

A.W.O.L., 184, 186

Bail, 212–222; origin of, 217

Bail, bondsmen, 212–217

Baker, Wilson, 83, 87, 102

Baldridge, Holmes, 160

Baltimore and Ohio Railroad strike, 61–62

Baltimore and Potomac Railroad Co. v. The Fifth Baptist Church, 148

Baptists, 109, 112, 117, 118, 121, 130, 131, 132

Barenblatt, Lloyd, 30–32

Barenblatt v. United States, 30–32

Barton, Clara, 55

Beauharnais v. Illinois, 25, 26

Becker amendment, 117–133; quoted at, 122

Becker, Frank J., 124

Bell, John, 151–153

Bennett, James V., 220

Betts v. Brady, 225–226

Biddle, Francis, 179

Bill of attainder, 30

Bill of Rights, *see* the Introduction; the Bill of Rights summarized, 136–137; its relation to the states, *see* Fourteenth Amendment *and see also* Due process; *see also* the Amendments to the Constitution by number

Bingham, John, 92, 93

Black codes, 91

Black, Hugo, 14, 15, 17, 25–28, 41, 99, 109–114, 168, 182, 185, 198, 225, 226

Blackstone, Sir William, 17, 50, 136, 200

Blair, William A., 146–153

Bloomer, Amelia, 53

Borchard, Edwin M., 228
Boycotts, 73
Boyd v. United States, 40
Boynton, Amelia, 79, 83
Bradley, Joseph P., 98
Brandeis, Louis Dembitz, 20, 25, 29, 142, 143–144, 166
Breach of the peace, 69, 86
Brennan, William J., 13, 14, 17, 19–21, 24, 27, 41, 114, 115, 120
Bronner, Edwin, 125–128
Brosman, Paul W., 194–196
Brown v. Board of Education, 76
Brown v. Mississippi, 224–225
"bugging," *see* eavesdropping, 43, 44
Burton, Harold H., 168, 183
Bus service for parochial pupils, 108
Bushel, Edward, 127
Butler, Mac S., 87

Cahill, William, 124
California, 53, 118, 130
Camden, Lord, (Charles Pratt), 39, 43
Carney, Daniel F., 187–189, 196
Carpetbaggers, 94, 95
Carr, Max, 33
Catholic, 26, 37, 109, 112, 114, 121, 128, 132
Cato, 18
Catt, Carrie Chapman, 58
Celler, Emanuel, 88, 119–132
Censorship, 12; history of, 16–20; by suit, 15, 18, 19, 27; by investigation, 30–31; of books and magazines, 14, 36–37, 42, 43; by favoring majority, 113–115; of mail, 34–35; gag rule, 48
Chaney, James E., 84, 100
Chaplinsky v. New Hampshire, 14
Charles I and James II, 38, 163
Charles II, 38, 110, 127
Church of England, 110, 112
Churchill, Winston, 190
Citizenship, 91–93, 184, 185
Civil Rights Act: of 1957, 77; of

1960, 80; of 1964, 84; of 1866, 92, 93
Civil Rights Commission, 77–80
Civil War, 91, 182, 191
Civilian supremacy over military, 172–197
Clark, James, 82, 102
Clark, Tom, 115–116, 167, 234–235
Clay, Raymond, 193–195
Clayton Act, 66
Clear and present danger, 24, 25
Code of military justices, 191–197
Cohen, Sheldon S., 203–205
Colonial period, 18, 37–40, 110–111, 117, 172, 183
Command control of courts-martial, 186–187, 192, 195–196, 197
Communist party, 28–32, 36, 68, 70, 165
Complicity, 228
Congress: plans Bill of Rights, *see* Introduction; passes Alien and Sedition Act, 17; passes Espionage Act, 24; investigates subversive activities, 29–32; outlaws wiretapping, 43–44; passes gag rule, 48; passes Antitrust Act, 65; investigates denials of labor's right to freedom of speech and assembly, 69–70; sets fair labor practices, 66, 67, 73, 75; on Negro rights, 77, 80, 84, 88, 89; sends Twenty-fourth Amendment to the states, 88; deals with Reconstruction era, 91–96; on Fourteenth Amendment, 93; on Fifteenth Amendment, 95; passes Enforcement Acts, 94, 95; and habeas corpus, 96; considers prayer amendment, 117–133; regulates interstate commerce, including air traffic, 147; on wartime labor disputes, 155, 157, 158; fights inflation, 155; criticizes the President, 159; limits wartime seizures of private property, 160, 166; and eminent domain, 138, 167; has tax power,

167; legislates for Hawaiian Territory, 175–176, 182; makes rules for armed forces, 188, 189, 191–197; and gun legislation, 198–205; reforms bail procedures, 212–220

Congress of Industrial Organizations (C.I.O.), 69, 71, 72, 154, 155, 161

Congress of Racial Equality, 84

Constitution, ratified, *see* Introduction; forbids bill of attainder, 30; on habeas corpus, 96; on religious tests, 108, 122–123; protects contracts, 140; operates in wartime, 149, 164; on powers of President, 160–168; on powers of Congress, 147, 164, 167, 188; *see also* Amendments by number

Continental Congress, *see* Introduction; 188

Contracts, 66, 140, 141

Coolidge, Calvin, 141

Counsel, right to, 189, 225–226, 228–231

Court of Claims, 149, 159, 161–162

Courts-martial, 184–197

Cox, Harold, 85, 90, 100

Craig, Walter E., 119

Cramer, William C., 124, 125

Davis, John W., 141, 142, 145, 162–165

Debs, Eugene V., 66

DeCarlo, Carmen, 195

Decker, G. H., 197

Declaration of Independence, 136, 183

Dehoney, Wayne, 117, 118, 120

De Jonge v. Oregon, 68

Dennis v. United States, 28

Depression of the thirties, 66, 99

Dix, Dorothea, 55

Doar, John, 80–81, 85

Dodd, Thomas, 205

Double jeopardy, 192

Douglas, William O., 25, 27, 28, 35, 41, 43, 73, 116, 150, 153, 166, 185, 215

Dow v. Johnson, 182

DuBois, W. E. B., 97–98

Due process of law, 99, 100, 141, 142, 224, 225, 229; protects against despotism, 183; *see also* military due process, 196

Duncan, Lloyd C., 177–184

Duncan v. Kahanamoku, 175–184

Eavesdropping, 43–44

Education, of women, 49–51; of Negroes, 51, 76, 91; *see also* academic freedom, *and see* schools

Eighth Amendment, 170, 185, 208, 217

Eisenhower, Dwight D., 77, 172–173, 201

Emancipation Proclamation, 55, 91

Emergencies, 160–162, 164, 167, 172, 184

Eminent domain, 138, 142–145, 148, 153, 160, 167

Employer free speech, 71, 73

Enforcement Acts, of 1870 and 1866, 85, 94, 95, 101

Engel v. Vitale, 109–113

England, Bill of Rights, *see* Introduction, 38; Magna Carta, 38, 150; law above King, 38; Blackstone, 17, 50; early censorship, 16–17; religious dissenters, 37, 109–110, 125–127; self incrimination, 39, 223; warrants, 37–40; judicial review, 40; Charles I, 38, 163; James II, 38, 163; Charles II, 38, 110, 127; trial of William Penn, 125–128; habeas corpus, 127; judges not to punish juries for their verdicts, 127; George III, 163, 181; bail, 217; *see also* Star Chamber

Episcopalians, 130, 132

Ervin, Samuel J., Jr., 215, 216

Escobedo, Danny, 227–231

Escobedo v. Illinois, 222–231

Espionage Act, 24, 25

Everson v. Board of Education, 115, 116
Ex. Parte Milligan, 182, 184
Ex. Parte Virginia, 101–102

Feinsinger, Nathan, 155, 156
Field judiciary, 197
Fifth Amendment, 30; and the property owner, 135, 136–168; and the accused, 170, 178, 192, 223–231
Fifteenth Amendment, 56, 83, 95, 101–102
Fighting words, 12, 14
First Amendment, 11–135, 137, 226, 233–239
Florida, 100, 103, 229
Flowers, Richmond M., 86, 87
Fong, Hiram L., 212–213, 216
Foote, Caleb, 218
Forrestal, James V., 194
Fortas, Abe, 100, 101, 229, 232
Fourteenth Amendment, 15, 43, 56, 83, 93, 94, 99, 108, 109, 144, 224, 226, 229–231
Fourth Amendment, 11, 36–44, 135, 137, 191–192
Frank v. Maryland, 40
Frankfurter, Felix, 26, 113, 166, 183, 226
Franklin, Benjamin, 136
Free press, 12–45; *see also* Press
Freedmen's Bureau, 91
Freedom of Religion, 108–133
Freedom to err, 12, 21, 31

Gag rule, 48
Garrison, Jim, 22–27
Garrison v. Louisiana, 22–27
Garrison, William Lloyd, 53
Gary, Joseph E., 64
George III, 163, 181
Georgia, 55, 110
Gephardt, Ernest T., 33
Germany, 57, 109, 167, 185
Gerry, Elbridge, 200
Gideon v. Wainwright, 100, 229

Gilbert, Jacob H., 121
Glass, Carter, 97
Glide angle, 147
Goldberg, Arthur J., 18, 25, 27, 156, 165, 166
Gompers, Samuel, 60–66
Goodman, Andrew, 84, 100
Graham, Billy, 121
Grand jury, 30, 85, 178, 192
Grant, Ulysses S., 96, 114
Graubard, Seymour, 123–124
Gray, Fred, 14
Greeley, Horace, 53, 92
Green, William, 66–67
Griggs v. Allegheny County, 145–153
Griswold, Erwin N., 119–120
Group libel, 25–26
Guinn v. United States, 98
Gun laws, 200–203

Habeas corpus, 96, 127, 175–177, 179, 181, 187
Hague v. Committee for Industrial Organization, 72
Hamilton, Andrew, 18, 127
Hand, Learned, 20, 28–29, 71
Hannah, John A., 77
Harlan, John Marshall, 32, 232
Hawaii, 175–180; Organic Act, 175, 176, 180, 182
Hayes, Rutherford B., 62, 97
Haymarket affair, 63–65
Haynes v. Washington, 229
Heilberg, Leif, 34, 35
Hitler, Adolf, 167
Hoffa, "Jimmy," 74
Holmes, Oliver Wendell, 25, 35, 142, 143, 152
Holtzoff, Alexander, 159, 187–190
Home Building and Loan Association v. Blaisdell, 138–169
Hooe v. United States (1910), 159
Hoover, J. Edgar, 201
House Judiciary Committee, 119–135
Howard, Jacob, 91

Hughes, Charles Evans, 68
Hunter, Andrew William, 79

Illinois, 25–27, 63, 65, 113, 131, 199, 219, 227–231
Illinois ex rel. McCollum v. Board of Education, 113
Indictment, 30, 85, 210
Injunction, 65, 66, 69, 159
In Re Oliver, 210
Internal Revenue, 198, 200, 203–205
Interstate Commerce, 68, 99

Jackson, Robert H., 24, 72, 116, 165, 167
James II, 38, 163
Japanese attack on Pearl Harbor, 175–177, 180, 182
Jefferson, Thomas, 19, 20, 32, 112, 138
Jews, 109, 110, 121, 129, 131, 132
Johnson, Andrew, 92, 182
Johnson, Frank M., Jr., 83–86, 103
Johnson, Lyndon B., 88, 204, 220
Johnston, Olin D., 212, 216
Judge Advocate General's office, 189, 193, 195
Junior Bar Section of the District of Columbia Bar Association, 215, 219
Justice, Department of, 80–85, 96, 100, 160, 161, 165, 177, 199, 213–214, 216, 219
Juvenile courts, 231–233

Kahanamoku, Duke P., 179–180
Katzenbach, Nicholas de B., 82, 89, 199–200
Keating, Kenneth B., 217, 219
Kenealy, William J., 128
Kennedy, John F., 27, 114, 198
Kennedy, Robert, 74, 213–217
Kilday, Paul J., 196
King, Martin Luther, 13, 14, 83, 87

Knights of Labor, 62, 63–65
Kohler Act, 139–144
Korea, 154–164, 193–195
Ku Klux Klan, 87, 95

Labor's Bill of Rights, 75
La Follette Committee, 69–70
La Follette, Robert M., 69–70
Lamont, Corliss, 28–30, 33–35
Lamont v. Post Office, 33–35
Landrum Griffin Act, 75
Latimer, George W., 194–196
Lawlessness, in the name of progress, 142, 144; in crime detection, 41, 100, 225–226
Legalized nuisance, 148
Lemnitzer, Lyman L., 197
Lewis, John L., 68–70
Libel, 13–27
Lichter v. United States, 163–164
Lilburne, John, 223
Lincoln, Abraham, 91, 92, 158, 182
Littell, Franklin H., 129
Little v. Barreme, 164, 169
Lobbying, 28, 48; women, 54, 55, 58; labor, 62, 66, 74, 75; employers, 70–71; Negroes, 86, 88, 91; on prayer amendment, 117–132; veterans, 131, 186–189, 190–191; gun owners, 200–203
Locke, John, 18, 19, 136
Lord, John Wesley, 118
Louisiana, 22–27, 55, 80, 89–90, 115
Louisiana v. United States, 89–90
Lovejoy, Elijah, 26
Lovett, Robert A., 155, 157
Lutheran, 132
Lyon, Mary, 50
Lyon, Matthew, 19

McCarthy, Joseph R., 29, 30
McClellan, John L., 74, 75
McGowan v. Maryland, 115
McIntire, Carl J., 117
McLaughlin, Frank, 179

Madden, J. Warren, 149
Madison, James, 17, 19, 20, 111–112, 116, 172
Magna Carta, 38, 150
Mahon, Margaret, 139–145
Mallory rule, 226
Malloy v. Hogan, 230
Manhattan Bail Project, 218–220
Mapp v. Ohio, 42
Marcus v. Search Warrant, 42, 43
Marshall, Howard, 234
Marshall v. United States, 234
Marshall, Thurgood, 76
Martial law, 176–185
Maryland, 40, 225
Massachusetts, 49, 50, 54, 59, 110, 127
May 1 work stoppage, 63
"Memorial and Remonstrance against Religious Assessments," 111–112
Memphis riot, 93, 94
Methodist, 112, 118, 130, 132
Metzger, Delbert E., 180–181
Michigan, 131; one-man grand jury, 210
Military justice, for civilians, 173–185; for servicemen, 185–197; before code, 185–191; after code, 191–197
Military necessity, 172, 173, 180, 181, 183, 191
Military, under civilian authority, 172–197
Mill, John Stuart, 12
Milligan, Lambdin, 182, 184
Mills, Wilbur D., 202
Milton, John, 16–17
Minton, Sherman M., 167
Miranda v. Arizona, 230–231
Mississippi, 55, 80, 81, 84–85, 97, 99, 100, 224–225
Moody, William H., 224–225
Mormon, 26, 118
Mott, Lucretia Coffin, 49–55, 57
Murphy, Frank, 69, 183–184
Murray, Madalyn, 115, 121
Murray, Philip, 69, 155, 156
Myers v. United States, 166

National Association for the Advancement of Colored People, 76, 83, 98, 99
National Firearms Act, of 1938, 198; of 1934, 200
National Council of Churches, (Board of), 121
National Labor Relations Board, 67
National Rifle Association, 201
Negro voter registration drive, 76–89
News media, *see* Press
New York, 54, 58; Board of Regents prayer, 109–114; Assembly report on bail, 216; Manhattan Bail Project, 218–220
New York Times Co. v. Sullivan, 13–22, 27, 28, 35
Nimitz, Chester W., 180
Nineteenth Amendment, 58
Ninth Amendment, 30, 137, 202
Norblad, Albin W., Jr., 186–187
North American Aviation Company pickets, 155
North Briton, 39
Northwest Airlines Inc. v. Minnesota, 147
Norris-La Guardia Act, 67

Oahu, 175
Obscene publications, 14, 42
Office of Price Stabilization, 156
O'Hara, William J., 22, 24
Oregon, 68
Organic Act for Hawaii, *see* Hawaii
Oswald, Lee Harvey, 198, 204
Otis, James, 37–38
Owen, David Robert, 84–85

Pace, W. L., 140
Parades: women, 58; labor, 63; civil rights marches, 83–84, 86–87
Parliament, 17, 30, 38, 40, 110, 223
Patterson, Robert, 187
Pearl Harbor, 175

Penn, William, 125–128
Pennsylvania, 127, 128, 139–145, 145–148, 150–153
Pennsylvania Coal Co. v. Mahon, 139–145
Penn Township, 151
Perlman, Philip, 161, 165
Petition, right to, 48; women, 54–59; labor, 61, 65, 66, 67, 74–75; employers, 70–71; civil rights, 77–89; worshipers, 117–132; property owners, 137; veterans, 186–191; riflemen, 200–203
Pine, David A., 160–161
Poindexter, Joseph B., 175–176
Police methods, 202, 214, 228, 229; brutality, 100, 224–225; restrictions on, 41, 43, 72, 100, 137, 205, 225, 226
Police power of state, 118–119, 138, 140–144, 199, 202–203
Ponder, William H., 24
Powderly, Terence V., 63
Powell v. Alabama, 226
Preliminary injunction, 159
Presbyterians, 112, 118, 132
Presidents: on Bill of Rights, 13, 19, 129; on Reconstruction, 91, 92, 96–97; on Negroes, 77, 88, 91; on separation of church and state, 111–112, 114, 115; powers under the Constitution, 160–168; on military power, 172, 173; on guns, 201, 204; restraints on, 160, 161, 163, 164, 166–168; on military justice, 193; on bail, 220
Press, freedom of, 11–45; and public opinion, 13, 26, 61, 88, 116, 131, 233–239; relation to freedom of religion, 37, 125, 127; relation to a fair trial, 233–239
Presser, Herman, 199
Presser v. Illinois, 199
Price, Cecil Ray, 84–85, 99–101
Privacy, 37–38, 41, 43–44
Property rights, 136–169; women's, 50, 51, 54, 57; protected by Fourteenth Amendment, 99, 144; limitation on, 137–138, 143–144,

147; relation to rest of Bill of Rights, 137
Provost Court, 178–181
Puritans, 37, 109, 127

Quakers, 49, 51, 109, 112, 125–128
Quinn, Robert E., 189, 194–196

Reconstruction period, 90–97
Reeb, James J., 83–87
Reisman, Leonard E., 202, 203
Religious freedom, 107–135; relation to other rights, 119, 120, 123, 127
Reynolds, Joshua, 39
Reynolds v. United States (1879), 115
Richards v. Washington Terminal Co., 148
Richardson, Robert C., Jr., 180
Rights of the accused, a jury trial, 180–184; a counsel, 189, 192, 194, 225–226, 228–231; an impartial jury, 183, 233–239; to be informed of the charges, 194; considered innocent, 183, 194, 213, 216; to call witnesses, 195; to cross examine witnesses, 192, 194, 231; to remain silent, 192, 221, 223–231; against double jeopardy, 192; a speedy trial, 196, 217; bail, 212, 217; a public trial, 210, 232–233; *see also* juvenile courts
Riots, 26; Cicero, 26; religious, 26; labor, 62, 64; Memphis, 93–94; New Orleans, 93–94; Negro, 103
Roberts, Owen J., 72
Robinson, David W., II, 89
Rogers, Byron G., 124
Roosevelt, Franklin D., 67, 153, 154, 157, 165, 175–176, 226
Roosevelt, Theodore, 114
Roth v. United States, 14, 20
Rousseau, Jean Jacques, 200
Runkle v. United States (1887), 188
Rutledge, Wiley B., 81

Sawyer, Charles, 157, 159, 160, 163

Scalawags, 94–95

Schenck v. United States, 25

School prayer, 109–133

Schools, public, 49, 60, 76, 91, 129

Schweitzer, Louis, 218–220

Schwerner, Mickey, 84, 100

Search and seizure, 36–44, 191; and free press, 37, 39, 42

Search warrants, 36–44, 191–192; and general warrants, 37, 38

Second Amendment, 137, 170, 173, 174, 198–206

Seized property, 14, 153–168; unauthorized, 159; in wartime, 157, 160, 162; *see also* Eminent domain and search and seizure

Self-incrimination, 222–231

Selma, march, 83–87

Seneca Falls, 52

Senner, George F., Jr., 125, 128

Separation of powers, 111, 112, 164, 166, 167

Seventh Amendment, 137

Shaw, Anna Howard, 58

Shaw, Lemuel, 59

Sheppard v. Maxwell, 235

Sheridan, Philip, 94

Sherman Antitrust Act, 65

Sherman, William T., 191

Short, Walter C., 176

Sisk, B. F., 130

Sixth Amendment, 100, 107, 137, 170, 178, 179, 192, 208, 225–226, 229–231

Smith Act, 28

Smith, Darrell F., 231

Smith, Joseph, 26

Smith v. Allwright, 76

South Carolina, 55, 96, 97; Supreme Court case, 89–103

Southern Christian Leadership Conference, 83

Spano v. New York (1959), 226

Speech, freedom of, 11–35; and libel, 13–27; and clear and present danger, 25; and academic freedom, 31–35; and the mail, 34–35; and assembly, 48, 71–72; and property, 137

Speedy trial: denial of, 18, 210; military, 196; with crowded dockets, 217

Spellman, Francis Cardinal, 121

Spies, August, 63

Stainback, Ingram M., 176–177, 180

Standing armies, 172–173, 190, 200

Stanford, John W., 36–44

Stanford v. Texas, 36–44

Stanton, Elizabeth Cady, 49–57

Star Chamber, 16, 223

State Constitutions and laws: have libel laws, 14–15, 26–27; affect Negro voters, 76, 80, 82, 97; on voting and literacy, 89, 101–102; religious liberty, 108, 125; over property, 137, 138; on self-incrimination, 224, 225; on right to counsel, 225; gun laws, 198, 202–203; *see also* States

State of South Carolina v. Katzenbach, 89–103

States: leave the union, 55; have jurisdiction, 84, 101–102; and Fourteenth Amendment, 15, 43, 56, 83, 93, 94, 99, 101, 102, 108, 109, 224, 226, 229–231; States rights, 57, 92, 93, 101, 102, 224, 226

Steel case, 153–168

Stevens, Thaddeus, 92

Stewart, Potter, 42–43, 116, 129

Stomberg v. California, 20

Stone, Lucy, 50–57

Stoneman, George, 93

Storey, Robert G., 77–80

Sturtz, Herbert, 220

Suffrage, 28; women, 52–59; and property, 60; and Negroes, 56, 76–103

Sullivan, L. B., 13, 14, 21

Sullivan Law, 202–203

Sumner, Charles, 55

Supreme Court, on freedom of speech and press, 14–45; on libel,

20–22, 24–27; on obscenity, 14; on Communist conspiracy, 28, 31, 32; on Congressional investigations, 32; on academic freedom, 32–35; on enforcement officer's discretion, 43, 72, 205; on early wage laws, 66, 68; on freedom of assembly, 68, 71, 72, 86; on poll tax, 88; during Reconstruction, 98; on Voting Rights Act, of 1965, 101–102; on States rights, 101–102; on religion, 109–117; on property rights, 99, 138, 143, 144, 147, 150, 152, 153, 159, 162, 166–168; on military trials of civilians, 182–185; on citizenship, 185; on carrying weapons, 195–200; on contempt of court, 210; on self-incrimination and right to counsel, 224–231; on witnesses, 231; on juveniles, 232; on fair trial and free press, 233–239; on jury selection, 238

Taft-Hartley Act, 73, 155, 157–158
Taft, Robert A., 73, 157
Taney, Roger B., 91
Tax power, 167
Tennessee, 91, 94, 117
Tenth Amendment, 30, 137, 202
Texas, 36–44, 55, 71–72
Third Amendment, 135, 137
Thirteenth Amendment, 91
Thomas, Daniel H., 81
Thomas v. Collins, 71–73
Tillman, Benjamin, 97
Torcaso v. Watkins, 108
Touro Synagogue, 129
Transcript, 231
Trial examiners, 67
Trial by jury, 18, 180–184, 233–239; *see also* rights of accused
Toth v. Quarles, 185
Trop v. Dulles, (citizenship), 184–185
Truman, Harry S., 77, 153–168, 193

Tuskegee, 78, 79
Turkish massacre, 130
Tuttle, Charles H., 122–123
Twenty-fourth Amendment, 88
Twining v. New Jersey, 224–225

Udall, Morris K., 128, 129
Undercover agents, 23
United States Court of Military Appeals, 192–196
United States v. Causby, 149–150
United States v. Louisiana, 89–90
United States v. Miller, 199–200
United States v. North American Transportation and Trading Co. (1920), 159
United States v. Pee Wee Coal Co., 162
United States v. Price, 84–85, 90, 99–100
United States v. Russell, 162

Vanderbilt, Arthur T., 187
Vaughan, Sir John, 127
Venue, change of, 235
Vera Foundation, 218–220
Vermont, 19
Vinson, Fred, 28, 167
Virginia, 97, 111–112
Vote, *see* suffrage
Voting Rights Bill of 1965, 88–90, 101–102

Wage Stabilization Board, 155
Wagner Act, 67–68
Wagner Robert F., 67
Waite, Morrison R., 188
Wallace, George C., 82, 86, 87
War and the Bill of Rights: Espionage Act of 1917, 24, 25; clear and present danger, 24, 25; woman's rights and civil war, 55; World War I and women demonstrators, 57, 58; habeas corpus, 96, 175–177; war and the Constitution, 149, 164; inflation and

War and the Bill of Rights (*cont.*)
  strike legislation, 155–158; sei-
  zure of private property, 157,
  160, 162; martial law, 175–184;
  courts and a war, 176, 181–184
War Department, 177, 187–188
War of the Roses, 223
Warrants, 36–44, 191–192
Warren, Earl, 20, 41, 42, 101–103,
  185
Washington, Booker T., 97
Washington, George, 129, 172
Weeks v. United States, 41
White, Byron R., 21, 22
Whitney v. California, 25
Wiener, Frederick B., 190, 191
Wilkes, John, 39
Wilkins, Roy, 76
Williams, Roger, 110

Williams v. United States, 100
Williams v. Wallace, 83–86
Wilson, Charles E., 156
Wilson, Woodrow, 57
Winthrop, William, 189
Wisconsin, 114–115, 131
Wisdom, John Minor, 89–90
Women's rights, 49–59
World War I, 24, 57, 58, 66, 188
World War II, 70, 149, 157, 165,
  175–181, 185–187, 190, 201
Wright, J. Skelly, 214
Wyoming, 56–57

Youngstown v. Sawyer, 153–168

Zenger, Peter, 18, 127, 210
Zoning, 137

THE AUTHOR

MARJORIE FRIBOURG was born in a 150-year-old house in Chappaqua, New York. At an early age she exhibited a marked ability for elaborate storytelling which she believes explains why most of her earlier works were fiction. A graduate of Columbia University Teachers College, she has taught off and on through the years and read her husband's law books avidly to get a better background in American history. In doing research for an earlier nonfiction assignment, she discovered to her joy that her experience in writing fiction could help to bring alive the vivid, true-life experiences behind great historical events.

Her careful use of the narrative style proved successful in her previous work, *The Supreme Court in American History,* to which the present volume is a sequel. The development of the Bill of Rights unfolds in terms of its impact on the lives of American citizens, past and present.

Mrs. Fribourg is the wife of a Trial Examiner at the Federal Power Commission and a resident of both New York and Washington. She keeps up an active membership in national, civic, and literary organizations. This summer she will serve for the second time as a member of the staff of the Georgetown University Writers Conference.